The N

Roomma

second

And 107 Other Issues Y
Might Run Into in College

The Naked Roommate:

second edition

And 107 Other Issues You Might Run Into in College

Harlan Cohen

SOURCEBOOKS, INC.
NAPERVILLE, ILLINOIS

Published by Sourcebooks, Inc.
P.O. Box 4410, Naperville, Illinois 60567-4410
(630) 961-3900
FAX: (630) 961-2168
www.sourcebooks.com

Library of Congress Cataloging-in-Publication Data for the first edition:

Cohen, Harlan, 1973-
  The naked roommate : and 107 other issues you might run into at
college / Harlan Cohen.
    p. cm.
  Includes index.
  ISBN-13: 978-1-4022-0909-3
  ISBN-10: 1-4022-0909-6
 1. College student orientation. 2. College students--Conduct of life.
I. Title.

LB2343.3.C62 2007
378.1'98--dc22

COHEN   2007001793

Printed and bound in the United States of America
VP   10   9   8   7   6   5   4   3   2

For Stephanie,
my higher education in love and in life

Acknowledgments

To my wife, Stephanie (my lifelong naked roommate), thank you again for all of your love and support throughout this entire process—pieces, pieces. To my parents, Eugene and Shirlee—thank you for opening the door to college life and always offering all the opportunities and love a child could ever want or need. Thank you to my brothers, Victor and Michael, and my sister, Irene, for loving me, guiding me, and always being there for me (and to Phoebe and Rae, too). Thank you to Marvin, Francine, Daniel, Rozi, and Moose for all of your love and support.

Thank you to my agent, Eliot Ephraim, for your endless commitment and continued support on this amazing journey. Thank you to my brilliant editor, Peter Lynch, and the entire team at Sourcebooks for pouring so much passion, wit, and wisdom into this project. Thank you to Glenn Mott and the entire team at King Features Syndicate for helping to make Help Me, Harlan! one of the most well-read advice columns in the country. A special thank-you to all the newspaper editors that run Help Me, Harlan! and to all those people who read it and write to me with questions, comments, and suggestions (even the ones who write about my ears).

A heartfelt thank-you goes out to all the students, professionals, and contributors who offered information for this book! Thank you for being so open, honest, and candid about your lives. Your stories will impact millions of students. I couldn't write without you. Thank you to all the high schools, colleges, organizations, and associations that have hosted my speaking events over the years and enabled me to conduct such detailed research.

A special note of gratitude is extended to Janet Cox and the BACCHUS Network, Linda Sax and the Higher Education Research Institute at UCLA, Dr. David Adams and the *Indiana Daily Student*, Tom Rolnicki and the Associated Collegiate Press, the National Orientation Directors Association, the National Association for Campus Activities, Indiana University, Alpha Epsilon Pi fraternity, Krishnan Anantharaman, Larry Rout, *The Wall Street Journal Classroom Edition*, and all the people who have been in my corner during this journey over the years. I can't thank you enough for all of your kindness and support.

Contents

Chapter 1
Arriving on Campus:
So Real You Can Smell It, Touch It, and Taste It 19

Chapter 2
Residence Halls: Living, Eating, and
Bathing with Hundreds of Strangers. 49

Chapter 6
Greek Life: Behind the Doors, Windows,
and Walls of Fraternity and Sorority Life 143

Chapter 7
Life Inside the Classroom:
Assuming You Wake Up and Go to Class 161

Chapter 8
Dating and Relationships:
Your Higher Education in Lust, Love, and Loss 213

Chapter 9
Sex:
Having It, Not Having It,
Hearing Other People Having It 253

Book Orientation

The Stuff before the Tips

Welcome Students

Welcome to *The Naked Roommate*. It's so nice to have you here on page one. I'm Harlan. I'll be your author and host throughout this book. I've included a picture of myself on the back of the book so you can see what I look like. And yes, I've actually been wearing that same outfit while writing this entire book (but I have gained about five pounds). As your host and author, I'd like to offer you something to eat or drink, but I don't know where to find you or if you can eat or drink where you are. If you're reading this at a place where they're serving food or drinks, please get yourself something. I can't pay for it, but if I were there, I would. I just want to make sure that you're comfortable.

So please, slip off your shoes, unbutton the top button on your pants if they're snug, find a comfortable place to sit if you're standing. Do whatever it takes for you to get comfortable, as long as what you need to do to get comfortable isn't prohibited by any indecency laws. If it is prohibited, please take this book home with you. I'm not trying to get you to buy it (well, maybe I am a little), but what is more important than you owning this book is that you are as comfortable as possible while reading it. Because when it comes down to it, that's what this whole book is all about—and it's really what the college experience is about. It's about helping you to get comfortable for what can be an uncomfortable (at times) journey ahead. Now, I'll give you a break to get comfortable. And please, feel free to browse through the book after you settle in.

—A Break in the Book—

Welcome Back

Hi, Harlan here again, your author and host. As you can tell by browsing through this book, you are probably expecting a lot of tips. When it comes to "tips," there are many different kinds in the world. There are good tips, bad tips, informative tips, tips that touch the surface, tips that give you something to think about, tips you leave on a table after eating at a restaurant, rib tips, finger tips, tiptoes, and various other miscellaneous tips. This is a tip book unlike any other tip book. It's a book that goes far beyond the tip and leaves you with something to think about, and when applicable, even offers you places to go for help on and off campus. I'd like to go so far as to say that this is the best tip book in the history of tip books (minus the 1762 classic, *Ten Tips for Settlers to the New Country*).

This might come to you as a surprise, but I wasn't a fan of "tip books"—that is, until I wrote this book. I don't just like this one because I wrote it (although that is part of the reason). It's because this book is genuinely different. It's based on what today's college students are honestly thinking, feeling, and doing on today's college campuses. It's their voices sharing their stories and experiences that will expose the uncensored truth about what's really going on in college. Not only will you get page after page of telling tips from students on over one hundred college campuses across North America, you'll also get the latest facts, stats, resources, support services having to do with college life, and some advice from me—someone who has been a freshman twice, has visited over two hundred college campuses, and has interviewed over a thousand students. Whether you're living on campus or commuting from home, whether you're going to a big school or a small school, whether you're the first person in your family going to college or the last—I wanted to make sure this book has something for everyone.

About the student-offered tips—one thing that I've discovered while writing my syndicated advice column and interviewing students over the years is that it's the rest of the story, the story of how someone came up with his or her tip or advice, that is the most telling. And that's exactly what you'll find here—the tips and the stories behind them. That's just not something you see every day. (Assuming you own this book, you now can see it every day if that's what you enjoy doing with your spare time.)

Speaking of time, I appreciate yours. I promise not to waste it. This book will be helpful. At the very least, it can always be used as a doorstop, a coaster, or a way to level out a shaky table. The actual information written on the pages of your new doorstop/coaster/level will also prove helpful. Whether you're heading to college as the star of your high school or you're one of those students who blended into the cement block walls in the back of your classroom, this book has something for you. And that includes all those people who fall somewhere in between blending into the cement blocks and being a star. This is the book that I only wish someone had written for me when I went to college.

High schools do a great job of getting students into college, but once on campus, few students know what to expect. That's what this book is all about—to help you expect the unexpected so that when the unexpected shows up, it won't be so hard to handle. When I went to college, I thought it was going to be an easy transition. I had two older brothers who had both been to college (one is five years older, the other eight years older). I also had a long-distance girlfriend who was a senior in high school. I went to a big college after graduating from a big high school, and expected everything to just fall into place. But instead, I only felt out of place. It took almost two semesters and my transferring from the University of Wisconsin at Madison (an awesome school) to Indiana University in Bloomington, Indiana (another awesome school), to figure it all out. At IU, I experienced a second freshman year and discovered what I should have done differently the first time around. That's what this book is about—it's all the things that no one ever tells you about your college years, things that will make college life easier to handle. Whether you're on a commuter campus, a college near home, or a university far away from home, so much of the college experience is universal. It's a higher education in love, in life, and in finding passion—inside and outside the classroom.

I'm so happy that you finally have your hands on *The Naked Roommate*. I hope you will keep this close to you through your college career. You might not need everything on the pages to follow today, but you'll use different parts of *The Naked Roommate* during different times in your college career. When you do need it, it's here. I know it will help.

Please note—you probably won't encounter every single issue and obstacle discussed in this book (and if you do, you should write your own book). That said, you will encounter many of them; if not in your own life, then in the lives of your friends. When that happens, you can share this book or get them their own copies. One thing I should mention before continuing: I promised many of the college students who offered advice for this book not to just talk about the bad parts of college; they didn't want this to book to scare you because the truth is that most of college is great. It's just not always easy. And with that, I've fulfilled my promise.

As you read this book and live out your own college experience, please send in your thoughts, tips, and stories. *The Naked Roommate* is an ongoing project. Submit your tips, advice, and stories via www.TheNakedRoommate.com or via my Help Me, Harlan! website at: www.HelpMe Harlan.com. You can also send email to me at: harlan@help meharlan.com.

As your author and host, please let me know if there is ever anything I can do to help you along your college journey. I know you have a choice when it comes to books about college life, and I appreciate you choosing this one. Thank you.

Welcome Parents

Hi, parents. This is Harlan. It's a pleasure to meet you!

I wanted to include a personal note to you because you are so important to the college experience—even more so than ever before. As parents of college-age students, many of you are college graduates from the 1970s and 1980s. In other words, you're the college students who set the standards in terms of bad behavior. If you weren't the ones doing it, you were the ones seeing people doing it or hearing them doing it. If you're a parent who never attended college, what you've seen and heard about college life has largely been what the media has offered—binge drinking, parties, danger, and generally irresponsible behavior. As a result, most parents, regardless of their college history or background, are concerned about their kids starting life in college. One thing that I'm always reminded of while sharing parent presentations and conducting research with students is how active parents have become in their children's college experiences. Ten years ago, a parent was lucky to get a call from their kid once a week. Now, with the help of email, text messaging, and cell phones, communicating problems to parents is nearly instantaneous. Never before have parents been so connected to their students' college experiences moment by moment as they unfold. Many parents are literally pulled onto campus. This can be a good thing, but also a not-so-good thing.

First, the good. Being so connected means that you can now offer more support than ever before. College can naturally be a lonely and difficult transition, so just knowing that you're close by can be helpful to your children. You also can know what's happening in your children's lives—or at least you know all is well when you get a return email or text message with the words, "Love ya—I'm alive."

Now the not-so-good: because parents are so accessible, students have a tendency to share more details about daily life with parents than ever. Because parents know more, they tend to get more involved. It makes sense. It's hard to not get emotionally involved when you hear bits and pieces of all the things your children are encountering on a day-to-day or even minute-to-minute basis. College professionals tell me that more and more parents are getting actively involved in their children's college experiences—and *calling campus* looking for answers to their children's problems. On top of that, the students who are having a difficult transition are more likely to use technology to become more dependent and more in touch with parents (and friends on other campuses, and long-distance boyfriends and girlfriends)—leading to homesickness and a lack of urgency to get involved on campus.

And that's where this book can be helpful. The tips, expert insight, resources, and support services offer a never-before-seen look at college life that can help you get a sense of what to expect—what's typical and what's not. It can give you a baseline to help ease your fears and anxiety while helping you to better guide your children through the normal obstacles that are part of college life. When a problem arises, instead of wanting to fix it yourself, you'll know what's normal and be able to point your child in the right direction. One suggestion: visit your son's or daughter's college website to see specific resources and support services on campus.

When visiting campus, introduce yourself to the people who will help your student. Knowing the people and places online (and on campus) will help when you point them in the right direction to find answers. My hope is that you pick up a copy of this book for your son or daughter, and then keep one for yourself. Keep it close by, and when a problem comes up, you can use it as a tool (or if a door needs to be held open, it's a great doorstop). This can be your study guide/cheat sheet for college life. In addition, you can find resources, tips, and information on the *The Naked Roommate* website at www.TheNakedRoommate.com and on my personal website at www.HelpMeHarlan.com. Feel free to share your comments and questions in the Naked Roommate forums in the parent's area (please invite other parents to share). Also, I invite you to please send in your comments, tips, questions, and feedback to me. You can reach me via the websites or at harlan@helpmeharlan.com. Thank you for reading *The Naked Roommate*. I hope it helps!

Welcome High School and College Educators

It's a pleasure to have you here! I wanted to take a moment to visit with you—specifically.

The Naked Roommate is the culmination of over ten years of research. It's my second book about college life, and I believe one of the most unique and helpful perspectives on college life inside and outside the classroom. This updated edition takes the latest trends, facts, and stats and combines it with the voices of students and college professionals. The information has been accumulated while talking with experts and speaking on and visiting more than three hundred college campuses. Also included in *The Naked Roommate* are resources, support services, recent data, the latest government information, hotlines, websites, and places for students to find answers to their questions. While gathering materials for this book project, I contacted the offices of the National Orientation Directors Association, the National Resource Center for The First-Year Experience, The BACCHUS Network, the Higher Education Research Institute at UCLA, the National Association of College and University Residence Halls, the National Panhellenic Conference, the North American Interfraternity Conference, and member schools of the National Association of College Activities. My goal was to create the most complete and fact-based look at college life ever presented. I'd like to think of *The Naked Roommate* as an encyclopedia of what may or may not happen to students in college. It's a tool to help ease students' anxiety while helping them find their places once in school.

In addition to this book, there is an online companion—TheNakedRoommate.com. This online forum delivers information in a similar style to the book, but offers opportunities for students and parents to contribute to the nakedness. If you visit the site, you'll discover daily college news, college blogs, the Naked Roommate blog, the Naked Roommate forums (for students and parents), the Naked Roommate eNewsletter (a free weekly newsletter distributed via email during the academic year), and advice from my Help Me, Harlan! syndicated advice column and speaking programs and tour. You'll also find video elements (many generated from students). In addition to TheNakedRoommate.com you can find me on Facebook and on MySpace. And yes, I'd like to be your friend. As my Facebook friend or MySpace friend you can stay with me when traveling through Chicago (or at a hotel close to me). You'll also get invited to participate in Facebook Groups throughout the year.

Note to High School Professionals
The Naked Roommate offers a window to the world of college life unlike any other. It's a look inside and outside the classroom that will help to ease the anxiety of college-bound students and answer their questions regarding the experience ahead. It provides a needed look into all aspects that make up college life—the social, academic, and emotional sides. In addition to helping students for life once in college, the information, resources, statistics, and facts offer them a list of issues to consider when selecting a college. It's a great tool for those thinking about college and those already in college.

Note to College Professionals
The Naked Roommate has been designed for professionals who are seeking a text for First-Year Experience programs or a text for student leaders such as residence life professionals, orientation leaders, and student mentors on campus. Facilitators of such programs are encouraged to incorporate resources and support services unique to each campus (i.e., people, places, phone numbers, and organizations) that can address the needs of students. Students in FYE classes are encouraged to share their tips in class and via *The Naked*

Roommate website (see Tip #107). For more information regarding a facilitator's guide and additional information that might be of help in this capacity, please visit *The Naked Roommate* website at www.TheNakedRoommate.com or send an email to harlan@helpmeharlan.com with the subject line Facilitator's Guide.

A Trend Worth Noting

There's one trend I want to highlight for you before going on to the rest of the book. I call it "The Fifth Wall." From cell phones with free nights and weekends, to instant messenger, to email, to blogs, to text messages, to video games, to digital cameras and personal websites, it's never been easier to be physically in once place, but mentally and emotionally somewhere else. It's changing college life.

As a result of The Fifth Wall, students talk to their parents more than ever, making the role of parents during the college transition increasingly important. Students talk to their hometown friends more than ever, too, making it easier to lean on old friends rather than getting out and making new friends. It also makes it easy to compare one college experience on one campus to another—and it's not always a fair comparison. In addition, it makes it easier to maintain a long-distance relationship with a boyfriend or girlfriend. Students can avoid meeting professors face-to-face (they can just send an email instead of asking a question in class). And all the ways to stay busy without ever having to interact with another person make it that much more challenging to connect with people on campus. More than ever, students need to make an effort to map out their path in college. They need incentives to get involved. They need educational professionals and student mentors on campus to actively involve them in life on campus.

My Reason for Writing This Book

I was the last person I ever thought would have a difficult time dealing with the college transition. My two older brothers had both been to college before me and didn't seem to have a problem. It seemed easy. While life in high school did a great job of preparing me to get into college, once I got to college, I was lost. There was so much I didn't know, so much no one told me.

I didn't know that I had to work to find my place. I didn't know it took time to find my place. I didn't know that I had to be patient. I didn't know that I had to leave with a map to get where I wanted to go. And I ended up transferring. It wasn't the college, though—it was me. According to ACT, Inc., roughly one in four students doesn't return to the same campus for their sophomore year. Less than two-thirds of students who start college will finish with a degree (percentages vary by type of college). It's a trend that continues, but I strongly believe that the tips, information, insight, resources, and support services on the following pages can help lower these numbers over the years. If students can come to college understanding and appreciating what it takes to get comfortable on campus, they won't be as likely to leave. That's what this book is all about: helping students get comfortable in college and making the most of life inside and outside the classroom. I hope it helps your students. Thank you!

About the Editorial Content

The Naked Roommate was compiled over nearly ten years during visits to over three hundred college campuses. The tips and stories behind the tips were compiled during face-to-face and phone interviews, via written request forms, and collected through my websites (www.HelpMeHarlan.com and www.TheNaked Roommate.com), email, and professional organizations that requested students forward their stories and tips. The latest facts, figures, and information were provided by the Higher Education Research Institute at UCLA using the CIRP Freshman Survey and Your First College Year data (2003, 2005, and 2006), The BACCHUS Network, and various U.S. government websites. Some of the quotations cited in *The Naked Roommate* were excerpted from articles I've written for *The Wall Street Journal Classroom Edition*.

Please keep in mind: the tips on the following pages are in no way a fair and accurate representation of the entire student population at each institution or of the institutions themselves. Due to the sensitive nature of some tips, and to protect free-flowing information from students, proper names could not be used. If a student had strong concerns, his or her year in school was changed (but not the name of the school). The tips and the stories behind them are not direct quotes, but are as accurate as possible.

The Updated Edition: 10 Percent More Nakedness

If you're reading this book (and you must be, unless someone is reading it to you), then you are reading the most updated version of this book. What I've learned about college life is that trends are always changing. To help highlight these trends, I've updated the stats and facts, added a few new websites, taken some away, included more voices from more students, and generally freshened the nakedness. Consider this a toning of the naked roommate. In addition to the changes just mentioned, you'll find various references to Facebook and MySpace. (Please, be my friend. Seriously.) Also, at the end of the book, you'll find several entries from the Naked Roommate blog. You can subscribe to the blog and add comments by visiting www.TheNakedRoom mate.com (yep, it's all free). And please check out TheNaked Roommate.com. You can post questions and comments, share videos, read comments, watch videos, hear music, and generally have a front seat to all the nakedness.

A Final Note to All Readers

The Naked Roommate is an ongoing experience. This is the second of what will be many editions of this book. Please send me your feedback, suggestions, and insight while reading through these tips. If you have a story, advice, or a tip that could help other students, just send it my way. If you have a book title that you think might be helpful to include in future editions of *The Naked Roommate*, please send the title. Send feedback by visiting www.TheNakedRoom mate.com or via email to harlan@helpmeharlan.com.

WARNING!!!

THE TIPS ON THE FOLLOWING PAGES ARE IN NO WAY A FAIR OR COMPLETE REPRESENTATION OF THE ENTIRE STUDENT POPULATION AT EACH INSTITUTION OR OF THE INSTITUTIONS THEMSELVES

not even close to it

no way, not at all

that means no

no, no, no, no

seriously, no

again, no!

last time

no, no,

no

wow, you have really great vision if you can read this

First Page, First Tip, and First Days of College

Welcome to the first page, the first day of college, and my first tip.

There are a lot of firsts happening here—first time away from home, first time living with a stranger, first college class, first college professors, first pages of textbooks, first college hookup, first love, first loss, first time possibly having sex (or not having it, or just hearing other people have it), maybe your first pregnancy scare, first sexually transmitted infection (also called sexually transmitted disease), first time seeing people use drugs, first time borrowing thousands of dollars and first time spending thousands of dollars, first time managing your money, first time having to make choices on your own, first time staying out all night, first time having to make a new life for yourself, and the first time when you can do as much as you want or as little as you want and have no one to answer to but *you* (assuming you don't answer your phone).

Naturally, the first time you do something, it's normal to not be completely comfortable doing it. Comfort takes time. So understand that it will take time to find your comfortable place in college. Be who you are, not who people want you to be (or who you *think* people want you to be). Work to find what you love to do inside and outside the classroom. And along the way, appreciate that no matter what happens, no matter what you're feeling, no matter what obstacles you encounter—you are never alone. As someone who has lived it, seen it, and heard about it in my advice column and from students on college campuses around the world, I can tell you: it's a fact. You are never alone in college.

As one resident director and recent graduate said to me, "They always say that college students deal with the same issues, but until I was a resident director, I never realized it was true. So many people are going through the same things, but don't know it." Each day is unpredictable. You never know what's going to come your way. That's part of the wild ride. In the words of an advisor I interviewed, "In college, you can have the best day of your life and the worst day of your life—and all within the same hour."

Welcome to your college experience.

Arriving on Campus

(1)

So Real You Can Smell It, Touch It, and Taste It

Dear Harlan,
How much of a change is college from high school
life? Is it a hard change to make?

—Curious about College

Dear Curious,
If you grew up sharing a room with a total stranger,
eating breakfast in a cafeteria-style kitchen, going to
classes with hundreds of people, coming home whenever you want, staying out as late as you want, bringing random guys or girls back to your room, and
being accountable to no one but yourself twenty-four
hours a day, college life should be little if any different than life in high school. If you are not doing these
things—it's different, very different.

The biggest difference between high school and college life is that you're in control. What you do in college is your choice. Who you want to do it with is your choice. When you want to do it is your choice. It's adult life, but with a safety net. Some people move too fast, some people move slowly, but no matter the speed you choose to go, if you find yourself losing your footing or heading out of control, you are surrounded by people who will help and support you.

As for change, I have a hard time with it. The only things I felt comfortable changing in college were my socks and underwear, assuming they were clean (a rare occurrence). The secret is to know yourself well enough to know what to expect. For example, if you're someone who has a history of having a hard time with change, expect college to be a challenging transition. If you can handle change well, expect fewer problems. Experiencing so many firsts so fast isn't always easy. But once you find your place in college, you'll probably *never* want to leave! College can be the best four, five, or six years of your life—but I hope it doesn't last six or more.

Tip #1
Expect the Unexpected

The Tip

Don't create too many expectations. You might think that you
know what will happen in college, but really, you don't.

The Story

I left for college expecting my
high school boyfriend and I to
stay together forever. Well, we
ended up breaking up in December of my freshman year. I had
always gotten A's in high school
classes. It was easy for me. I left
for college expecting to do the
same amount of work in college
as I did in high school (not all
that much) and to get the same
grades. In reality, I've never had
to work harder and no longer
always get the A. I thought my
friendships in college would be
the same as they were in high
school. But I soon learned that it
takes time to develop those same
kinds of friendships. Once I

Expectations versus Reality

96.9 percent of students
expected to make at least a
B average.

77.0 percent of students
actually did.

(But this book will help you
to get an A average.)

84.5 percent of students
expected to participate in
student clubs or groups.

48.8 percent of students
actually did.

(But this book will help
make it easier than ever
to get involved.)

33.8 percent of students
expected to seek personal
counseling.

10.7 percent actually did.

(But this book will make it
easier than ever to get help
along the way.)

—Higher Education
Research Institute
at UCLA

stopped expecting so much and started expecting the unexpected, college got so much better.

—freshman, Northwestern University

* * *

I know, you didn't expect this to be the first tip.

Welcome to your college experience. Right now, you're on that upward climb, preparing for what is guaranteed to be a wild ride. It's like a roller coaster moments away from running at top speed down the tracks, and unless you're able to handle the unexpected twists and turns ahead of you, you risk running off the tracks or just getting sick to your stomach. Not good.

While it's unnatural to leave for college with NO expectations, try leaving with flexible expectations. If your expectations are too rigid, when the unexpected pops its head up (and it will), you'll snap or possibly break. If you begin college with flexible expectations and can move with the unexpected twists and turns, the ride ahead will take you to places you never imagined. (I ended up as an intern at *The Tonight Show*, and then as a syndicated advice columnist—nothing I had ever imagined.)

If you and I were close enough that I could reach out and grab you by your shoulders (without you thinking I was making a move) and talk to you, I'd tell you exactly what I wish I could have told myself before heading to college.

Just relax.

Have fun.

Enjoy it all.

Your job is simple:

Be your personal best,

Meet lots of people,

Make new friends,

Make smart decisions,

Possibly find a career,

Possibly find love,

And take risk after risk after risk so that you can figure out what you love and what you don't love. Expect that all the risks you take will not always go as planned. Some will, but not all. When it doesn't go as expected, don't go on the attack, don't give up and hide—instead, look inward, look outward, and then move forward. If you do this, you'll leave college with more than a degree. You'll leave knowing what it takes for you to be happy. Really, what more could you want?

Bottom Line

When you expect the unexpected, you're better prepared when the unexpected arrives. Should it throw you, lean on the professionals on campus who have seen it all (or at least most of it) before.

Tip #2
Patience, Patience, and More Patience

The Tip
Don't expect everything to happen at once. It takes time.

The Story
Freshman year, I came to college expecting everyone to be

friends right away and for it all to be great, because that's the way they built it up in high school. They made us think college was going to be a perfect place. I got here and expected to wake up in the morning and love my classes, love my roommate, and love my friends, but I didn't—everything was not perfect. It took me a while to realize that it takes time. It took me a while to find friends—and I mean real friends, not just acquaintances. One of my friends lived in my hall, another one was in my classes, and another one was in theater crew. There was a defining moment our sophomore year when we realized we were such close friends. It happened on Valentine's Day; we were having dinner because none of us had a boyfriend. That's when we realized how close we had become. It still took a while before we could have screaming fights and know that it would be all right. Now, they are like family. It all took time. It also took me until junior year to realize what I wanted to do with my life. It might sound stupid, but I had to learn to chill out. I had to relax and let it all happen.

—junior, Brandeis University

* * *

I wanted to put this tip at the beginning of the book for those of you who are impatient and are contemplating skipping ahead to some of the more exciting tips—dating, drugs, sex, relationships, managing your checking account...

Most people get to college and want it *all* now. They want friends, grades, and the good life as soon as possible. While you might want it right away, appreciate that it doesn't always happen that way. New takes time. Like breaking in a new pair of shoes, a new pair of jeans, a crisp textbook, or a firm mattress fitted with extra-long twin sheets, it takes time for it all to feel right.

When you get to college and begin discovering that everything doesn't feel comfortable immediately, know that it's normal. Things like finding your way around campus, finding your classes, finding professors you like, finding a major that keeps you awake in class, finding great friends (or good ones), finding a roommate you actually like being around, and finding the best and cheapest wings, breadsticks, and pizza takes time.

If you're looking to speed up the process, leave for college with a plan. Head to school with a map of what you want to do and where on campus you can do it. (No, this isn't something you can find on MapQuest or Google Maps.) Use what you did in high school as a compass to guide you. There's more about this in Tip #4, but just understand that it can take weeks, months, and even years to find your place. That's why you need to be patient. It took me three semesters, two campuses, and *two* freshman years to figure it out. I was totally impatient. I either tried way too hard or just stopped trying. Had I only known, I could have been so much more patient and kinder to myself.

Bottom Line

Take good shoes, a favorite pillow, and lots of patience with you to college. You'll need them all to get comfortable.

Tip #3
Finding Your Place on Campus

The Tip

Get involved, join something, and meet as many new people as possible.

The Story

My senior year of high school was amazing. I was the prom king, president of my senior class, and King of the Year. I was dating a beautiful runner who was a state champion, I received more scholarships than I could count, and I set a school record in backstroke—as the first student from my school to go to state in years. Needless to say, I was feeling good!

> "Try not to allow your fear to consume you. If you follow what's in your heart, then you're on the right track. Just don't hold back."
>
> —junior, St. Peters College

Yet, immediately when I went to college, everything tottered and fell apart. No one knew me, not many of my friends went here, and my girlfriend broke up with me within two weeks. I wandered around pining and depressed for weeks, trying to figure out what had gone wrong. The moment I got involved with freshman orientation, a student organization on campus, everything turned around. I had new friends, a sense of purpose, and found my place at a huge university. Get involved with something that feels right and make as many new contacts as possible. It opens up a world of opportunity and creates strong new friendships. College went from a scary and foreboding realm to a place that I can call home.

— junior, Indiana University

* * *

Given that this is only the third tip, it's not a good idea for me to call this the most important tip of the book—then you might decide not to read the rest, throw the book away, or just return it. I'll just mention that this tip is extremely important.

The truth is that you might not find your place right away when you start college. It takes work and time. Everyone seems to forget to mention this to you. Finding your place is so important—because if you have no place, you'll

"When I first came here, they gave us a book that had events to go to. I went to a step show, I went to an ice cream social, and I went to some parties at the union and ran into some people I knew from a summer college program that I went to when I was in high school. I went to a poetry reading with my roommate and girl I met through her. We also met a couple new girls who were sitting behind us."

—freshman, Ohio State University

end up lost, and if you're lost with no place, there isn't anywhere to go, and that's when you will want to go home.

In high school, everything seemed to just kind of fall into place. You might have found your place by participating in athletics, the student council, plays, debate, a student newspaper, academic clubs, or some kind of other activity. Your parents might have pushed you in a particular direction, or maybe it was a friend or older sibling who helped you get involved. But in college, you have to work to be the one to help yourself find your place. Without as many friends around and without as much structure to your day, it doesn't all just happen right away.

Start with what you know and go from there. Seek out the places where you were most comfortable in high school. If you're athletic, figure out how you can get involved with club sports and intramurals (see Tip #31). If you're into academics, figure out how to get involved with academic clubs and organizations (see Tips #30 and #32). When in class, talk to your professors. Allow them to know you. Work to make new friends. The goal in doing all this is to make college comfortable. The more comfortable you can be, the better college will become. No matter the size of your school, leave for it with a plan. Visit your campus's website, talk to your resident assistant in the residence halls, talk to the people in the student activities office and counseling office. Talk to older grads from your high school who are already on campus. Just don't sit around waiting for the world to make you happy. You have to be the one to get up, get out, and get involved.

Bottom Line

Attending college is like attending a live event that has general seating. The ticket gets you inside the venue. You have to be the one to make the extra effort to find the place where you can be closest to the action and you're most comfortable.

Tip #4
When Lost or Confused, Ask

The Tip
Ask questions when you get confused. You'll be surprised at what you learn.

The Story
I came to campus not knowing very many people. It's easy to get lost. When I did get lost, I'd ask anyone who I thought could give me an answer. I'd ask my questions and the answers would lead to even more answers. When I got lost on campus, I'd ask for directions and find new places I didn't expect to find. People would give me their maps if they had an extra or direct me to a website. When I got tired of eating at my residence hall, I didn't know where to find other places to eat. So, I asked, and some guy told me about other places that I didn't know were part of my meal plan. When it came to preparing for classes, I asked people who had already taken the class in my major how to get through a class and how to study for certain professors. I asked questions and found answers.

—freshman, Ohio State University

* * *

Please note. This tip should come with a map, but there is no way to put a map of every college in every book. So please refer to your campus's website, print out a map, and staple or glue the map to this page (punch staple here _____).

Whether you leave with a plan for college or not, there's a good chance that you'll need some help getting around. You might need directions to a location on campus, you might need directions for getting involved in a club or organization, you might need directions for finding some new friends, or you might need directions for rushing a fraternity or sorority (see Tip #35). You might need directions for how to find the best defense attorney or bail bondsman (that would be bad). If you get to college and find that you need directions on how to find your place on campus, do not hesitate. Ask for directions. Most people will stop and help. Most won't steer you wrong.

"Moving to a new city my first year of college at age seventeen was a huge challenge. I was implanted into a new environment that was unfamiliar and surrounded by people that I wasn't sure how to communicate or relate to. I had to overcome financial and social challenges on my own. The strength these events contributed to my character is overwhelming and undeniable—something every college student should experience."
—senior, Cal State University–Fullerton

If you want to get somewhere quickly, ask for directions even before you get lost. Talk to all the support staff on campus to help you map out a course, and then check in with the same people while on your journey.

For example, map out where you want to go academically and where you want to go outside the classroom. Check out your campus's website and brochures before leaving for college. Contact students on campus via Facebook doing the things you want to (yes, this is cool). These people and places will be the maps to help guide you. And again, when you do find yourself getting lost or confused, turn and find help. It's all around you. Turn to people who look like they know where they're going for directions around campus (hint: they tend not to be people also looking at maps). Turn to your academic advisor for an educational map. Turn to professors to help you travel through each class. Talk to your resident assistant or an older friend on campus to help guide you socially. Turn to a religious club or organization to guide you spiritually. If you're looking for direction, you're lucky because there are so many people who want to help. Just do *not* be afraid to ask when you get lost along the way.

Bottom Line

If someone gives you wrong directions on purpose, don't feel like an idiot. Find the person again and thank them. Say, "Thanks, GREAT directions! Awesome short cut!" Then walk away before he or she can speak. This way, they'll either waste time trying to find the "short cut" or feel stupid for actually having helped you.

Tip #5
Be Yourself: Not Me, Not Him, Not Her

The Tip
Relax! Be yourself.

The Story
I was a freshman in college and knew virtually no one at my university. So, I decided that the best way to fit in was to fit in with a bunch of different groups and act like them

when I was around them. Well, what I didn't count on was the fact that a few people from each of the groups knew each other and started talking about me. It turned out that in the process of trying to fit in, I ended up with no friends and I didn't know who I was anymore. After that, I was just myself and people liked me a lot better that way. Now I have tons of friends and am happy with the "myself" I found in the process.

—graduate student, Eastern New Mexico University

* * *

A little story on this tip. It was a late addition to *The Naked Roommate*. It happened after most of this book was already written. After interviewing more than a thousand college students, researching hundreds of hours, and putting together all the ingredients that make up this book, one theme came through again and again. It's simple, but it's important—just be yourself. Don't be me. Don't be that guy sitting across from you. Don't be the girl over there.

> "Stay true to yourself and don't do what other people want you to do just because you want to fit in."
> —sophomore, Allegheny College

While there's nothing wrong with wanting to redefine yourself once you get to college, don't lose yourself. Start with who you are now and go from there. It's nice to run away from the past, but go slowly. Take small steps in new directions. A perk of attending to college is that, usually, there are more people than there were in your high school and more space. This means you can avoid the idiots you couldn't avoid in high school and can surround yourself with the good people who you want to be around. This also means less pressure to "fit in" because there are so many more places to fit.

Whatever you do, avoid becoming the person you think people want you to be just so they will accept you. When you change to be liked, you end up doing stupid, regrettable things that lead you to bad places and bad relationships (examples: getting into drugs, sleeping around, and crawling through dumpsters late at night while drunk looking for old hamburgers). This also tends to be when you start feeling lost and confused. Relax, and be true to yourself. If you don't know yourself, be patient, take smart risks, and figure it out. You've got time to find you.

> "Don't be afraid to do things that interest you even though other people don't think they're cool. This isn't the same as high school."
>
> —junior, University of Pittsburgh

Bottom Line
Try too hard to please the world and you end up pleasing no one. Be yourself and the world will be your friend—or at least the people who matter will.

Tip #6
About Your Parents...

The Tip
Work out a plan for when you're going to talk to your parents once you get to school. If you don't, plan on having problems.

The Story

I'm the older of two daughters. When I left for college, my parents and I didn't talk about when I would call or when they would call. I moved about five hours away. From the first day, they called me *every single night*. I'm not kidding. Please, we sent email and instant messages every day! They wanted to know what I was up to. They would ask me the same annoying questions night after night after night. There were questions about how specific classes were and about every single detail of my whole day. After a few nights there was nothing new to talk about. Still, they kept calling. A month or so into the semester, I started getting upset. It had built and built up. I didn't tell them sooner because, me being the oldest, and being five hours away, I was being nice to them. I didn't want to hurt their feelings.

One night, I lost it. I just kind of blew up at them. After getting in trouble for giving them so much attitude, they asked me, "Do you want us to call every night?" I was like, "No, I'll call you when I'm free." They were fine with that. It shocked me, but they're pretty understanding parents. A semester later, things are much better. We talk two to three times a week—and we regularly send email and instant messages.

—freshman, Texas A&M Commerce

* * *

Parents of college students can be categorized as follows: those who never leave you alone, those who leave you alone, those who want you to be thirteen forever, those who continue to check up on you to make sure you're home, and those who try to control you by using guilt, money, or hypnosis (although hypnotist parents are rare). All have their own approach, but it's all out of love (and not a love of making you miserable). They miss you. They love you. They want to hear from you. Appreciate that this whole college thing is also a transition for them. Appreciate what they're dealing with—debt, aging, your new independence, and for the first time, you possibly not living at home.

No matter what category your particular parent(s) fall into, there is a three-step approach to dealing with them.

1) Listen to them carefully.
2 Tell them you appreciate what they're saying and repeat their advice while doing so.
3) Then do what makes you happy.

Please note—this approach only works if you're being reasonable. If you're doing things like skipping classes, selling drugs, and drinking to the point of blacking out, they have a good reason to interfere. You might not be ready to be at college on your own.

Helicopter Parents

You've probably heard this term, and if you haven't, now you have. Basically, helicopter parents are hovering parentals who circle around campus, getting way too involved in life on campus. When something is wrong, they make it right. Instead of having their kids fix the problem, they make the calls, make the trip, and attempt to make everything better. Sometimes you ask for them to help, other times they take it upon themselves to help. A lot of times they can't help themselves. But don't just let them fix your life for you when things go bad. Encourage them to point you to the people, places, and resources on campus that can help, but you need to be the one to solve your problems. Professors don't enjoy calls from parents, residence life professionals don't look forward to calls from parents, your friends don't appreciate calls from parents. When you talk to your parents about a problem, tell them that you will fix it and ask for suggestions. If they ask if you would like them to write, email, or place a call on your behalf, thank them for wanting to help and then do it yourself. This is your life—it's your job, and it's your responsibility.

A Quick Parent Checklist

○ Set a regular time and day of the week to check in (Sundays work well).

○ Regularly keep in touch via email and instant messaging, but avoid asking them to solve your problems by contacting people at school. That's not their job.

○ Regarding campus visits, plan in advance when your parents will visit you, and plan when you'll come home. If you're close to home, set up some parameters on when they'll visit. A call the day before isn't asking too much.

○ When getting advice from them—wanted or unwanted—ask yourself if what they're saying is right for you. Things like picking a college major, rushing a fraternity or sorority, and going abroad could be possible issues. If they don't agree with your choices, make sure you have a strong support system on campus to support you.

○ Send them a thank-you card or letter. Mailing a card to your parents will make them very excited (see the Bottom Line).

Bottom Line
If you want to surprise, shock, and floor your parents, send them a handwritten thank-you card. They eat that card thing up (not literally). Note: say thank you and avoid asking for money in the same card.

Tip #7
Homesickness: Breathe Deep, It's in the Air

The Tip
The brochures usually show you the best, but every college has the other side, too. First semester is not the easiest or happiest. It's normal to get homesick.

The Story
The brochures never mentioned grabbing meals and sitting on my own in the cafeteria and then not going out on the weekends because I didn't have good friends to hang out with. No one mentioned that I could get depression (see Tip #100). No one told me that it was normal to go get homesick. After Thanksgiving, I started hanging out with new

"I had a friend was really homesick and down. She was thinking of transferring out. One of her main problems was that she never got out of her room. She was upset that she hadn't met anyone, but I was like—you can't meet people if you're in your room."

—freshman, Salve Regina University

friends in the dorms. Sometimes it can take longer. This isn't something that just happens here, it's everywhere. All my friends said the same thing. This is my second college this year, and it's been the same experience at both schools. Knowing that it's normal and what to expect makes it easier to handle.

—freshman, George Washington University

* * *

College brochures are filled with shiny, happy pictures of smiling students appearing to have the time of their lives. It's giggles and good times with images of cheerleaders cheering, students studying, and everyone smiling in picturesque spots on campus, arm in arm in a multicultural snapshot with everyone donning their officially licensed college logo–branded clothes. Coincidentally, it never rains, never snows, and always appears sunny on campus. This is the shiny part of the college brochure.

Homesickness: Who's Catching It?

- 62.7 percent of surveyed freshmen "frequently" or "occasionally" felt lonely or homesick

The not-so-shiny part of college is something you don't see. The truth is that life in college can also be difficult, lonely, and sad at times (and it does rain, snow, and get cloudy). The emotional pendulum swings both ways. And when you're swinging in the other direction, and you start yearning for the things that you once had at home, just know that it's normal.

I'll say it again: getting homesick is normal. It happens to most students. In fact, 62.7 percent of surveyed freshmen "frequently" or "occasionally" felt lonely or homesick. It usually hits mid-fall—after the newness fades to normal. You miss your bed, your friends, home cooking, and walking to the bathroom without having to wear flip-flops (and for God's sake, always wear flip-flops in the bathrooms—I can't stress this enough).

"It hit me in late October. I missed my friends from high school. A lot of work was coming down on me, and I missed hanging out, riffing with my friends from home. I have an older brother who went to a different college and went through the same thing. Had my brother not prepared me for what would happen, I think it all would have been so much harder."
—sophomore,
Carnegie Mellon University

Remember, the things you miss are the things that have been part of your life for years, things that took time to establish. The knee-jerk reaction is to run back to the familiar. There's nothing wrong with visiting home once in a while, talking with a friend online or on the phone, visiting a friend at another campus, or bringing home cooking back to school with you. But do it in moderation. The cure to homesickness is not at home—it's realizing how you made your old home so comfortable and doing the same things in your new home. If you do it right, by the time you graduate college, you'll be

"The best advice for finding male friends is to learn how to play any EA sports game. It's an obsession for some people, but don't play too much. I have a friend who failed out because he skipped classes to master the game."
—freshman,
George Washington University

homesick again—only this time you'll long to be back at school, your other home.

Bottom Line
Medicate yourself with small doses of home, friends, and familiarity. Use your past experiences to make your new life a home—then you can have two homes to be sick about when you graduate from college.

Tip #8
Technology: The Fifth Wall

The Tip
Don't stay in your dorm and live online. It's hard enough to explore on your own without having the Internet, online dating, instant messenger, video games, and all the other electronic gadgets that make being alone much more tolerable. You'll miss out on so much.

The Story
I hated the first college I attended and the community around it. I didn't exactly help myself make it work. The campus was in a very urban place and I didn't know anyone on campus. I wasn't the most outward person, which didn't help.

I'd literally spend some of my weekend nights at home online. I'd have a couple of beers, open instant messenger, and download umpteen punk rock classics online—for me that was quite a good night. I kept talking to people I previously knew from high school instead of getting out of my room and making an effort to meet more people. I was quite apathetic. It's just so easy to get lost in it. I'd hear the "ding" or "door opening" sound and then have to see who was online. And now people have these elaborate profiles and these online journals. Be careful not to live your life online.

—senior, Emerson College

✻ ✻ ✻

Like pop-up ads that just won't go away, there's a big issue that came up again and again during research for this book. This tip is another late addition (actually, I had to shift every tip up one to fit this one in here). This is the only college tip book where you'll find this particular one—that is, until more people hear about it.

There are actually five walls in your dorm room when you arrive in college. No, The Fifth Wall is not a wall of dirty clothes (that would be the sixth wall). This wall is invisible. It's the wall I call technology. This includes the Internet, instant messenger, email, cell phones, video games, and anything that takes an electric current to play. Getting caught behind The Fifth Wall happens when you least expect it. It works like this—college is naturally an unfamiliar and uncomfortable place. When in an unfamiliar place, your urge is to spend time in your comfort zone. This includes talking to friends from home, chatting online, hanging out on Facebook and MySpace, spending free nights and weekends talking to a long-distance boyfriend or girlfriend, dating online, instant messaging, reading and writing blogs, emailing the people closest to you, or playing video games. The Fifth Wall is easy to get stuck behind without even realizing it.

The risk is that you end up missing out on the moment. You risk missing out on meeting people face-to-face. You risk not getting involved with clubs, activities, and organizations because you're running back to your dorm room to jump online. You risk not knowing your professors because you just email them when an issue comes up rather than talking to them (they know your username or email address, but not your face). You risk depending on your parents for everything because you're in contact with them every day via email. You risk not being as patient or as flexible when twists and turns come up (instead of dealing, you'll just hide and complain to anyone who will listen). You risk getting homesick more easily because you're still so deeply rooted in everything that is part of your old life. You risk avoiding making new friends because all you do is talk to old ones. And should these old friends who are attending other colleges be having a better time than you, there's a decent chance you might start thinking about transferring. This is not what college is supposed to be.

I'm not saying that you should avoid the computer, email, instant messaging, calling friends, and playing video games. Just be careful not to overuse them (some people get addicted). Use, but don't abuse. Never before has it been so easy to physically be in once place but mentally in another. Watch out for The Fifth Wall—don't get stuck behind it.

Facing The Fifth Wall:
Facebook and MySpace

I don't know how to say it, so I'll just come out and say it. Be my friend. I'd really like for you to be my friend. Seriously, please be my friend. I need your friendship. I want your friendship. Give me your damn friendship...

What's in it for you?

As my Facebook and MySpace friend, you can look at pictures of me on the road. You can keep tabs on my mood swings. You can also keep up-to-date on my relationship status. At times, I will let you know what I'm eating for selected meals and what I'm wearing. Once in a while, I will post updates regarding competitive eating contests (I make those up). Last fall I provided regular updates on a candy corn eating contest sponsored by the Milwaukee Chamber of Commerce. I finished second with 54,543 corns in twenty-four hours (again, just a joke). Best of all, as my friend, you have a place to stay when you are traveling through Chicago (not with me, but I know a lot of hotels and city parks). I'd like for you to be my friend. Not only do I want your friendship, I'd also like you to join *The Naked Roommate* Facebook Group. You can find links at www.TheNakedRoommate.com or just look my profile up on Facebook and MySpace.

If you're not familiar with Facebook or MySpace, you are probably from another planet or your parents have locked you away. Basically, these online communities allow people to stay connected, hook up, and get rejected (but not face-to-face).

The good, not so good, and really not so good

The good

It feels good to get poked. It's nice to read the writing on the wall or posts on the profile page. There are so many ways to find out so much about people you would never talk to in real life without ever opening your mouth. You can find out personal interests, academic interests, and social interests. Not only do you get to read about it, there are pictures as well (I love pictures). You can see the people and the people in their lives. On top of that you can join interest groups, send out invitations to events on campus, and communicate via email. For someone who is looking at college or is new to college, online networks are a window into the world of college life that has never been visible before. And it's totally acceptable and not weird at all to send a note to someone on Facebook or MySpace. It can be the president of a club or organization, someone on a team sport, or a professional who can help you out. This is good.

The not so good

The problem is that some people use online networks as a substitute to actually approaching someone (shy people, strangers, stalkers). Facebook and MySpace should NEVER be a complete substitute for a face-to-face conversation. It should only be a first step. For example, even if you're checking someone out to consider hooking up, if you discover that person is in a relationship via their profile, this should only make it more comfortable to make a move. That's right—still get to know that person. You can use their profile to find out if that person is in a serious relationship, you can find out if the person is a cheater, or you can use it as a chance to say, "Of course you're in a relationship. I couldn't expect someone like you to be single for long." Then you can start a friendship with the person. Too many people assume too much based on these profiles. NEVER BEFORE HAS IT BEEN EASIER TO JUDGE SOMEONE BEFORE EVER MEETING THEM. It happens with friends, roommates, members of organizations. Be careful what you assume and be careful what other people assume. Use Facebook and MySpace as a way to meet people, not fantasize about or secretly follow people (aka, stalking).

The really not so good
Be careful what you post. If you're underage, don't post a picture of you drinking. If you're a leader on campus, don't post yourself doing something stupid. If you're doing something illegal, don't post yourself doing it. If you're a pageant contestant, don't post pictures of you flashing your thong at a bar. Potential employers, professors, friends, stalkers, and family have access to your information. Expect EVERYONE you don't want to view your pictures to view them. **Make sure to set your privacy settings.**

Another thing to keep in mind—Facebook and MySpace can become addictive. College life shouldn't mean spending hours on your computer living in online communities. With all the changes that come with college, online communities can become a substitute for real life communities. Use your online relationships to initiate real relationships. And one last thing before I'm done with this one—be careful you don't get expelled. Hate speech, groups that violate student codes of conduct, and illegal activities can get you in trouble. Students have been expelled and even arrested by the police because of their Facebook activities (see the Naked Roommate eNewsletter archives for links to stories).

Bottom Line

When you email me with questions (harlan@ helpmeharlan.com), please don't sit around for hours in front of your computer waiting for a reply. Get out. The reply will be there when you get back (give me a few days to a week). If I take too long to respond, write me again (I mean it).

Harlan's Tip Sheet

Arriving on Campus Resources, Support Services, Websites, and Additional Info

- *Visit your college's website.* Seriously, spend a few hours getting familiar with all the different parts of campus. You'll be surprised at what you'll find on the campus website. The more you know about your campus, the more comfortable you will become once you're there. Do this and you'll be totally prepared. If you don't do anything else on this Tip Sheet, do this.

- *Visit the Student Activities Office in person or online.* The Student Activities Office is similar to the student activities office in high school—it's where you'll find lists of student organizations, activities, and clubs. Pick organizations that you want to get involved with before you even get to campus.

- *Get in touch with former graduates from your high school who are attending the college that you'll be attending.* Don't hesitate to find them on Facebook or MySpace and send them a message (it's not weird). Ask them any questions you have. They've been there and done that. Don't hesitate to call. Then you will know someone on campus.

- *Attend summer/fall orientation.* Whatever type of orientation program your school has, absolutely go to it. It helps. It's a way to meet students and professionals on campus and become familiar with the place that you'll call home for the next four (or more) years.

- *Visit your campus before classes begin.* Take advantage of the campus tours organized through the college. At the least, take a trip there with a few friends.

- *Visit the counseling office (in most cases therapy is free).* If you're a little uncomfortable before going to college or uncomfortable once you get to college, it's helpful to have a contact on campus who can help you. If you're going to school with a medical condition, make sure that you identify people who can help you and a plan should you need medical attention.

- *Read your college's campus newspaper.* In most cases, you can find them online. If you don't have a great newspaper on campus, check out the local newspaper. This will give you a feel for what's happening on campus and in the community, and an idea of how you can participate.
- *Set your privacy settings on Facebook and MySpace.* You never know who's checking you out.

Residence Halls ②

Living, Eating, and Bathing with Hundreds of Strangers

*Commuter students: feel free to flip ahead to Tip #24 or keep reading for fun. I just wanted you to know that I was thinking about you.

Dear Harlan,

I can't decide on where I want to live in college. The problem is, I have a two-year-old puppy that I love very much and I want to take her with me. However, many people have told me that if I don't live in a dorm I won't make friends that easily. I am a very shy person, so it would be benficial to me to be around people my own age in a dorm. On the other hand, if I could choose between sharing a bathroom with twenty girls or having my own bathroom and own apartment (money is no problem), I would choose the apartment. Plus, I would get to bring my puppy.

What should I do?

—Dilemma

Dear Dilemma,

If your puppy went to college and she were given the choice to either live in a residence hall for a year, where she could meet different breeds of puppies from around the world, or live off campus in a cage far away from everyone else, what would she do? While all the other puppies are eating together, walking to classes together, playing together, and sniffing each other, your puppy would be isolated, away from the activity, sniffing herself. Sure, your puppy could visit, but being a shy puppy makes it more difficult.

The best choice is to live with all the other puppies. Sure, the living conditions might not be as comfortable at times, but the positive side of life far outweighs the negative—at least for a year. Residential life helps freshmen with the college transition. In addition to being with all the other new students, there are RAs (resident assistants) who live in the residence halls to help answer questions and address issues and obstacles. There are floor activities, flyers on the walls to recruit new students for new activities, and plenty of people to hang out with. There are sometimes even classrooms in the residence halls. Living in an apartment is the perfect way to isolate you and your puppy from the college experience, making you both sad puppies.

Tip #9
Residence Halls:
A Cruise without the Water

The Tip
At all costs, live in the dorm your freshman year!

The Story
The words "girls' dorm" not only sent chills up my spine, but made me want to puke as well. So when I found out I had no choice but to live in the dorm, I wanted to shoot myself in the foot. I have never been what you call a "girly girl." When naming my friends, I would almost always name more guy friends than girls. I had no desire to live in a building with a bunch of giddy girls. Boy, was I wrong. The girls on my hall have truly been one of the highlights of college life, much to my astonishment. They always have a willing ear to listen when I need to talk, and we have made some wonderful memories such as doing cartwheels down the hall, having midnight ice cream parties in our rooms, and representing our dorm in intramural volleyball. (Go North Russell Rockers!) As corny and cheesy as it may sound, they are no longer the giddy girls that I had stereotyped in my mind; they have become more like my sisters whom I have grown to love and cherish. So if you are considering not living in the dorm your freshman year, consider it no longer. Live in the dorm. It is only for a

year, and you will be surprised at how many fantastic people you will have the opportunity to get to know.

—freshman, Baylor University

* * *

Residence halls, dormitories, dorms, campus housing—whatever you call it, these are the places most new students who live on campus call home. They are long halls filled with hundreds of mostly clueless people on a common journey. It's like a cruise, but without the swimming pools, room service, spa, casino, alcoholic drinks, ports of call, free midnight buffets, fine dining, all the water, and the boat. See, exactly like a cruise.

Bonus Tip

ALWAYS wear flip-flops in the showers. If the floors could talk, they wouldn't speak, they'd just scream!

Living in a residence hall is a once-in-a-lifetime experience, so you should experience it at least once in a lifetime (more if you enjoy it). Living in campus housing is so important the first year that some campuses require new students to do it. It's required because not living on campus means missing out on so much. The logic is to put all new students in a place where everyone is equally as clueless, naïve, lost, and seeking to find their own place in one place. There's an electricity that buzzes in first-year residence halls (if the buzz is too loud, call maintenance, but don't expect them to come right away). And if that doesn't excite you, appreciate that it's just easier living. There is enough going on during your first year of college to not have to deal with things like paying bills, paying rent, setting up utilities, dealing with landlords, getting cable, getting groceries, finding a place to live, getting to classes, and setting up Internet connections.

Yes, it's true that living with so many people can get annoying, irritating, and disgusting, but the alternatives do not compare to what you do get. If you're a commuter student, look into living on campus. Between the cost of traveling, the inconveniences of driving, and the challenges of feeling connected to campus life, you might be better off living on campus. Talk to a financial aid advisor and see if you have any options. But everyone should do it at least once.

Perks of Residence Life

- Meet people without even trying.
- Possible amenities include cable, Internet, heat, bathroom suites, a gym close by, air conditioning, coed floors, study suites, libraries, on-site counseling, free tutors, twenty-four-hour computer access, mini food marts, and dining options.
- Help, support, and answers to your questions are just a few doors away.
- Great location—usually near classrooms, campus, and transportation.
- Floor activities on the weekends (and often on weeknights) and opportunities to participate in residence life student government.
- Flyers, notes, and general information flows on bulletin boards, on walls on the way to the cafeteria, and in any common area.
- Reasonable cost (in most cases).

Bottom line
Live in a residence hall. It's worth the cramped quarters. (For more information on quarters, see Tip #96 about doing laundry.)

Tip #10
Meet People without Even Trying

The Tip
Always leave your door open. Close it only if you're sleeping or not at home.

The Story
I was the kind of person who, unless I knew someone or was comfortable around them, I wouldn't be around them. At first, when I got to college, I was like, I'm keeping my door shut, because I didn't know anyone. The second day after keeping my door shut, I started to hear people outside my room. It happened all the time. I felt like I was missing out on college life. That day when I opened my door I literally started to meet people. People would just come in and say hi. They just stopped in. I lived in a six-floor high rise and it was coed by room. Keeping my door open helped me make so many friends (a lot of them athletes that lived on my floor). The friendships I formed those first few weeks on campus have lasted throughout my college life. I made a group of friends that all lived in the same hallway. Four years later,

a few of them transferred, some moved off campus, but we're all still in touch, even today.

—senior, University of Akron

* * *

Living in campus housing makes meeting people as simple as waking up, eating lunch in the cafeteria, going to classes, coming home, eating dinner in the cafeteria, and going out at night. It's easy because most freshmen come to college without friends at the same school. Considering that most people need friends, meeting people and making friends becomes pretty easy. Even if you're shy or antisocial, you'll meet people while living in a residence hall who will become part of your life (to the antisocial people—sorry).

It all starts with being forced to meet your roommate(s). Then there are all those friends of your roommate(s) you'll meet. Then there are the people in your hall. Then there are people in your classes who live in student housing (you can walk back to your room together and study for exams together in the study lounges). Then there are all the people in the dining hall that you see again and again, many whom you'll eat with. Then there are people at parties who look familiar from seeing them in the residence halls. Then there are opportunities like floor events, hall events, and all campus events. Familiar people from the residence halls will become the people with whom you become friends. And another perk worth mentioning—with coed dorms and even coed floors, you can find more than friends by living in student housing.

The opposite of on-campus housing is off-campus housing or private housing. And yes, living in an apartment off campus, living with a boyfriend or girlfriend, or living in a place other than a residence hall means missing out on an opportunity to meet people.

Quick note to transfer and commuter students: try to live on campus your first year. Even if you end up with freshmen, it's worth it. If you just can't live on campus, find friends who do live on campus. It will give you a place to crash and a way to meet other new friends. This can give you the best of both worlds.

Bottom Line
It's hard not to make friends while living in the residence halls (but if you really want to avoid making new friends, it's possible. For help on not making friends, see Tip #8).

Tip #11
Resident Assistants:
Your Personal Assistant

The Tip
Don't be afraid to talk to someone else's RA. If you don't mesh with your RA, find another one who can help.

The Story
When I first moved into the residence hall freshman year, my roommate and I didn't get along very well. I went to the RA on my floor and she wasn't supportive at all. She didn't listen to me and didn't help very much. It

was extremely frustrating. That's when I started spending more time on my friend's floor. She lived below me. I mentioned my problems to the RA on my friend's floor. She not only listened, she helped me find ways to deal with my impossible roommate, and kind of took me under her wing. She adopted me as one of her own residents. It made life so much better. One time she called me to invite me to a floor program she was running. They were making homemade chapstick and she called me up. She said, "You should really join us because you practically live here." Second semester, after moving out of the room with my roommate from hell, my surrogate RA from the floor below continued to check in to make sure I was happy with my new living situation. She turned a hostile situation into one that was livable. She made living in the residence halls a lot more enjoyable. This year, I got lucky enough to get on her floor. Now she's my RA for real!

—sophomore, University of Miami–Coral Gables

* * *

Some people call them Resident Assistants. I've heard them called CAs, and I've also heard them called other names (but I can't publish those). For this tip, I'm going to call them RAs, but you can change the RA if you get confused—grab some Wite-Out, cover up RA, and fill in the appropriate initials that represent your RA.

Your RA is typically a student employee who lives, eats, and showers in the residence halls with the students (no, he or she shouldn't actually shower with you). Your RA's job (and it's a paid job) is to make sure those living in the residence halls are comfortable in their homes and following the rules. It's a best friend–worst enemy relationship—best friend if you follow the rules, worst enemy if you break them.

Most RAs are there for the right reasons: to make your life comfortable. If you have a question or concern, talk to your RA. Should you need help dealing with a difficult roommate, talk to your RA. Should you need to find a new roommate, talk to your RA. Talk to your RA if you need directions to class, suggestions for a place to order in food, help dealing with dropping or adding classes, help adjusting to college life—the list goes on. If your RA doesn't have an answer, he or she can direct you to the people who can help you. If your RA is too busy or apathetic to help you with your problems, try an RA on another floor, your residence hall staff, and the office of residence life.

If your RA is a miserable lump and ignores you and your floor's needs—don't let it go. Report him or her. They are supposed to be there for you. Every RA has a supervisor and those supervisors have supervisors. Don't stop until you get answers. Should you find that your link to campus is an RA looking for a free ride, don't hesitate to make noise.

Bottom Line

Resident Assistants are paid friends who are there to help you (although they can bust you). They know the campus, know professors, and know how to navigate the system. Take advantage of them, but don't let them take advantage of you. Never date your RA.

Tip #12
Not All Residence Halls Are Created Equal

The Tip
Figure out what your campus has to offer in the way of student housing before getting to campus, and get your housing application in as soon as possible. When it comes to housing, it is often first come, first served.

The Story
As a senior resident assistant, I've seen a lot. I had one student who came down to school and was the last one to move into the student housing. She realized she was going to the get the bed that was up high and also the smaller closet. She ended up moving to another housing unit and then came back to the original one. If she had investigated the student housing, she would have known what she was getting into. Some of our students live in eight-person town houses, and we also have four-person campus views with doubles and singles. What living arrangement you get also depends on pricing and when you sign up. This is pretty much standard at most campuses where I have friends. Another suggestion to new students is to get there early. A lot of students will come the night before and stay in a hotel. It helps to get there early if they want to get the good closet, the right bed, the desk near the window, and the dresser on the right side of the room. Also, if you get there earlier, there's a better chance of changing your room. Whomever gets there first gets to put their stuff all over the room.

—senior, Shawnee State University

This tip is pretty self-explanatory, but I'll explain it anyway.

Not all residence halls offer the same amenities and crea-ture comforts. Each has its own look, feel, and personality. Shop around. For example: dorm rooms come in singles, doubles, triples (the most I've heard is four in a room). Bathrooms are community, suites (two rooms sharing one common bathroom), or private. Some residence halls are all men or all women. Some are coed by floor or by room (that's every other room, although some schools are considering coed rooms for couples). Some halls have visiting hours and/or quiet hours. There are ones with dining halls, ones with no dining halls, ones with little mini-marts inside, and ones with only vending machines. Ones with dining halls might offer different dining options (like fast food franchises as opposed to just fast food) and different dining hours (some are closed on the weekend). Some halls are gigantic and others are tiny. Some are close to campus, others are far away. Some are newer, others are older. There are ones filled mostly with freshmen, ones with sophomores, and ones with upperclassmen. Some allow alcohol, but most don't. There can be parking or no parking. There may be class-rooms or no classrooms inside the buildings, big study lounges or no study lounges, computer labs or no computer labs, RAs on every floor, RAs on every other floor, or just one RA per building. Some are more liberal and others are more conservative. Some are filled with athletes, some with international students, some with students in living and learning communities (programs where students attend class together and live together). Some are more diverse.

Some lack total diversity. Some are less expensive and others more expensive. You get the idea.

Clearly, not all dorms are created equal. To get the inside info, one idea is to talk to the people already living in the places you want to live. You can do this during a campus visit (make sure you're there at a time students will be on campus). Just hang out near the residence hall and ask people questions. If you're not going to be on campus or feel like a freak stopping people, don't. You can also find students to contact via Facebook (people share their residences in their profile). Just send them a note (no, not weird).

When you arrive on campus, give your hall a try, and consider switching if you really don't like it. Contact your RA or the office of residence life. But before running to switch residence halls, remember that sometimes the newer halls are for the upperclassmen. While they might be nicer, it's better to live with freshmen. You can try to switch second semester, if you must. Each campus has different types of residence halls and different rules on when and how you can switch rooms, but you can usually work something out. Once you get to campus, you'll get a better sense of what the right fit means for you.

Bottom Line

The best place to live on paper might not be the best on campus—talk to upperclassmen from your high school or get in touch with current students via the admissions office, orientation office, and housing office and find the best places to live.

Tip #13
The Ugly Side of Residential Life

The Tip
I don't care where the dorm is or who lives there—always lock your door and your window when you're not in the room.

The Story
The old not-locking slapped me twice my freshman and sophomore years, at two different dorms. My roommate and I used to forget to lock our room's door—we knew our suitemates a little, so maybe the fear wasn't there. I woke up one October morning and saw the door wide open, a pile of weird sweats and tube socks on the floor. Turns out a drunken suitemate had disrobed in our room, thinking it was his, and later passed out naked in the right room. The lock was checked by each of us every night thereafter.

   The next year our room was broken into, along with a dozen others, over Thanksgiving Break. The guys were never caught, and they went through all the rooms with unlocked windows. Apparently the screen wasn't enough security. Weirdly, they left the TV, my roommate's computer, all of my CDs (I was offended), and my PlayStation, taking only my roommate's old Super Nintendo and games. Completing a collection, no doubt. But they also searched through my underwear drawer, a deep violation I'll never shake. The moral? Whoever you live with, no matter where, check the locks. Often. It's a dog-eat-Super Nintendo world out there.

—sophomore, University of
North Carolina at Chapel Hill

* * *

In all fairness, I needed to include a tip that exposes the underbelly of residential life.

Most of the time, the ugliness is minimal, but the following highlights potential ugliness and ways to prevent the problems.

Narrow-minded people, selfish people, stupid people, arrogant people, ignorant people, people who steal, people who vomit in the bathroom sink, people who cut their hair and/or nails in the bathroom and leave trimmings on the floor, people who don't flush, shouting in the hallway, ridiculously noisy neighbors, weird floaters on the bathroom shower floors, odd odors, garbage in the hall, cigarette smoke, pulled fire alarms (yes, always evacuate), absurd rules, bizarre roommates (see next chapter), and RAs who think they're on an episode of *COPS* can be a serious nuisance. Should you have problems (and moving is not possible), instead of letting these things worsen or idly bitching and moaning, talk to the people on campus who can make things better (no, do not let your parents fix the problems—you do it). If the people who are supposed to fix the problem become a new problem, then talk to the residence hall director. If that doesn't work, then talk to the director of residence life. Get names. Document your journey through what can be a bureaucratic mountain of manure. Keep going until you reach the college president's office. And if that fails, get the media involved as a last resort—the campus newspaper, the local newspaper, the local TV news. The last thing a college wants is for parents, future students, and alumni to hear about how terrible life is on your campus—that's bad PR. Do not get pushed around.

And be smart with your stuff—keep your doors and windows locked at all times when you're not around. Even if you're leaving for five minutes to shower, lock your door. Also, consider getting a footlocker to keep your expensive electronics, games, and other valuables (keep it locked). People who want what you have will work fast to get it. Put your name and ID on your personal items (I engraved my license number into digital equipment). Keep your electronic passwords protected and change them frequently. Don't leave jewelry, cash, checks, credit cards, or bank statements sitting out. Keep valuables hidden in a small locked box in your closet or buried in a drawer.

Bottom Line

Appreciate the ugly side of residential life for all its beauty. It's all part of what makes this a once-in-a-lifetime experience.

Harlan's Tip Sheet

Residence Hall Resources, Websites, and Additional Information

- *The office of residence life.* This is the place where the director of the residence halls works. If you have issues that need to be resolved, this is the place to go. If your residence hall has an information desk, you can talk to your hall director.
- *The dean of students office.* The dean of students or president's office is where you can find the people running the college. If you can't get answers to your question, concern, or problem in the office of residence life, head to the higher-ups.
- *Residence hall student government.* Check out the residence hall government. This is great way to get involved and make new friends.
- *Floor activities/hall activities.* Attend these events. At least check them out. Go alone so other people who go alone can meet you and not be alone.
- *Get your housing application in early.* The sooner you apply the better your chances of living where you want.
- *Changing residence halls.* Every college has a different policy. Talk to your RA, the director of your residence hall, and then the head of residence life. If you find yourself in the wrong residence hall for whatever reason, talk to someone immediately. There are often

waiting lists to change rooms. Do not stop making noise until you get results that will ensure your comfort.

- *Dining options.* Different residence halls often offer different dining hours and food options. Some residence halls have fast food options in different dining halls. What you have at your hall isn't necessarily what's being served in other halls. Ask your RA.
- *Put your name on everything.* Engrave your electronics using an engraving gun. Put an ID number or your name on it. It makes it easier to identity it should it get stolen.
- *Rules and regulations.* If you follow the rules, there's no problem. Most resident assistants are cool about things. Most of them follow the motto: "We just don't want to see it, hear it, or smell it," because they don't want to have to deal with it.
- *What to bring.* Don't bring everything. Leave your "maybe" pile at home. You can have it sent to you or you can get it on a quick trip home. For example, don't bring all your winter clothes in fall. As for CDs, burn them into MP3s. People love to steal CDs. As for jewelry and irreplaceables, leave them at home, or at least most of them.
- *About pets.* Start off with a plant. Keep it living for a semester, then move onto fish. Check out rules about pets, but college isn't the best atmosphere for pets that you want to live long and healthy lives.

3

Roommates

Good Ones, Bad Ones, and Everything in Between

Dear Harlan,

My roommate and her boyfriend are driving me crazy. They fight constantly and then they have make-up sex every day. I try to keep my nose out of it and ignore them, but they are constantly in our room. They never go to his place because she doesn't like his roommate. If I'm in our room alone watching TV or studying, they come in and take over the whole place. They'll change the channel or be loud and wrestle while I'm working. If I leave the room for even a second, they put up our "signal" on the door, which means they're having sex, so I can't come back in. I've tried talking to her, but she just laughs and denies being rude. I'm at my wit's end. What do I do?

—Ready to Move Out in Wisconsin

Dear Ready to Move Out,

A roommate who denies being rude is a roommate stuck in rude denial, one of the rudest forms of roommate rudeness. The question is, how can you you get her out of rude denial? You can try being equally rude, but then she'll just think you're being rude and then have a reason to be rude on purpose, which will probably be far ruder then the way she's acting now, considering she doesn't think she's rude.

Try this approach—tell her that you want to talk, but don't accuse her of anything. Explain in the friendliest way that something has been weighing on your mind and that you wanted to talk to her about it. Ask her if she could try to put herself in your shoes. Then explain what has been happening that's so upsetting to you. Pick out specific examples when this has happened. Then ask her, what would she do if she were you? Ask what the best way to approach you would be. The hope is that she will begin to see the problem from your perspective and come out of rude denial. Then she can even help come up with solutions to the problem.

You might want to then add in a few of your own ideas. Ask her to keep the "signal" to a maximum number of times a week. Also, consider creating another "signal" that means you need time to yourself. If she's still unresponsive and rude, then talk to your resident assistant. Have him or her help you find a way out. If your roommate wants to get along, your roommate will find a way to get along. But first, she needs to come out of rude denial. Then you'll find out if she wants to get along.

The Tip
Respect each other's differences and make rules before you need rules.

The Story
My roommate was totally different from me in more ways than I can ever even explain, but we always had college in common. That was enough to help us get along. We respected our differences and wanted to get along. We created room rules together to avoid uncomfortable situations that could become big problems in the future—things like smoking in the room, overnight guests, sharing food, and cleaning needed rules to avoid big problems. Lastly, I knew coming into this that not all personalities mesh. You can be great roommates and not be great friends. As it happens, we turned out to be great friends.

—sophomore, Bay Path College

* * *

Assuming you've never spent time in prison and don't intend on spending time in prison, this could be the only time in your life that you'll spend a year or more living with a complete and total stranger. Until you've experienced living in an eight-by-eight-foot room with someone you've never met before,

"If you have a conflict, you need to work it out as soon as possible."
—senior, Bentley College

it's hard to understand what it takes to get along. Even if you're living with someone you know extremely well (this tip applies to college students of all ages), even the most compatible roommates will have disagreements. Whether it's in a residence hall, an apartment, a fraternity or sorority house, or even at home, conflict is unavoidable. How you and your roommate deal with it makes all the difference.

The best way to start the roommate relationship is to set a precedent early. Have a conversation and make it clear that you want to get along. Then ask your roommate to let you know when you do something that makes him or her uncomfortable. Then ask if it's cool for you to do the same. This will let you get comfortable with the uncomfortable. Then, when a problem comes up, instead of a confrontation, it's a conversation. If you want to get along and your roommate wants to get along, you'll get along. If not—welcome to roommate hell.

And that's the ultimate tip to remember when living with a roommate: *roommates who want to get along find a way to get along.* You don't need to be best friends. You don't even have to be friends. You just have to want to get along.

It's always helpful to try and gauge if your roommate wants to get along before moving in together. For example, when you talk on the phone for the first time during the summer, mention a minor concern that you might have. It

---

How Much Trouble Are Roommates?

48.6 percent of students surveyed reported "frequently" or "occasionally" having difficulty getting along with roommate(s)/housemate(s)

—Higher Education Research Institute at UCLA

could be people smoking in the room (blame it on allergies), strange people spending the night in the room (blame it on your parents), or concern over getting to sleep for your 7:30 AM classes (blame it on not wanting to fail). Casually mention one thing that concerns you most. Do not go through a list of every single small issue on your mind. Just test the waters. If you sense that your roommate neither cares nor wants to get along with you, be concerned. Responding to you with, "Too bad. Sounds like your problem, not mine," is a bad sign. Try having another conversation or two and give your future roomie another chance. If he or she doesn't have a better attitude when you arrive on campus, consider finding a new roommate. Be careful not to confuse likes and dislikes as fundamental issues. A roommate doesn't need to be your best friend—just someone who will respect you, your space, and your stuff.

> **"Someone didn't pick up this little candy wrapper that was sitting out...it was there for four days and then the dam broke. That's when they had a blowout."**
> —sophomore, Thomas College

> The Naked Blog:
> The Roommate Honeymoon Ends.
> See www.TheNakedRoommate.com.

Bottom Line

Roommates who want to get along will find a way to get along. As a rule, make rules before you need to make rules.

Tip #15
The Random Roommate

The Tip
Avoid judging your roommate based on first impressions.

The Story
The summer before I entered college, I remember getting really excited about who I was going to live with, who my "random rooming person" would be. The day finally came when I got her name and contact information in an envelope. I was so excited. I ran straight inside and called her. She didn't seem as enthused as I was, and it didn't seem like we had anything in common. We talked a few times before school, and still there was no real connection, so I was scared. On move-in day, her stuff was already in the room, so I looked at her shoe and movie/CD collection to try to get a feel for the type of person she was. I got mixed messages from the dozen Disney movies and the stack of Metallica CDs that took up her bins. We were different and I didn't know if we would be friends. As the days went on, we got along fine, respected each other, and had fun. It's funny, because we don't know when exactly it was that we clicked, but we became friends—best friends, even. We joke around that

> "Don't spend all your time freshman year with your roommate that you just met. I did everything with my roommate my first year only to realize that I had no other friends. As I found out more about her, I didn't want to spend time with her."
>
> —junior, UC–Davis

we'd never have been friends in high school. We have different interests, but we connected on the same level. After freshman year, I had to transfer to a school that was in-state because of financial reasons (and then I was ten hours away from her). Leaving her

and my hall of friends that I had grown to know and love was so hard. It has been three years since I lived with her, but we talk at least two times every single day, and I've been to visit a few times each year. She is still my best friend.

—senior, George Mason University

* * *

For your entire life, you're told to avoid complete strangers, then you're thrown into a room with one (sometimes more than one). It's a strange phenomenon. It's like *The Real World*—only this time it's real and no cameras are rolling (you hope). For some roommates, all you'll find that you have in common is college, breathing, and the same clothing (until you realize your similar tastes in clothing is actually your roommate stealing your clothes). No matter what kind of roommate you find living in your room with you, remember this—strangers are only strange until you get to know them better. Then they're just weird.

It's normal to pass judgment on a new roommate when you first meet; chances are that your roommate will do the same thing. Actually, with Facebook and MySpace it's easier than ever to pass judgment on a new roommate without ever meeting. You might decide not to get along before even seeing each other in person (don't do that). The user profile doesn't tell the story. There's the heavy metal roommate who turned out to be the clean, kind, and sober roommate; the pretty cheerleader roommate who turned out to be anything but the self-indulged popular girl her roommate expected her to be; and the roommate who he thought was a cool guy, but turned out to be anything but cool. It works both ways. It can take months to honestly know your roommate. Give him or her a chance before slapping on a label.

That said, not all roommates will get along and become best friends. A lot learn to tolerate each other. If your roommate doesn't want to be your new best friend, don't let it keep you from getting along. Living together isn't about becoming best friends, it's about getting along well enough to go to school. If you turn out to be friends, it's a bonus. Creating too many expectations will only leave you disappointed or forcing friendships that shouldn't happen.

Bottom Line

Don't judge your roommate until you live together for a couple months. Then judge your roommate and invite your roommate to judge you. When judging, it's sometimes more fun to actually dress up like a judge. Then your roommate knows that it's judgment time.

Tip #16
The Naked Roommate

The Tip
Realize that all people have different comfort levels with themselves and their bodies.

The Story
My first roommate in college was a very nice and interesting girl. Then, out of nowhere, she began to walk around without her shirt on. Not just in my room, either! She would walk in the halls, other people's rooms, boys' floors, and even in the office area of our dorm. To say the least, everyone has seen the girl in her bra. At first, it kind of bothered me, but after a few months, I have realized that it's just how she is. Plus, it could be worse—I mean, at least she wasn't walking around completely naked.

—sophomore, Loyola University–Chicago

> **Recommended listening while reading this tip:**
> "My Roommate Stu"
> (Available at www.TheNaked Roommate.com, iTunes, and CDBaby.com).

✳ ✳ ✳

Nudity is like the cafeteria food served in the residence halls; everyone reacts differently. Some get completely disgusted, others delight in the experience. The bad experiences can spoil your appetite. The good can leave you hungry for more.

> "My sorority sister walked in early and her roommate was sprawled out on the futon, totally naked. The next week the naked roommate moved out. I guess she needed her own space."
> —junior, University of Georgia

Nakedness in a room is unavoidable—we are all naked at some point. Some of you might be naked right now (please, put something on). While researching the naked roommate tip, I came across three forms of roommate nakedness.

Category I: The "I'm Naked, Look at Me" Roommate

This category of the naked roommate likes to walk around as if nudity were normal. They work in the nude, order take-out food in the nude, play video games in the nude, chat online in the nude, and lounge on your furniture in the nude. When someone says something to the naked roommate about his or her nudity, this roommate tends to be surprised. These roommates can be considered borderline or all-out nudists. Nakedness is freedom. Should you live in this environment, make it clear that it's not about his or her body, it's just that you're not quite comfortable with their level of nakedness. If you have to come to a compromise, perhaps your roommate can wear boxers, or a thong. Should you find yourself in this situation, take the top bunk and put plastic on the furniture.

> "My roommate likes to change when the door is open. She doesn't seem to care that boys from other floors are walking by—come to think, that's probably why they're always walking by our room."
> —freshman, University of Georgia

Category II:
The "I'm Naked, Do Not Look at Me" Roommate

This naked roommate doesn't like being nude. They don't like to be looked at or to be near anyone while they are nude; this includes themselves. This roommate is highly averse to any shape or form of nakedness. Their extreme uncomfortableness with their own naked bodies spills over into the common living situation. These roommates often exhibit behavior such as dressing in the closet, performing the "underwear under" maneuver (putting on his or her underwear while still covered by the towel), making an announcement such as "I'm changing, turn around," or directing your attention elsewhere by pointing out the window ("Wow! Look! A rainbow!"). If you're afraid of nudity, the best approach is to get comfortable with your own nudity. If you're living with someone who can't handle nakedness in any shape or form, don't force them to change—let them change where, when, and how they want to change.

> "I got sick of looking at my best friend's face, hearing my best friend's voice, and smelling my best friend's gas."
> —senior, University of Illinois

Category III:
The "I'm Naked, But Didn't Mean for You to See Me (Or Us)" Roommate

Two words—surprise nakedness. It's a shock to the nude and the clothed. It can happen after a shower, while in a sexual situation (with or without a partner), while changing, or while lounging. The best approach is to laugh (but not while pointing at any particular body part) or to apologize and never mention it again. If it happens more than once, say something sooner rather than later. If not, this will evolve into the "I'm Naked, But My Roommate Doesn't Care That I'm (We're) Naked, So I'll (We'll) Continue Being Naked" Roommate.

Whatever the level of nakedness in your room, the more you allow it to happen, the more likely it will become a habit. (And if it makes you uncomfortable, follow the precedent in Tip #14 and address the undress.) As a general rule, someone will be naked at some time. It's the law of roommate living. Address the undress or accept the naked truth.

> "There is nothing to gain by living with a friend. It's a lose-lose situation."
> —senior, Bentley College

Bottom Line

When finding yourself living with a naked roommate, ALWAYS take the top bunk, put towels on the furniture, and request that there is no eating in the nude (for your health and his or her safety—cheese pizza can be hot and dangerous). If you are the naked roommate, then be kind and courteous while naked.

Tip #17
The Best Friend Roommate

The Tip
Do not live with your best friend from high school.

The Story

I made the mistake of living with one of my best friends from high school. We got along, but we got so sick of each other. We just got on each other's nerves. It's not like we ever threw down or anything like that—at the worst it was throwing a plate of French fries at him, but no punches. The biggest problem with living together was that it was harder to meet new people. We were always chilling in the room. It was way too easy to stay inside and do nothing. I did meet some new friends, but we shouldn't have lived together our first year. It could have waited. Honestly, I do feel like I missed out.

—junior, DePaul University

> "Don't live with a large group of friends. It sounds like fun but by the end of the year we wanted to kill each other. We constantly talked behind each other's backs and could barely communicate. Since moving out, we've become friends again, but I would never again live with people that close to me."
>
> —senior, UCLA

* * *

Living with a best friend in college is like eating ten pounds of chocolate every day for ten months out of the year. What once made you happy can make you sick. (If you don't like chocolate, please substitute ten pounds of your favorite candy or food.) No matter what you think about rooming with friends, there is definitely much more to lose than there is to gain (yes, it can work, but that's not the point of college). Here's why:

1. Best Friends Don't Try as Hard to Get Along

When you've known someone for most of your life, they don't always try as hard to please. A best friend is more likely to leave the room messy, expel gas at will, and abuse your stuff. The more comfortable the relationship, the more complacent the people in the situation tend to become. Cleaning, respecting each other's space and things, and following rules become optional. Not that a stranger is guaranteed to respect your space and your things, but at least with a stranger, there isn't much of a loss if you never speak to each other again after moving out.

2. College Is about Making NEW Friends

Living with a best friend is *not* what college is all about. You know your friend. You'll continue to know your friend. Living together is just a security blanket that can end up suffocating the relationship. Living apart helps you branch out and get to know each other's new roommates (and their friends). Should you or your best friend want to hang out, you can always choose to be together. But it's a choice. Living apart means keeping your best-friend relationship intact and allowing for some space to make new friends.

3. Living with a Best Friend Means Missing Out

Being forced into a room with someone forces you to learn how to compromise, how to communicate, how to deal with conflict, and most important, gives you a deeper appreciation of another person's culture, lifestyle, and family dynamics. Never again will you have the opportunity to see the inner workings of a stranger's world (and you might never want to see the inner workings again). It's a once, twice, three, four, or five or more times in a lifetime experience depending how many roommates you have. Living with a best friend means missing out on living with someone you don't know—and that means missing out. No question about it!

Bottom Line

If you live with your best friend and hate it, you'll lose a best friend. If you live with a stranger and hate it, you'll lose someone you hate living with and never liked—not a loss.

Tip #18
The Gay, Lesbian, or Bisexual Roommate (pick one)

The Tip

To roommates who aren't gay: listen to other people's stories and try to learn. Everyone is unique. To those roommates who are gay: don't be afraid to be yourself. The people around you will respect you—the ones who don't will lose out.

The Story

When I moved into a dorm freshman year, I swear everyone had a boyfriend. They would talk about them all the time. The pictures overwhelmed their counters and desktops. My pictures were of family and friends. In the bottom drawer of my closet sat a picture of my girlfriend, hidden so no one would find out. After dodging the boyfriend question for a while, I found the courage to put her picture on my desk. Nobody seemed to notice for a long time until my roommate said, "Is that your sister?" After a short pause, I answered in a manner sure not to offend, "That is my girlfriend. We have been dating for about a year." "Oh," was all I got. She was only my roommate for two more weeks.

One thing I want to tell gay/lesbian/bi-questioning people is that it's not that bad. Being yourself is so much better than being the person you think people want you to be. It took me a long time to accept myself and show my true colors. I went from being a freshman that hid the truth to a junior who has a rainbow flag and other icons up in my room. People respect me more now that I am completely open and honest to myself and everyone else. A lot of the time, friends and floormates knock on my door and ask if they can come in and talk to me about my life and what I've dealt with. They want to know what it's like and what offends me. One friend walked into my room and asked how my parents dealt with my homosexuality. After a long discussion, she went home and talked to her parents about it. The interesting part? She wasn't gay, not even bi. She just wanted to tell her parents about me. If you're not gay, talk to people who are and listen, listen, listen. If you are gay, lift the veil and let your true self breathe! Show the world the beauty underneath.

—junior, Bemidji State University

* * *

Some of you will have gay, lesbian, bisexual, or transgender roommates. If the statistics are correct, about one in ten students are GLBT (gay, lesbian, bisexual, or transgender). Some of you might be the gay, lesbian, bisexual or transgender roommate. Assuming that your college doesn't have an all-GLBT residence hall (and it doesn't), there's a fairly decent chance that you or a friend will end up living with someone who is gay, lesbian, or bisexual. If you are gay or lesbian, whoever lives with you will have a 100 percent change of living with a gay or lesbian roommate.

If you're not gay, lesbian, or bisexual and find yourself living with a gay, lesbian, or bisexual roommate, there are three ways to react. The first is to run and hide from the problem. The second is to alienate your roommate by verbally (or physically) attacking him. The third is to look at this situation as a unique once-in-a-lifetime experience. Unless you're gay, lesbian, or bisexual, this is probably your first opportunity to live with someone who is. And considering the huge number of people in the world who are GLBT, this is an opportunity to learn about something totally foreign to you (the situation would be extra foreign if living with a gay, lesbian, or bisexual international student).

If you think your roommate is gay, but you're not sure, leave it alone. It's not your sexual orientation, so it's not your business. If your roommate is out (signs can include rainbow posters, pictures of gay icons, and wearing T-shirts reading, "Gay, Proud, and Your New Roommate"), casually talk to him or her about it. Start with, "I don't want to be insensitive, but I've never lived with someone who was gay before. (Note: if you set a precedent from Tip #14, this all become a lot easier.) Can I ask you a few questions?" If your roommate is cool with that, then ask away. Don't be offended if you express your concern about your roommate possibly making a pass at you and he or she answers with, "It would never happen—I don't find you attractive at all. Besides, I'm already involved."

If you're gay and living with a roommate who isn't, consider letting your roommate know that you're open to answering any questions. You can say something as little as, "You might have guessed from the pictures of my boyfriend/girlfriend that I'm gay. I don't know if you've ever had a gay roommate before or if you have friends at home who are gay, but I don't mind if you ask me any questions…"

Should you find yourself living with a gay, lesbian, heterosexual, or bisexual roommate and find that it's too much for you to handle, consider changing rooms. But please, be respectful. It's *your* problem that you can't handle the situation, not your roommate's problem. He or she is just being him-or herself. For those who are gay, lesbian, or bisexual and are concerned about finding your place on campus, find out if there is a GLBT group or organization on campus (or find one on another campus nearby and take advantage of their resources).

The Naked Blog:

A Very Good Year to Be Gay.
See www.TheNakedRoommate.com.

Bottom Line

Residence hall request forms do not come with a box to check listing preferences regarding your roommate's sexual orientation. Therefore, there's a fair chance that you might end up living with a gay, lesbian, or bisexual roommate. If you're the one who is gay, lesbian, or bisexual, there's an extremely good chance that someone in your room will be gay, lesbian, or bisexual.

Tip #19
The Noisy, Naughty, and/or Nasty Roommate

The Tip
Say something to your roommate immediately if there is a problem or it will only get worse and worse. Don't be afraid to speak up!

The Story
My roommate was disgusting. She never put anything away. She left crumbs, pizza stains, and random spots on the furniture. She didn't want to clean, she didn't care to clean, and she didn't know how to clean. We had our own bathroom attached to the room and she would leave used items wherever they landed (use your imagination). It was so disgusting. I made the mistake of not saying anything until later in the semester. It was too late. I exploded. She stopped talking to me. And we still don't talk. My advice—don't let it get out of control. If it gets bad fast, say something or get out of the living arrangement.

> "Every evening at 9:01 p.m. her cell phone rang (free nights and weekends). She would spend hours talking on the phone. She never stopped talking!"
> —freshman, Mount Union College

—sophomore, Wheelock College

* * *

Like a growing mold on a half-eaten chicken finger under your roommate's bed, the noisy, naughty, and/or nasty roommate can be hard to spot at first. It can take weeks before becoming a serious problem. The master tip—deal with it before it gets ugly. The longer you let it go, the more out of control the situation will become. Most roommates are reasonable if you deal with the issues right away (and you've set a precedent already for dealing with the uncomfortable).

Deal with the Noise Factor

It's about common courtesy. If you have early classes, let your roommate know what nights need to be early nights for you. If your roommate wants to talk on the phone during late-night hours, suggest he or she talk in the hall or lounge.

> "I was asleep; they were in the next bed having sex."
> —sophomore, University of Michigan

If your roommate wants to listen to music, suggest headphones. If your roommate wants to watch TV at night, then find a way to work it out without making him or her leave—it's their room, too. But considerate roommates will minimize the noise.

Deal with the Naughty Factor

Once you discover that you have a naughty roommate, make some rules. Don't just let it go and complain to your friends. Find a system to let each other know if you're "busy." This includes a system for roommates who insist on getting it on while they are alone (yes, it happens). Try to limit

> "Every residence hall I've ever supervised has a smelly roommate situation; it's the roommate that doesn't shower, doesn't clean, and doesn't care. Talk about it when the stink starts—if not, it will only start to smell worse and worse."
> —experienced college professional

the "I'm getting it on" signal to a certain number of nights a week. If having sex while you are in the room is unacceptable, say something the first time it happens. If your roommate ignores you or loses control, talk to your RA (assuming your RA isn't the naughty partner). Oh yes, if your roommate insists on doing things with someone while you're in the room, you DO NOT have to pretend to be invisible. You have every right to stand up and watch. You can even make comments. Shouting, "Wow, that was fast!" is not inappropriate. Inviting friends over to watch can be a quick way to get things to end.

Deal with the Nasty Factor

By week four, you'll smell it, see it, or step in it. If your roommate smells funny, suggest deodorant. For bad gas, ask that you at least get fair warning. For the nude or sweaty roommates, ask them to put down a towel on the couch when lounging. Whatever the situation, try and approach the problem the way you would want your roommate to approach you. For super nasty roommates, see if your RA can get the roommate to sign a roommate contract that includes a hygiene clause.

> "Watch out for the crazy roommate that has a 20,000 volt Taser, eats catnip, and entangles his testicles, causing them to be surgically removed. It happened!"
> —sophomore, Juniata College

Bottom Line

Noisy, nasty, and naughty roommates make for great stories. First you have to live through it. The funny part starts about three to five years later (depending on the nasty factor).

Tip #20
The Your Girlfriend/Boyfriend Doesn't Live Here Roommate

The Tip
If your roommate has a girlfriend/boyfriend, discuss up front when the significant other will and will not be allowed in the room. There's nothing worse than having an extra roommate.

The Story
My freshman year in college, I lived with a sophomore. He had a girlfriend that he had been seeing for years. She used to come by all the time. She even had a key. It got so bad that she was there when I left and there when I came home. She was even there by herself. Because I was new at school and he was older, I didn't have the courage to tell him what I felt. I just let it go. It got so bad that I wouldn't even change in the room because she was always there. She ate my food and smoked cigarettes in the room. He did ask if I minded once or twice, but I told him that it was fine, it didn't matter. I didn't want him to get upset. I didn't have the courage to tell him. It all got even worse after that. I ended up moving out after a few weeks, so it never got too heated. I should have told him when I had the chance, but I didn't.

> **"Freshman year, I lived in a triple. We had to sit one of our roommates down and tell her that she needed to get our permission to have her boyfriend spend the night."**
> **—sophomore, Boston University**

—sophomore, University of Illinois

* * *

There are few things more uncomfortable than finding yourself stuck with an extra roommate—like finding yourself stuck with two, three, or four extra roommates. Typically, it unfolds in one of two ways:

1) Your roommate comes to campus with a significant other. From day one, he or she thinks that their boyfriend or girlfriend can come over and do whatever he or she wants. The significant other even gets his or her own key.

2) Your roommate falls in love during the year. It starts out with a night here and there, and then quickly turns into endless nights *here* and never there. You are the third wheel living in your own home.

Both situations are problematic, but both can be avoided by preemptive planning. For those moving in with a roommate who has a significant other, ask your roommate how often he or she plans on having the significant other spend the night. Mention that it makes you very uncomfortable having someone else hang out in your room alone (assuming it does). If it's a problem, find a way to compromise or find a new roommate.

> "My freshman year, my roommate would leave sticky notes on the door that always said he was 'studying.' That was always the tip-off—he never studied."
> —junior, University of Minnesota–Twin Cities

If you're moving in with a roommate who isn't attached, make sure you have a plan to avoid gaining an extra roommate (or two). Agree not to make a copy of the keys for boyfriends or girlfriends. Insist that a significant other can't be in the room alone. And mention that if it ever gets to be too much, you'll let the other roommate know.

Again, promise that if and when something bothers you or your roommate, you'll both talk about the situation. That way, it's not as if either of you is attacking the other and nobody will be put on the defensive. Just talk it out. It doesn't have to be a confrontation, it can be a conversation. If you can't do that, someone will just have to move out. Or you can just happily ignore each other. My roommate did that to me. Seriously, he stopped talking to me, but I never stopped talking to him. It really pissed him off. I'd ask him, "Do you want something from Taco Bell? If you're not hungry, then don't say anything." He said nothing. I guess he wasn't hungry.

Bottom Line

The only good thing about having an extra roommate is that if you get locked out there's a better chance of someone being there to let you in.

Tip #21
The Lying, Stealing, Klepto Roommate

The Tip

If your roommate takes, borrows, or steals your stuff, say something—don't just let it go. You might never get it back.

The Story

I had one particular roommate who was extremely hard to live with. Besides being messy (she would smear peanut butter on the couch), she'd steal my stuff and then lie to my face about it. It got so bad that I was forced to put my initials on everything, including food, clothing, CDs, toothpaste, and even tampons. Still, she would take things. I tried to make rules, but it was too late. My biggest mistake was not saying something sooner. One time, I went into her closet and saw a few of my friend's missing sweaters. Later, she lied to us about it, and this was while they were still hanging in her closet. It's important to set ground rules early when you move in together, like what you'll buy together and what you'll share and what can be borrowed. It's a trust issue, and until you know your roommate, it's hard to trust. Even then, you can't be totally sure that things of yours won't end up in her closet.

—senior, University of Wisconsin–Madison

> "One day, I discovered that she had been 'borrowing' my underwear. I moved my underwear to my desk drawer. She stopped sharing, but I sometimes find paper clips and other office supplies in my underwear."
>
> —sophomore, Bay Path College

***

You might not realize it, but this book could get stolen (yes, a scary thought). Sadly, some roommates like to steal. Some take clothing. Some take jewelry. Some take

"Put your name on all your stuff!"
—sophomore, Curry College

money. Some take your food. Some take your condoms. Know that most roommates will not take your things, but some might—and do. And if it's not your roommate doing the stealing, it could be someone coming and going in and out of your room.

To minimize risks:
- Put your initials on *everything*. Use a permanent marker for CDs, clothing labels, food (on the wrapper, not the actual food), toiletries, condoms, and tampons (again, on the outside

"She actually did me a favor by stealing my Hanson CD."
—grad, Ohio State University

labels, please). For electronics, consider using an engraving tool and put your driver's license number or something else that will distinguish it into the actual casing. It makes recovering and identifying stolen stuff easier should anything get stolen (you can rent or buy engraving tools at hardware stores).
- Do not bring valuables or irreplaceable things to campus. If you're afraid of having something stolen that can't be replaced, leave it at home. If you do have valuables, make sure they are put away in a place that is hard to get to, like in a small safe that has a lock.

- Keep anything you do not want to get stolen out of sight. If it's in plain view, someone can easily be tempted to take it without you ever noticing. Put it away.
- Lock your dorm room door (that's double lock) whenever you leave the room. It's easy to open doors with credit cards (I've done it when locked out). It's even easier to get in when the door is unlocked.
- Get a footlocker and keep it in your room (under a bed or in a closet is optimal). With thousands of dollars in electronics, video games, and valuables, a footlocker is one more layer of protection from someone looking to make a quick grab.
- Don't hesitate to tell. Alert your RA or an authority in the residence hall if something is stolen. Mention to your roommate that you think someone is stealing and he should put his stuff away. It's not accusing your roommate, but it's telling him or her that you're aware.

Bottom Line

I'd like to take this opportunity to confess that I still have a CD I "borrowed" from my roommate in college.

Tip #22
The Drunk and/or High Roommate

The Tip

When you have a roommate who comes in drunk, don't try to deal with it when he or she is drunk and you're sober. It will annoy you, and he or she won't be able to comprehend it. Instead, wait until the morning when he or she sobers up…or build yourself a canopy.

The Story

My roommate loves going out; it doesn't matter what night of the week it is. It's not that she's inconsiderate; she's just not really "there" when she drinks. During the first few weeks of school, almost every night, she would come into the room after I was sleeping and yell something—not a word, just a weird "ohhhahhhh." Then she'd turn on the lights, see that I was sleeping, and realize that she'd woken me up. Then she would begin to apologize for waking me, not realizing that she's now keeping me up later. After her nightly apology, she'd stumble all over the room and finally go to sleep. My first approach was to get her a night-light. When that failed, I decided to build a canopy. I went to the fabric store and spent $80 (I got carried away—the whole interior designer part of me). I then suspended the fabric with little shower curtain connected to a wire hanging across the ceiling. I took matters into my own hands. It works great. She stills come in at night, but she's quieter. Building my customized noise barrier helped her get the hint. People could take a much easier approach by talking to their roommate. I went a different route.

> "He was the nicest guy and most considerate roommate, but he sold drugs."
> —junior, Indiana University

—freshman, University of Georgia

✳ ✳ ✳

If your roommate uses this book as a coaster for beer or uses this page as rolling paper for a joint, you might have a drunk, high, or just incredibly stupid roommate. The ultimate roommate rule holds true with drunk and/or high roommates: roommates who want to get along will find a way to get along. That's assuming your roommate isn't too drunk or high to remember to try to get along.

There are those that are considerate drunk and/or high roommates, and then there are those that are inconsiderate drunk and/or high roommates. For example, the considerate roommate leaves the room to vomit. The inconsiderate roommate lets it fly wherever it lands (hopefully you're not on the bottom bunk). Until you live with your roommate, it's hard to know which one you might encounter. Also worth mentioning: you may not have a drunk or high roommate—he or she might be a completely sober roommate. Imagine that.

Again, make sure to deal with the problems when they come up because issues involving alcohol and drugs tend to get worse as the term progresses. The biggest mistake roommates make is saying nothing. When dealing with a roommate who is impaired, wait until he or she is sober to discuss the situation. If the roommate vomits, urinates, or

> "My roommate jumped off his bed, opened the middle drawer behind my bed, and started urinating. It went all over me, my bed, and all my pictures from home. I was pissed."
> —recent graduate, Ohio State University

defecates in the room, take videos and/or pictures. Your roommate won't remember and might need evidence to help jog his or her memory. Talk about it sooner rather than later. Avoid letting it brew inside you because one day it will boil over. The first time is the best time to deal with it. As for problems like using or selling drugs or alcohol in the room, if it's in the room and it's against the rules, then you could be busted, too. If you're uncomfortable with your living situation, talk to your RA. And if you happen to be the one bringing drugs or alcohol or into the room, don't be irritated or surprised when your roommate asks you to keep it out of the room. It has as much to do with him or her as it does with you

One more thing to keep in mind—if your roommate is ever nonresponsive, unconscious, or vomiting blood, please *seek medical attention*. Do not let him or her just "sleep it off." There's always the chance that your roommate might not wake up.

> "We were total opposites. I'm the kind of roommate who likes to hang out in my room and do my own thing. He was the kind who liked to party and wanted to be popular. Mostly, he took his partying to other places. When he did come home, he was wasted and usually just passed out. It wasn't a problem. Second semester was even easier. He disappeared or probably dropped out."
> —sophomore,
> Loyola University–Chicago

Bottom Line

Chances are that your roommate's partying will only be a temporary problem—that is, until he or she fails out, passes out, or forgets where he or she lives.

The Tip

When you live with someone, talk to a professional when you see signs that he or she needs help.

The Story

I had a really emotional roommate. We had talked to her parents and tried to get help, but there was only so much they could do. One day, I came home and found that she was trying to commit suicide. It was relationship-related. She was dating someone long-distance and he had dumped her a month before college. She just had downhill depression. She wasn't enjoying school. She didn't settle in and make friends. I actually came home and walked in and found her really emotional. She had gone to the bathroom—and I just knew that something was happening. She had taken pills and was trying to cut herself. We had to call the ambulance. She was pretty angry and violent, but they got her under control and took her to the hospital. My friend and I followed her. She was taken to another hospital. She came home a couple days later. She survived, and she's doing a little better, but she is still having a

> **Quick Tip Fact**
>
> Suicide is the third leading cause of death for young people aged 15–24.
>
> —National Center for Injury Prevention and Control

hard time dealing with everyday life. College is full of emotionally unstable people.

—senior, University of Virginia

* * *

I hate to end this roommate section on such a downer; getting someone help can be such an amazing gift (see, this isn't such a downer). It's a tough tip, but this could happen. I know, it's not fair that you should be the one to have to get someone you barely know the help he or she needs. But when you're a roommate, you see things that most people don't see. You see more than family. You see more than boyfriends and girlfriends. You see more than the RAs. You see a lot of things you don't want to see, but if you see it, you shouldn't ignore it.

For depression information, see Tip Sheet on page 414.

For alcoholism information, see Tip Sheet on page 321.

For drug risks information, see Tip Sheet on page 344.

For eating disorder information, see Tip Sheet on page 415.

If you think that your roommate is in danger, get other people involved who can help keep him or her from hurting him- or herself. While researching this book, I heard story after story about roommates attempting suicide, getting dangerously drunk, and doing other stupid things. If it happens, approach your roommate (when he or she is sober). Talk to your RA. Talk to people in the counseling center, and talk to your roommate's parents if possible. In an emergency, call 911. Remember, passed-out roommates might not get up, meaning they may be dying. Help them.

Your roommate might not appreciate your help, but people in these situations aren't usually the happiest people to begin with. So, don't let her reaction deter you. If you can save your roommate from a dangerous situation, at least try. And if you find that you just need to get away from the situation because your roommate is too messed up too much of the time, then do it. Not everyone can save the world and take care of themselves at the same time.

> "My roommate cut herself all the time. She was a cutter. I once took her to the emergency room and sat with her."
> —junior, UCLA

And if you should find that you're the one who is being spoken to by a concerned roommate, don't just brush it off. Listen. Chances are that you're the one who is wrong and your roommate is right. At least listen.

Bottom Line

You never asked to be your roommate's keeper, but it can work both ways. Hope no one needs to be a hero, but don't hesitate to get outside help, such as RAs, paramedics, or the police.

Harlan's Tip Sheet

Roommate Resources, Websites, and Additional Information

- *Check in with your new roommate.* Talk before leaving for school. Figure out what you each of you should bring. Avoid two microwaves, two game systems, and two TVs. (That is, unless you have a microwave that's really special to you that you don't want to share.)
- *Avoid judging your roommate via their MySpace or Facebook page.* Wait to meet them before deciding not to like them.
- *Make it a rule.* Talk about the things that concern you when they become problems. Ask your roommate to do the same. When something is a problem, you will both promise to say something to the other before whatever it is becomes a habit or gets out of control.
- *Changing rooms.* Typically, you have to wait a certain period of time before moving. Talk to your RA or resident director if you need to move. Every school has its own rules and regulations. If it's an emergency, there are always exceptions to the rule.
- *Give it a few weeks.* Don't be so quick to run away from your roommate because he or she is different. You might be "different" to someone you're living with. Unless you're in danger, give it at least a few weeks.
- *Campus police.* Report any illegal happenings to the

campus police. If they don't seem to be very effective, call the local police and get them involved.

- *Campus counseling center.* If your roommate needs help, if you need help, or if you want to know how to handle a situation, talk to a counselor or therapist.

Websites Worth Visiting

- Parents, Families, and Friends of Gays and Lesbians
  www.pflag.org
- The National Coalition for Gay, Lesbian, Bisexual and Transgender Youth
  www.outproud.org
- Al-Ateen—Offering hope and help for friends and family of alcoholics
  www.al-ateen.org
- Half of Us—a newer site offering help and support to a college-age audience
  www.halfofus.com

Hotlines

- National Hope Network
  1-800-SUICIDE (1-800-784-2433) twenty-four hours a day, seven days a week
- Gay and Lesbian National Hotline
  1-888-843-4564
- Need Immediate Help? Call 1-800-273-TALK

(See Tip Sheets in Chapters 9, 10, and 13 for alcohol, drugs, and depression info.)

Finding Friends

4

Your Social or Antisocial College Life

Dear Harlan,

I started college a month ago, and I haven't made any friends. I have a roommate, but she has friends from her high school and doesn't seem to want to make any new friends. All of the people on my floor seem to have their own groups already, and I don't think I can fit in with them. I think this is a problem for me, because I am very shy, and people see me differently because of it. I just can't seem to get over my shyness, and it is affecting my whole life. I need some advice on how to make some friends, because I don't think I can go through school without them.

—Friendless

Dear Friendless,

Unless you start a club on campus called "Shy People On Campus" and hold meetings in your room, you'll actually need to leave your room to make new friends. (Even if you did start the SPOC club, most people would be too shy to come to the first meeting.)

Considering that most shy people don't like attention and work to avoid situations where they feel like they're being judged, you should work to put yourself in group situations where the activity, not you, is the focus. Activities like sports, academic associations, performing arts, fraternities and sororities, religious organizations, and various clubs and activities will work. The idea is to put yourself in the same room with the same people over a long period of time. As these people become more familiar, you'll become more comfortable and will naturally make friends. It just takes time, work, and patience. If attending an activity alone is too difficult, think about this—other people are going alone too, so no one is really alone. Should you arrive and discover that your fellow shy people let you down, talk to an experienced member in the group. Trust that someone around you has been in your place before and that someone will be there for you. And if none of this advice works, head to the counseling office and get help. The problem might be more than just being shy.

Tip #24
The Snow Globe Factor

The Tip
Take advantage of the new beginning. Do not let who you were in high school determine who you will be in college.

The Story
In high school, I was more of a floater, with some redeeming traits. In truth, I was not the most outgoing guy. Yeah, I was sociable, yet only had a small circle of friends. I tried to be involved in school activities, but I did not always belong.

Once I got into college, however, my eyes were opened to a new world of opportunities, friendships, and romance. Because everything was so new and so different, I didn't feel that others judged me as much. Once I figured out that all these people were as out of place and as afraid as I was, it all became so much easier for me to be open, friendly, and receptive to the people around me. I have now become a leader in the classroom, and thankfully in my own life, with all my friends who share the same awkwardness that I once had. The harder the lessons learned, the greater the reward earned.

> ### A Friendly Fact
> 39.2 percent of surveyed freshmen "frequently" or "occasionally" felt worried about meeting new people.
>
> —Higher Education Research Institute at UCLA

—junior, Stephen F. Austin State University

* * *

Imagine being trapped inside a life-size snow globe—one of those small souvenir globes with water and fake snow inside that resembles an instant blizzard when shaken. If you're unfamiliar with the snow globe, go to Google or Yahoo and do a search for "souvenir snow globes." I just did the search and found a New York snow globe that would look perfect in any dorm room. A great conversation piece.

Okay, now imagine yourself inside that snow globe. Instead of the "I Love New York" image, substitute your college campus inside the dome. Now, imagine taking that snow globe and shaking the hell out of it. The frenzy that results inside represents the first few weeks of college. It's controlled chaos; everyone scrambling to find friends, to find their classes, and to just find their place on campus. This is all totally normal. This is what the first few weeks (or even months) of college life are all about. If you know there will be a storm, you can come equipped to weather the conditions.

> "Roommates and friends of roommates are easy to be friends with at first—it's convenient. But I think they should be one of two groups of friends. I missed out on meeting a lot of cool people that I realized I was more compatible with because I clung onto the first people I met."
> —junior, UCLA

You're dealing with a lot—new friends, new classes, new reputations, possibly new roommates, new clothes, and new professors. It's all so new that people don't know you at all—you start off as a stranger. Who you were in high school no longer matters. If you were someone popular, you have to start over. If you weren't all that popular, you also get to start over. There is no such thing as popular or unpopular now, because no one here knows who you are or what you were in high school. Everyone gets a new start, and what you make of it is up to you. That said, starting over can be lonely and confusing at times.

When it comes to making friends during the first few weeks of college, it can be overwhelming. So, instead of trying too hard to figure it all out, do what you love doing and you'll naturally meet people with whom you

"It was very hard to transition from having friends in high school to making friends in college. It was painful my first semester. I never tried to make friends and ended up hanging out by myself a lot. My second semester, I ended up joining a few clubs and meeting new people. After that, I became more sociable and made lots of friends."
—senior, University of Alabama

share something in common. When you get confused and uncomfortable, lean on what's familiar, like the things you participated in back in high school. Once the snow settles—and once the friendship storm settles—your world will be easier to navigate and you'll find your new friends. Just expect it to be a little stormy at first.

Bottom Line

If you don't like the snow globe analogy, imagine a bobblehead doll with its head bobbing uncontrollably. It takes a while for things to settle. Once things calm down, you can find balance and move more easily through college life.

Tip #25
Shopping for New Friends

The Tip
Do not be afraid to take a risk once you arrive on your college campus. Approaching someone at the food court might be intimidating, but a friendship is the best result!

The Story
Unlike most college students, I did not move away. I went to a university within driving distance from my home in order to save money to go abroad, amongst other reasons. None of

> "I'm trapped between going to class and returning to my apartment to study, and I can't make friends this way."
> —sophomore, University of Georgia

my high school friends went with me, and for a long time, I was depressed because I wasn't having the "college experience." Going to a commuter college often means that students go to class, then go home. It wasn't until my second semester (of loneliness) that I realized no one was going to approach me, and I needed to put myself out there! So I started looking for people in the food court eating alone who I thought would be friendly. It took some guts, but I asked them about the book they were reading, and if they responded nicely, they usually asked me to sit down. I met two of my best friends that way. Try it. Most commuter students (and even noncommuter students) feel lonely and will never turn down an invitation for company.

—junior, San Jose State University

For those of you who have friends from home going to college with you, you may think you don't need this tip. You might think you already have enough friends. If you're looking for new friends in addition to your old friends (and you should be), keep reading. If you want college to be a bigger version of high school, then just surround yourself with people you already know, and skip to the next tip. Go. Now. I mean it!

Still here? Okay, then read on...

Some students leave for college panicked that they won't find new friends. If they're not going to a school with friends, they're not sure how they'll make friends. This is a big worry, but most of the time it's a waste of energy. The reason it's a waste is because most people come to college without friends, and the friendless need friends. That's why making friends the first few weeks is so easy.

If you're out of your room, living life, and getting involved with college life, doing what you love to do, you'll make friends. It just happens. It happens when you go to class, in the residence halls, at parties, with friends of friends, when working campus jobs, when involved with student government, when playing intramural sports, when joining fraternities and sororities, in the laundry room or the library. Like catching a stomach flu or an STD/STI, if you expose yourself to the action, it's much more likely to happen.

> "Involvement on campus, nonalcohol related, is the way to true friendships."
> —junior, Western Illinois University

It doesn't happen if you stay in your room. You need to get out of your room (or at least keep the door open). If you're too shy to approach a stranger, find a study group in class. If you aren't living in a place where there are lots of other freshmen, join clubs, activities, organizations, and religious groups. These are all easy places to make friends. After you take part in an activity, you'll get to know the people there. Then you'll have new friends.

> "If you want to meet new people, join as many clubs and organizations as possible. I came into college completely alone. None of my friends were attending the same school and I missed my freshman orientation. I didn't think I'd meet anyone. After complaining to my mother about feeling so out of place, she suggested that I see what kinds of organizations there were on campus. I looked into some and ended up joining three clubs my freshman year. It was the best thing I ever did!"
> —sophomore, Eastern Connecticut University

Bottom Line

Most students come to college friendless. They need friends and unless you're accessible and available to be met, they can't meet you. Beware: not all friends you make the first year will become lifelong friends (see Tip #27).

Tip #26
Why College Friends Are Different

The Tip

It might seem like you know someone, but it takes time to really know new friends. Be careful.

The Story

I was really good friends with a girl down the hall. My roommate and I had gotten into a fight that weekend. I was talking to one of my new good friends over IM about the situation. Later that night, the roommate of my new friend comes into my room and tells me that my roommate, the one that I had been fighting with, had been allowed to see the IM message that I thought was only being seen by my friend. I couldn't believe that she would do that to me. That's when I learned that it takes a while to trust new friends. From that point on, I've been much more careful with what I tell people. I only tell others the things that I don't mind other people finding out about. New friends are different than high school friends. It takes a while to find people that you know you can trust. In high school, you've known your friends for years. In college, you've only known them for a few months, and you don't really know everything yet.
—freshman, Cazenovia College

> **"You really learn who your friends are and aren't when you get into trouble—the ones who talk behind your back aren't your true friends."**
> —recent graduate,
> University of Michigan–Ann Arbor

> **"College friends offer a false sense of family."**
> —sophomore,
> University of Nevada–Las Vegas

* * *

College friends are different than high school friends. They look different, sound different, dress different, talk different, smell different, and have different names (in most cases); they are different people and you haven't had a lot of time to get to know them well.

The friends you have from high school are the friends that you've shared so much with over the years. In a lot of friendships, you've gone from a boy to a man, girl to woman, bike to car, home-coming to prom, une-ducated to educated, single to involved, virgin to nonvirgin (in some cases; see Tip #66), innocent to guilty, and so on. Some friends have even been through elementary and middle school together. High school friends are the only friends you've ever known with whom you've shared a lifetime of memories.

> **"Do not judge people right away. Labels don't hold. Stereotypes don't fit."**
> **—freshman, Northwestern University**

And then you leave for college.

Assuming you don't know people on your new campus, the transition can be anxiety-provoking. New friends take time to make. Facebook friends take time to make (find me on Facebook, I'm looking for friends). Just like with a new pair of shoes, or new hairstyle, it takes time to get comfortable with new friends. New friends can't compare to high school friends, so don't try to compare them.

A lot of people leave for college thinking they will make new friends immediately, and they panic if they don't. They think there is a big problem. But the real problem is thinking that it all should happen so fast. It's not normal. Friendships take a long time to form. Like fine wine, it's a process that depends on the essential ingredient of time (not to be confused with the spice thyme, which shouldn't be present in a good wine). If you don't feel connected to your new friends in college right away, don't worry. Get involved, meet people, live life, and you'll naturally build good, stable friendships—or bad, shaky friendships (depending on the kind of friends you're looking to find).

Bottom Line
College friends are untested. Until you've been friends with the people you meet at college through good and bad and good and bad again (say, at least three times), you don't know how strong your friendships are. It takes time.

Tip #27
Friend Today, Gone Tomorrow

The Tip
Don't be disappointed if the people you were best friends with your freshman year are not around by the end of college.

The Story
We met through a mutual friend and become close friends freshman year. We all lived on campus then, not too far from each other. We were such close friends; we'd even go home together once in a while. We went to parties together. We just pretty much hung out all the time. She was one of my best friends. Junior year we started to grow apart. There wasn't a fight or blowout. We just started to have more work to do. See, when you're a freshman, there's more time to hang out. As we got older, there was much

more to do and less time to hang out. When you have two different people and two different majors, you can't always connect. The people that I'm closest with are people that I share a major with. We go to classes together, we study together, and we hang out together. My freshman friend and I don't live near each other at all. It's important to not take it personally if you're not friends with the same people sophomore, junior, or senior year. Don't think there's anything wrong. People grow apart. It's not like high school. Friends come and go.

—senior, Farleigh Dickinson University

* * *

Take a good look around (assuming you're reading this while at college—otherwise, remember to take a good look around when you get to school). The people around you who you'll soon call friends the first few months of college might not be your friends next semester. Don't freak out. It's not just you—it's everyone.

Friends made the first few weeks are like seasonal clothing—some lose their appeal after a while. It's not until months into college that you begin to see who your friends are and are not. And that can change, too. It takes time to sort it all out. A lot of the friends you make the first year of college are what I like to call "friends of convenience." It works like this—the people you tend to be friends with the first couple months of college are the people you tend to be around a lot, like the people in your residence hall, people from classes, people you rush with (if you're pledging a fraternity or sorority—see Tip #35). As you branch out and get more involved on campus, you'll naturally meet more people, people with whom you'll have more in common. Along the way, you might find that the friends you made the first few weeks are no longer people you want to have as friends. That's normal. You don't have to be mean to them, you can just naturally distance yourself. And remember, you might find yourself on the receiving end of some distancing. Just understand, this is normal too!

Most new students go through friends like they go through toilet paper the first few months of college (that cafeteria food can be harsh on the system). Know that this friend-today-gone-tomorrow phenomenon is to be expected. At the same time, a lot of the people you meet those first few months will become great friends—even life-long friends. Not all of them are a temporary convenience.

Important note: should you find yourself without temporary friends those first few weeks, don't freak out. As you get more comfortable and more involved on campus, you will meet more people who will become your friends.

"Instead of trying to get involved in everything and be friends with everyone, be intentional about what you do. The deepest friendships develop with the people you spend time with. I spent my first two years juggling my time between many different activities. And as a result, I have many friends on campus that I see in passing—there's a reason we call them 'Hi' friends. My most meaningful relationships have come as a result of spending time with a smaller number of people."
—junior, Trinity Western University

Bottom Line

College friends the first year of school are like the weather—hard to predict. They blow in and blow out without notice, and they run hot and cold.

Tip #28
High School Friends, Cows, and Cats

The Tip
High school friendships will change, but not as much as you might think.

The Story
I went to the University of Michigan and most of my friends stayed close to home. My fear was that everyone would hang out with each other and I'd be left with no one. I was afraid I would be out of sight, out of mind. When I got to school, I got along with my roommate, which helped a lot. I also play some basketball, so I met some guys that way. After a few weeks, I had made some new friends on campus. I stopped worrying so much about being left out when it came to my high school friends. It was easy to stay in touch with friends from home through email and IM. Everyone has cell phones. When we all went back to our high school for homecoming it was like nothing had changed. Everyone had stories, but it wasn't much different. That's how it's been every time we've seen each other. They come and visit at least once a semester or I see them. I think they like it better here. I'm

surprised how little our friendship changed. It's cool—I have my college friends and my high school friends.

—sophomore, University of Michigan–Ann Arbor

* * *

Worried about your high school friends?

Don't be.

They aren't going anywhere. If you want to stay in touch with them, you can email, instant message, call on free nights and weekends, visit them, and have them visit you. You'll meet their friends and their friends will meet your new friends. Sure, your friendships will change, but they can change for the better. You can't stay in high school forever (you could try, but I don't know how long you can stay before they'd ask you to leave the premises). Between coming home for breaks (if away at school), seeing each other over the summers, and visiting each other at school, you can still hang out with your friends.

The most important part of this tip is this part: *do not compare your college experience to your friends' college experiences*. If you're having a crappy time and your friends are having an amazing time at another college, don't immediately give up on your college and think that you should transfer. They might be having a terrible time in a few months or in the next year (or they might be covering up the truth because they're having a hard time and don't want to admit it). It might take you a little longer to get comfortable. The dynamics of your college experience are completely different. They might know more people on campus than you. They might be more involved. They might have an RA that helps them meet people more easily. Who knows, and who cares—all that matters is what's happening with you.

My first semester at college was hard. I didn't know anyone. My friends were at a state school having an amazing time (so it appeared). College sucked. I started to feel sorry for myself rather than actually working to find my place in college. I compared my experience to those of my friends at other schools. But they can't be compared. It's like comparing a cow to a cat. Mine was the cow, and theirs were all cats.

See, the title of this tip now makes so much sense...

Bottom Line
Whatever anybody tells you, cow-tipping (pushing cows over while they sleep) is dangerous and mean.

Harlan's Tip Sheet

Finding Friends Resources, Websites, and Additional Information

- *Get out of your room.* Unless you order carry-out and become friends with the people delivering your food, friends won't come knocking on your door, begging you to hang out. Get out of your room. Study outside your room, get involved, and put yourself out there so people can find you.

- *Take advantage of student organizations.* These are great places to make friends. If you do what you have fun doing, the people you're doing it with naturally become your friends. (See the next chapter.)
- *Do not hang out with just your high school friends.* The biggest mistake is to go to college and remain in your former circle of friends. Branch out. Go with one friend to an event, club, or organization and talk to the other people there. Make sure you meet people during your first year. It's way too easy to use your friends that you came to school with as a crutch.
- *Get in touch with grads from your area.* Before leaving for college, get in touch with your high school college counselor or the department that deals with alumni relations. Email or call students who are at the school you're going to attend. Find them via Facebook or MySpace if you don't know them that well. Ask them any questions you have. Who knows, you might even make a friend.
- *Attend welcome week festivities/activities.* Do your best to attend as many of the welcome week events as possible. While you might think some of them seem boring, they're actually a good time. Go to the BBQ, see a band, watch a speaker. (It could even be me—I also play the guitar during my shows. Check out my music on MySpace: www.myspace.com/harlancohen.)
- *Attend summer and fall orientation programs.* If it's not required, pretend it is. At these programs, you meet the same people you will see around campus. Orientation is a ready-made opportunity to make friends.

- *Best places to meet new people on campus*:
    - gym/recreational center
    - student government
    - residence halls
    - fraternities and sororities
    - in classes
    - the library
    - religiously affiliated groups and organizations
    - outdoor/adventure clubs
    - club and intramural sports
    - special interest clubs and activities
    - a part-time job

Getting Involved on Campus

An All-You-Can-Do Buffet

5

Dear Harlan,

I'm going to college in a few weeks and I'm more scared than excited about going away to this school. I'll be pretty far from home. I am so scared that I will not find my place and end up quitting. There is no one that I know there. I sometimes get frustrated and depressed because I didn't choose a college closer to home. I feel so stupid.

—No Turning Back

Dear Turning Back,

If you had chosen a college closer to home because you were afraid of going off to college, you'd probably feel stupid. Either way you'd feel stupid (and you're not), so you made a smart choice.

The most common piece of advice offered by college students for this book has been to get involved. This is how you can find your place, find friends, and even someone who can be more than just a friend. Leave for college with a plan on how you will get involved. Put together your plan by visiting your college's website and checking out clubs, activities, and organizations. Use your extracurricular experiences in high school to guide you to similar experiences in college. Talk to older students already on campus doing the things that you might want to do. If you don't know any personally, search for clubs and organizations, find members via Facebook, and send a message. Also, make a list of what looks interesting, then get busy. If you have questions or can't find what you're looking for, contact the student activities office.

If you arrive at school and you don't have anyone to go with to these activities, just go on your own (you can meet other people who are also going alone). Activities like clubs, sports, intramurals, and student government are easy ways to make friends and keep busy. Relax, enjoy, and leave with a plan. And know that help at the counseling office is there for you if you find that it's too much to handle.

Tip #29
Getting Involved: What, Where, When, How, and Why (but not in that order)

The Tip
Get involved sooner than later. You'll have more time to explore opportunities and you'll gain a sense of belonging.

The Story
I always felt too afraid, embarrassed, shy—whatever you want to call it—to get involved with organizations on campus. I came to a university with the single focus on performing well academically. After two years of only minor involvement, I threw myself into two positions in my junior year. While I love the experience, I find myself attempt-

> "As a freshman at a small school, join as many clubs and activities as soon you get there. I've been a tour guide, president of the campus activities board, and a resident assistant."
> —sophomore, Endicott College

ing to cram everything into my last two years. Getting involved earlier connects you instantly to the campus community and allows you the amazing opportunity to explore practically what your skills and passion are.

—junior, Trinity Western University

* * *

This tip is among the top five most important tips of the book. And don't let the fact that it's Tip #29 diminish its value. The reason it's so important is because this one is connected to so many others—this is how you find friends, find yourself, branch out, find your place, get to know professors, and get to know campus. This is the master key that can unlock the door to the best college experience ever.

If someone should tell you to NEVER get involved in clubs, activities, organizations, and life on campus, trust that this person dislikes you and is trying to ruin you. He or she is your new enemy. Trust that they don't want you to make great friends. They don't want you to find your comfortable place in college. They don't want you to discover your passion. They absolutely don't want you to be happy or stay in college for very long. Maybe they want your bed, girlfriend, boyfriend, iPod, PlayStation 3, Nintendo Wii, Xbox, textbooks—it's something you have. Telling someone to NOT get involved is bad, horrible, terrible advice that should be ignored at all costs.

Why get involved? Find friends, find your place on campus, get out of your room, find an interest to pursue, find love (it happens), and find a way to impact campus life.

How to get involved? When you get to campus, ask your orientation leader, an upperclassman, or a professional in student life on campus. Keep an eye out for clubs and organizations at the fall activities fair. This is when most of the clubs and

> "Join a student organization the minute you start school. If you are lucky, the upperclassmen in the club will show you tips that would take you months or even years to learn."
> —junior, Devry University

organizations set up displays with information on how students can get involved. In addition, find the names of current leaders of the club or organization you like and send an email with your specific questions.

What to get involved with? Pick a club or activity that looks interesting to you, even before you get to campus (check out the college's website).

Where to find your chosen club or organization? Once you get to campus, they can typically be found by visiting the club or organization's website, emailing a member, or visiting the office on campus that oversees student organizations.

When do you get involved? According to the Institute of Higher Education, 84.5 percent of new students who come to college plan on getting involved in a club or group, but only 48.8 percent of first-year

> "Get involved, but don't go overboard. It's about finding a balance."
> —senior, Henderson State University

students actually get around to doing it. Start off college by picking one club or activity that interests you. Try it out your first semester (or quarter). If you have extra time, try another next semester (or quarter). Plan ahead and you can make sure you get involved sooner rather than later.

A quick note on going to meetings on your own: assume other people are going to meetings alone and depending on meeting other new members. Do not let them down by not going. And please, *never* judge a club or organization by one meeting. Go to at least three meetings, then judge (use the judge's outfit from Tip #15).

> "Getting out of my comfort zone was hard, but once I found something that I enjoyed, it was almost like the snowball effect. I met people, and then you meet their friends, and then we all became friends, and then I'd get even more involved. Start early, because I've found that the four (or five, or six, or ten) years go by quickly."
> —junior, Indiana University

Bottom Line

Get involved, make some friends, find your place, and figure out what you love to do—and the things you don't love to do.

Tip #30
Clubs and Organizations: A Smorgasbord of Opportunity

The Tip

There is a club or organization on your campus for almost every interest. Get involved with those you are interested in and learn more about yourself.

The Story

Getting involved in campus activities and organizations

was how I found my place in college, but it took a few years to get there. Freshman year was all about experimenting and finding my limits. Sophomore year was about finding a student organization that I could give something to and that could give something to me. It was my junior year that I really found my place—on student union board. It started by getting involved with student government my sophomore year in a program for new students. It was through that program that I met the advisor for union board. He had just started at the university and said to me, "Hey, you need to be on this board." And I said, "Okay." I've met so many incredible people—not just students, but also faculty who can help me in the future. It's helped me find my desire to be a leader and my need for people—I used to think that I wasn't a people person. I now realize that I can talk to people and work well with people. That's something I never imagined getting from college.

—senior, Iowa State University

* * *

Your college experience is like a buffet of opportunity—instead of all you can eat, it's all you can do. The only limitation is how much time you have to consume the experiences. Start slowly and pick one or two things you can commit to freshman year.

When looking at clubs and organizations on your campus website, search around. Each college lists them in different categories. The club and organizational categories can include pretty much everything. Some examples include clubs and organizations addressing politics, women's issues, diversity, public service, alcohol education, religion, athletics, abortion, right to life, singing, gun control, the death penalty, equal rights, gay/lesbian/bisexual rights, volunteerism, leadership, entrepreneurship, student development, campus pride, juggling, video games, and role-playing games. (I was recently at a campus and saw a group of students in the midst of some kind of medieval role-playing game in the quad. Either that or they were *really* going for a retro look.)

"Don't be afraid to do things that interest you if other people don't think they are cool. This isn't the same as high school. There are enough people in college who do things that are uncool to make them 'cool.'"
—junior, University of Pittsburgh

You'll find clubs and organizations unique to your campus and then you'll find national clubs and organizations with individual chapters on campus. If you don't find a club or organization that excites you, start your own. Usually, all you need are a few members and a faculty sponsor. Once you're recognized by the college, they sometimes offer funding. When I was at school, I was a founding member of an improv troupe called Full Frontal Comedy. They're still going strong on campus. Whatever your interests, consider starting a club—from a prayer group to a book club to a club that talks about the clubs on campus. Get creative. The idea might hit you when you least expect it, like while eating barbecue. Yes, the Barbeque Club is a real club at the University of Texas–Austin. Here is their mission statement:

> The Barbeque Club
>
> The purpose of the barbecue club is threefold:
>
> 1) to serve the University of Texas and Austin community through barbecue
> 2) to uphold and promote barbecue consumption and tradition
> 3) to provide culinary leadership through barbecue while maintaining high standards of barbecue excellence.

And yes, it's worth mentioning one more time—*go to meetings on your own*. Trust me—there will be people there to welcome you to your new club or organization.

"Join Alpha Phi Omega; it's a national coed service fraternity. We do community service around Fort Worth—blood drives, community rehabilitation, an event call PNO—Professors Night Out. For PNO, we baby-sit professors' kids so that they can go out on the town at night."
—junior, Texas Christian University

Bottom Line

Visit your college's website to investigate clubs and activities offered, and visit other colleges' websites to see what new clubs and activities are out there for you to start. Your campus never knew how badly it needed a Disco Bodypaint Club.

Tip #31
Sports and Athletics: Buckets of College Sweat

The Tip
If you played sports in high school but don't want to play at a highly competitive level in college, look into club sports. They are less intense, involve intercollegiate competition, and take up less time than varsity athletics.

The Story
When I was in high school, I played basketball and soccer. I knew when I arrived at Boston University that I wouldn't be playing either sport, but I still wanted that intense feeling of competition. The result: women's rugby.

> "I play football, softball, and basketball as part of a league. It's only open to people on campus and it can get extremely competitive."
> —sophomore, University of Pennsylvania

Before I got to Boston, I didn't know what rugby was; I had never touched a ball and knew nothing about the positions and rules. The returning players and coach taught me everything I needed to know. Most importantly, my playing time wasn't affected if I missed practice due to intense amounts of homework. Being involved in a sport helped me manage my time and be successful.

—sophomore, Boston University

* * *

Like sports? Scared of gaining the freshman 15 (see Tip #97)? Looking to tackle some people or rip flags from their bodies? If you were an athlete in high school, you can be one in college. And you don't even have to be great to play.

Whatever you want to play, you should be able to find it. On a decent-sized campus, you've got basketball, football, baseball, soccer, Ultimate Frisbee, golf, lacrosse, rugby, crew, field hockey, softball, fencing, bicycling, bowling, martial arts, archery, ice hockey, cross country, track and field sports, Rollerblade hockey, field hockey, ice hockey, luge, and bobsledding (luge and bobsledding are more common at Swedish colleges).

There are three levels of athletics at most colleges. Varsity athletics are for the elite athletes, club sports are for the serious athletes, and intramurals are for the rest of us. Varsity athletics almost always have tryouts. Club sports are competitive and open to most students who want to play (sometimes there are tryouts). As for intramurals, this is typically the lowest level of competition. While it can still get intense, it's the easiest (most accessible) of the three to participate in. To find out how it works, contact your school's recreational center or the student activities office.

And if you want to participate in a team sport and don't have a team, don't let that hold you back. Typically you can be placed on a team.

Team sports are also a part of residence hall life, Greek fraternities and sororities, and other student organizations (my campus newspaper at IU had a softball team). You may be thinking, *I'd love to get involved, but I'm a horrible athlete.* Unless you play, you'll always be horrible. Start now, and in four years (or more if you're on the seven-year plan), you won't suck so badly. You might even become a team captain—or at least not the worst player. Michael Jordan got cut from his high school basketball team. Remember Michael Jordan? The basketball player?

Bottom Line
Stay in shape, meet people, play games, hang out later with the team—and then get so amazing that you go pro. (Staying in shape doesn't apply to the World Series of Poker players and professional bowlers.)

Tip #32
Academic Organizations:
Where Smart People Gather

The Tip
There are more than just social fraternities. Talk to your professors to see if there are any professional organizations for your major.

The Story
I had never heard about an engineering fraternity before

coming to college. It was midsemester and two professors visited our engineering class with some students in the engineering fraternity. They gave us an overview on how to become a prospective member. Signing up was as easy as picking up a form in the engineering fraternity lounge in the engineering building. Inside there are books, magazines, and refreshments, all maintained by members of the fraternity. For the first two years, I'm a prospective member. It's not until my junior year that I can be admitted. Even then, I have to maintain a minimum GPA, get high marks in all my engineering courses, and get a professor recommendation. Once I'm a member, along with it looking good on my resumé, there are opportunities to contribute to publications and a national database of information that opens doors to internships, job opportunities, and other ways to network with students, professors, and professionals. I'm in a Greek fraternity, but had no idea that there were these types of fraternities, too.

—freshman, Bradley University

✱ ✱ ✱

You don't really have to be smart, as in GPA smart, to be in an academic organization, although sometimes you do need to have a minimum GPA to participate.

Academic organizations and/or fraternities (which include men and women) are professional organizations where students with similar interests gather. They offer great opportunities to get involved within your academic department. It's a way to tap into internships, work-study jobs, and help build relationships within your field of study. Many academic fraternities are part of a larger national organization that can open the door to opportunities for internships, jobs, research in your field of study, and networking with students and professionals on other campuses. If you're interested in going to graduate school or have a particular passion, you can use the database to ask members for informational interviews and to build relationships that can help you throughout your academic and professional life.

My girlfriend in college (now my ex) was in the psychology club called Psi Chi. She was on the executive board of the campus chapter. As part of the group, she helped host guest speakers, publicize events, and run the organization. Being in Psi Chi enabled her to get to know a professor who mentored her, helped her get published in a professional journal as part of a research project, and helped get her into graduate school where she earned a PhD.

How you can join academic organizations varies. Sometimes, you just need to be enrolled in a particular field of study. Sometimes, you need to carry a minimum grade point average. You might even need a letter of recommendation. There can be a required number of meetings you must attend. In addition, there can be a small membership fee. To find out about them, talk to your professors, visit the departmental website, and stop by the actual department office to speak with the dean of the department. This is a great way to introduce yourself to someone important, and it gives you something to talk about. One more thing to keep in mind—students in these organizations are leaders in the field. These are also students who will make great study partners in the classes you have together.

Bottom Line

Meet people with similar interests, find an internship, network to find a job, and eat pretzels and pound soft drinks in the lounge.

Tip #33

Religious Activities: Your Prayers Answered & the Culture Club (no Boy George)

The Tip

Check out the religious organizations your university offers and use them to help ground yourself.

The Story

When I arrived at college I was bombarded with so many different aspects of life and lifestyle choices that it could have been easy to be swayed without the right support system. My closest friends are all the people that I have met as part of the Christian Fellowship on campus. These have been the people who have helped me through turbulent years and my faith in God has been strengthened. It is no longer my parents' influence that has connected me with my faith, but it is something that I have chosen for myself and I'm so thankful.

—junior, Northern Michigan University

> "Hillel (the Foundation for Jewish Campus Life) has given me a place to go on campus and friends who are involved in so many aspects of college life. It made what was a big campus much smaller and friendlier."
> —junior, University of Iowa

* * *

There's nothing like a good prayer after a tough week (and more than half of students attending college are doing it, according to the Higher Education Research Institute at UCLA). If you have strong ties to your culture, or religion is running through your blood, then run to the religious organizations and cultural centers on campus. These centers are where students sharing a common interest come together. It's a place to attend prayer services, participate in outdoor activities, take part in public service projects, and get a chance to travel to locations near and far with meaning—from a trip to Jerusalem, to a trip to Vatican City, to a tour through Latin America. Locally, there are activities such as rafting trips, athletics, hiking, weekend dinners, prayer study, guest speaker events, and other group activities to help bring students together.

Religious Activities
• 64.8 percent of students are praying/meditating during the first year of college.

"Freshman year I was scared to death of joining any campus activity, but I began to take part in different ministry opportunities on and off campus. I eventually became the leader of senior adult ministry and I am now a freshman family leader. I have met so many different people and have been able to volunteer on my campus and in the community in ways that I would not have been able to if I had not joined."
—senior, East Texas Baptist University

Whatever your religion, whatever your culture, there should be a place for you (if not on campus, then near campus). A few examples of religious/cultural clubs—African

American Center, African Students Association, Asian American Association, Baha'i Friendship Club, Baptist Student Ministry, Black Student Union, Brazilian Association, Buddhist Club, Campus Prayer Ministry, Catholic Campus Ministries, Chinese Christian Fellowship, Christian Campus Center, Fellowship of Christian Athletes, Hillel Jewish Foundation, Indonesian Student Association, Islamic Center, Japanese Student Association, Latter-Day Saints Student Association, Lutheran Campus Ministry, Lutheran Student Fellowship, Malaysian Students Association, Muslim Student Association, Pakistani Students Association, Taiwanese Student Association, United Methodist Students, Zen Club—and for the ones I missed, I'm sorry (send me a note and I'll include it in the next edition). Whatever your

> ### Religiously Speaking...
> - 54.3 percent of college students reported "occasionally" or "frequently" attended a religious service
> - 78.0 percent of college students reported "occasionally" or "frequently" discussed religion

faith, have faith that there will be people and places to celebrate it with (and if your faith or culture doesn't have a club or organization on campus, just start one).

As for this whole going to meetings and events alone thing (I know, enough already), if ever there were a place that welcomes new students, religious groups are it. Members will welcome you with open arms. And then, when you find yourself dealing with tough issues, you'll have advisors, spiritual leaders, and new friends to help you along the way.

Bottom Line

You don't have to just pray that you meet people—pray AND meet people, or seek out groups with whom you have cultural ties. Have faith and make friends who can help make campus a comfortable place.

Tip #34
The Perks: Travel and See the World for Free

The Tip
Don't be afraid to go on an adventure with a club or activity if you don't know anyone in the van.

The Story
Last spring, I went off campus as part of an alternative spring break program. It was with ten strangers also from campus. We met up and drove twenty-four hours in a van to Miami to build a home for a low-income family. The owner was so happy to have us there. I'll never forget the look on the mom's face when she saw us helping fix her home. She was crying. When we weren't working, we spent time hanging out and walking around South Beach. It was all part of a program at school that only cost about $175. It was a cheap spring break. I

> "We get to go to educational conferences all over the country—Las Vegas is one of the best places. I can't complain."
> —sophomore, Emerson College

even got to wear a bikini. I loved it so much that I'm going on another spring trip as a project leader—despite the strange odor in the van.

—junior, University of New Hampshire

* * *

This is a perk I never knew about when I went to college. The idea that a college would have paid for you to fly across the country and hang out with thousands of students from hundreds of colleges seems too good to be true. Yes, it's true. Every year, students go to places like California, Chicago, New Orleans, New York, Cincinnati, Boston, Portland, Las Vegas, Seattle, and Boise (yes, even Boise). And the list goes on. I'm talking even international locations. There are conferences, conventions, symposiums, competitions, and educational trips to Europe (sometimes I might even be speaking at them). Usually, travel and a stipend for food are included.

> "Some of our students get to tour the sites in France that are associated with the life and works of the university's patron: Saint Vincent de Paul."
> —professional, DePaul University

If you're someone who doesn't travel much, this is your chance. I've met students who have never flown or even left their home states before. If you're one of those people, this can be your ticket. If you're in a club or organization that doesn't travel, talk to the faculty sponsor and see if you can be the first group to attend a convention. Departments have budgets for things like this. All you have to do is ask. Should they say no, then put together a fund-raiser and make it happen on your own. Here are some ways to get involved and see the world:

- *Sports on and off campus.* Travel with your team for away games and compete in national competitions in other cities, states, or countries.
- *Competitive clubs and activities.* Attend regional, national, and international competitions (like those competitions that air on ESPN2 at three o'clock in the morning).
- *Religious organizations.* Travel to other campuses for retreats and conferences. Take a trip to the homeland and tap into national funds. Project Birthright offers free trips to Israel.
- *Clubs and groups with national affiliations.* Investigate your organization's national conference calendar. Executives can often travel for free.
- *Greek life.* Attend regional and/or national conferences (these happen ALL the time).
- *Student leadership.* Attend national conferences, regional conferences, and educational meetings. Also investigate summer leadership retreats.
- *Study abroad and alternative spring breaks.* Go to your study abroad office and inquire how you can spend a semester in another country. Often, the price of tuition is the same (or even less). Inquire about scholarships to travel abroad.

"As part of program board, we've had students travel to Indianapolis, Boston, Cincinnati, then regionals in Portland, and next year they'll go to Reno, Nevada. We travel twice a year. Our students get their air, hotel, and some meals provided. And they stay in nice places, generally in four- or five-star hotels."
—advisor, Idaho State University

Bottom Line

Get into a club or organization and get out of town. Packages include free air, free hotel, and free food. Sorry—you'll have to spring for the Pay-Per-View movies.

Harlan's Tip Sheet

Getting Involved Resources, Websites, and Additional Information

Places on Campus to Find Information

- *Campus operator/student information desk*. It seems obvious, but these people know a lot about the campus. One college even boasted that the campus operator could give cooking instructions for a Thanksgiving turkey.
- *Student activities office*. The central hub that oversees campus activities. Typically, student-run clubs and activities need to be registered here.

- *Recreational center.* The gymnasium/field house where students can participate in organized and open sports. Take a walk down the halls and read about events, happenings, and ways to get involved.
- *Dean of students office.* The dean's office oversees all of campus. If you have questions, don't hesitate to call.
- *Department/academic offices.* Every area of study has a departmental office. Ask who can lead you to the information you seek.
- *Facebook and MySpace.* Locate and contact executive members of clubs and organizations via their website and find the executive board members' information via Facebook and MySpace. Then send a note with your questions.

Key Words

Activities fair: Most colleges offer organized events where students can visit booths with members of various clubs and organizations. At the least, watch for signs and posters advertising various activities in the Union, student center, or resident halls.

Call-outs: Watch for advertisements listed in the campus newspaper or posted around campus inviting students to take part in a club or activity.

Philanthropy: Participate in charity events organized by students and run by students.

Greek Life

Behind the Doors, Windows, and Walls of Fraternity and Sorority Life

Dear Harlan,

I'm going away to college next year and would like to join a sorority. I've heard stories of girls going away to college and not getting into a sorority. I wanted to know about the whole process and what happens if I don't get into a sorority. Please help!

—Sorority Searching

Dear Sorority Searching,

It's easy to get into a sorority house. The challenge is not being asked to leave by current members once inside. As a guy, I could never pull that one off.

The process of becoming an actual member and getting into a sorority (or fraternity) house differs from campus to campus. Generally, you arrive on campus and move into the residence halls. RUSH (the caps are for drama) is the process in which potential sorority members meet current members and check out the different houses. Generally, rush takes place in the fall or spring. The rush process consists of organized visits to the sororities on campus, interviews with members, events, and bids (invitations) offered by the sorority and fraternity members.

Rush isn't a perfect process. It can be nerve-racking to have strangers judging you, and it can get a little uncomfortable. Not getting in is *not* the end of the world. It can be hard at first, but then once you find your place on campus, you can still be friends with the sorority sisters and then rush again next year. Or you can just do your own thing and have the best of both worlds!

Tip #35
Greek Life: Getting In

The Sorority Tip

The Tip
Don't put on a show for the rush parties.

The Story

There are several girls in my sorority who, while going through rush, put on a huge act about who they were, what they liked, and so on just to get into the sorority they thought was cool. Now that they are in my sorority, they are really unhappy because they have none of the same interests as the girls and they feel like they have to continue to put on a show to fit in. That is not what being in a sorority is about. It is no fun going to functions if you have to act like someone else. College is the time when most people find themselves. How are you supposed to know who you really are when you can't act like yourself around your supposed best friends at school? Putting on an act might get you in, but this isn't about just getting in. It's about finding people that you want to be with.

—freshman, Clemson University

The Fraternity Tip

The Tip

Be yourself and find out what the fraternity is all about.

The Story

Most fraternities will drop a lot of cash and make you feel like you're the most important person during the rush process. There are boat cruises, paintball games, nice dinners, and bagels in the morning. I knew it all couldn't keep happening, but I thought at least there would be bagels in the morning. When rush ended, it all stopped. Don't lose sight of what's most important: the people in the frat. Talk to the brothers and ask questions. Some guys will be straight with you when asking what a typical weekend is like. Don't be afraid to ask. The brothers will respect you more for asking—and if they don't, you shouldn't want to be in that house anyway. Three years later, I'm into Greek life.

—junior, Massachusetts Institute of Technology

✳ ✳ ✳

You don't need to be Greek to get into a house. The term "Greek" comes from the letters of the Greek alphabet fraternities and sororities use for their names. If you're interested in getting an invitation to join a Greek fraternity or sorority, it all starts with rush (but please, no pushing to get in).

The Sorority Rush Overview

Typically, rush is called "formal rush" because it's a highly organized process lasting several weeks. Women are usually required to visit each sorority and meet current members. It's a way for those rushing and sisters in the house to gauge each other's personalities. The current members often sing, dance, and put on shows to welcome visiting potential members. There is usually a short interview with such probing questions as: Where are you from? Do you have any siblings? What do you do for fun? Have any pets? Once sorority members meet all the rushees, they invite certain people back for subsequent meetings (sometimes dinner or an activity). Eventually, bids are offered. Bids are invitations asking those rushing to become members. This is when things can get ugly. Some people who want bids don't get bids—only hurt feelings. Please, do *not* take the process personally.

These people have no clue who you really are and what you're all about. If you don't get in, at least you'll have friends you meet from the rush process. Then you can have the best of both worlds, and should you decide to rush again, you'll have a ticket in the door. If formal rush is too much for you, informal rush happens all year long, in which you and the members can get to know each other over time.

The Fraternity Rush Overview

Again, it varies from campus to campus, but fraternity rush is generally less formal than sorority rush. During men's rush, it's all about getting to know the brothers and finding out if you mesh with the guys in the house. Organized rush events like attending a sporting event, playing basketball with brothers, cookouts, dinners, and rush parties are typical. Once rush ends, the fraternity members hand out bids. If you accept, you become a pledge. Most fraternities have a fall pledge class and a winter pledge class. And again, if you don't get in (and you wanted to), at least you'll have friends who are in who can offer you a bid next semester (it happened to me).

Bottom Line

If you decide to rush, do not take the process too personally. These people don't know you and have no way of knowing you so quickly. Look at it like this—they should be more concerned about impressing you. They need new members.

The Sorority Tip

The Tip

Don't pass up on rushing or pledging the Greek system on your campus just because you think you're not "sorority material."

The Story

I thought the exact same thing when I started college. I told myself, "I don't need to pay to have friends." [Monthly dues are sometimes associated with Greek organizations.] I pledged a sorority on a whim during my second semester freshman year. I loved the girls I pledged with, and even wound up being elected vice president of the sorority my junior year. That brief tenure as vice president taught me quite a bit about running an organization of that size, and it also looks nice on a resumé.

> —graduate student, Montclair State University

The Fraternity Tip

The Tip

Frats can offer you much more than beer.

The Story

I never in a million years pictured myself in a frat. I soon discovered that some guys I met weren't the typical frat guys I thought they were. They were a colony, which is one of the first stages in the creation of a chapter. I wanted to join after one meeting. That was five years ago, and I have now held two different executive positions in the chapter and joined five other campus organizations that I never would have even known about if it weren't for my brothers. I am now a senior approaching graduation, and I have held five executive offices in four different organizations, and all because of a colony I helped build. I not only have a great group of friends, but I also have one impressive resumé.

—senior,
Pittsburg State University

According to the North American Interfraternity Council

48 percent of all U.S. presidents are Greek.

42 percent of U.S. senators are Greek.

30 percent of U.S. congressmen/women are Greek.

40 percent of all U.S. Supreme Court Justices have been Greek.

30 percent of Fortune 500 executives are Greek.

10 percent of all people listed in *Who's Who* are Greek.

* * *

Having pledged two fraternities, dated women in sororities, and unsuccessfully interviewed five times to be a live-in houseboy at sororities (not true), I've seen the good, the bad, and the ugly parts of Greek life. This is the tip about the good.

Personally, I think Greek life can be great. It gives you an instant group of people your age to hang out with, a social life, and a comfortable place on campus. Members often live together (not all fraternities and sororities have houses on campus or require living in the house), eat together, sleep together, party together, play together, study together, and go through pledging together—it all helps form a tight bond. You have a common identity—the history and the reputation of your campus chapter. And once you graduate, you have a network of support that can help you professionally. And no, it's not about buying friends—it's paying dues to help run an organization (locally and nationally) where you can make new friends.

The Best Parts of Greek Life

Leadership Opportunities. Each house usually elects an executive board consisting of a president, vice president, secretary, social chair, rush chair, philanthropy chair (for fund-raising and community involvement), and several other chairs or positions. Outside the inner workings of the house, representatives of fraternities and sororities work with other leaders on campus to organize campus events. Seasonal rituals like homecoming, alcohol awareness events, dance marathons, acting/singing competitions, and community service events are often opportunities for Greeks to get involved and to meet other Greeks and non-Greeks.

Social Opportunities. As a member of a fraternity or sorority, your social life is kind of just there for you. You just need to show up. There are date parties, formals, and other social events (where a fraternity and sorority may pair up). It's an easy way to make friends inside and outside your house. Besides these events, there are often team sports and campus-wide activities and philanthropic opportunities.

Diversity. Between national affiliations, volunteer work, service on campus, and other activities, you can meet as many people as you choose to. Most national fraternities and sororities have national conferences annually where you can meet people from chapters around the country with similar interests and a common bond.

Academics. Some houses have better GPA averages than others. On many campuses, Greeks are the most academically successful. It helps to be in a fraternity or sorority that values academic achievement. Whatever it is that your house is known for, chances are, when you become a member, you'll follow the same path.

> "Join a Greek organization! At the very least rush them and see what the deal is. I came to college with a very anti-Greek view of things. I was under the impression that all fraternities were just like *Animal House*, doing nothing but partying and hazing their pledges. I went through my entire freshman year uninvolved and not feeling particularly like a student. At the beginning of my sophomore year, I was finally convinced to rush. The moment I set foot into the house I felt a connection that I hadn't felt with anyone in years. The entire experience was remarkably life-changing."
> —junior, Drexel University

Bottom Line

Greek life can be a great life. Not all people love it, but most people outside the system don't always take the time to understand, appreciate, and see the good in it.

Tip #37

The Tip
Don't be afraid to de-pledge if it's not the right fit.

The Story
I became close friends with a girl through a team sport my freshman year. She was a year older and someone I liked hanging out with. She invited me to come to dinner at her sorority house a couple times. Then she invited me to rush her house. Once I got into the sorority, I was just friends with two or three people. The rest I didn't have much in common with. It's funny. They were supposed to be the "cool" sorority, but it was just a bunch of girls who weren't cool in high school, but then thought they were cool in college. I couldn't stand it. I found out that I'm just not someone who likes to be in a house with fifty other girls. I didn't like any part of it. And it cost money. They told me that I would have to move into the house, so I de-pledged. This all happened a few days ago. I just stopped going to chapter meetings and left a message on the president's phone. I'm not the sorority type and now I know it. Some people are, but it's just not my thing. They

> "Don't join a sorority. I joined a sorority my second semester of my freshman year. I wasted over $500 for 'fake' friends. Now that I am out of the sorority, 80 percent of those girls never even look my way these days."
> —junior, Henderson State University

might not understand, but that's not my problem.

—sophomore, college withheld

✳ ✳ ✳

Everyone and everything has a good side and a bad side (my left side in extremely dark lighting is my best). Greek life is no exception. In all fairness, this is the bad side of it all. If you can't handle it, then please, feel free to look away. And be forewarned, the ugly side is the topic of the next tip.

The Potential Problems

Isolation and lack of diversity. When you're in a house, it's easy to isolate yourself from the rest of campus. It takes effort to use the opportunities provided to you by being involved with Greek life to get involved outside of your fraternity or sorority. Some people go Greek and close off their social circles. It's much better to keep yourself open to the best of both worlds. It's great to belong to a group, but the group should never keep you away from meeting people—Greek and non-Greek.

Social pressures. When you're part of such a tight group, it's normal to feel intense pressure to do things you don't always want to do—like drinking, drugs, sex, and partying. Statistically, those involved in Greek life tend to drink more. It's a fact. That said, some fraternities and sororities like to party more than others. Find out which house fits your personality and set of values. Whatever the people in the fraternity or sorority do will most likely be the things that you'll end up doing. Most members buckle to the pressure (but still, a select few do not).

Loss of identity. It's easy to let the group define you. It's like this: you're in a new place, surrounded by new people, and all you want is to feel like you belong. Pledgeship takes unique people and can roll them into one ball of dough from which cookie-cutter members are formed. Some people lose their identities and become lost in the group. *Do not* let your Greek organization turn you into a cookie-cutter person. Define your Greek life. Do not let your Greek affiliation define you.

Complacency. It's easy to not get involved outside of the Greek circles when your social life is pretty much taken care of for you. It's easy to just go with the flow. Make a real effort to meet people and to participate in activities outside of the Greek circles.

False sense of superiority. Some people think they're better than others on campus because of the letters on their chests—the letters that will end up in a box once you graduate. It's the people who think they're better who are the most insecure.

Bottom Line

Greek life makes it extremely easy to be a leader, but just as easy to be a follower. Choose to be a leader.

Tip #38
Greek Life: The Ugly

The Tip

Pledging activities are always a choice. Don't demean yourself—especially to the point of physical harm—just to fit in.

The Story

Our college's pledging program is undergoing a crackdown from the administration. Many alleged pledging activities have been the focus of concern in recent years—such as pledges not being allowed to sleep, being kept outside all night, and so on. But when one fraternity's pledges were reportedly observed at a party covered in what appeared to be vomit and urine, and being kicked down stairs, another Greek group's members decided to alert authorities. I'm a member of a nonhazing sorority myself and we're suffering the consequences. As a result, the school is implementing an indefinite suspension of pledging pending appointment of a faculty-student-staff "task force." We think it's time— no student should be allowed to abuse another just for the sake of "belonging."

> "Don't do it if you think it's wrong in your gut. Brothers who give you a hard time aren't people you'll want as friends."
> —recent graduate, University of Illinois

—senior, Cornell College

* * *

And now, this is where the chapter gets ugly. Sometimes, people get carried away and "tradition" overrides rational, intelligent behavior. That's when members end up forcing pledges and other members to do stupid things. And if you're someone who wants to belong, you might do things you never wanted or expected to do, because not doing these things can mean not being part of the group. But please, *never* put up with hazing. In fact, hazing is a crime:

> Hazing
> The term "hazing" means any conduct or method of initiation into any student organization, whether on public or private property, which willfully or recklessly endangers the physical or mental health of any student or other person. Such conduct shall include whipping; beating; branding; forced calisthenics; exposure to the weather; forced consumption of any food, liquor, beverage, drug, or other substance; or any other brutal treatment or forced physical activity which is likely to adversely affect the physical health or safety of any such student or other person, or which subjects such student or other person to extreme mental stress, including extended deprivation of sleep or rest or extended isolation.

Every college and state has strict rules against hazing. If you're the one doing it, you could be arrested. If you're

"If someone is hazing you, report it to nationals or the proper authorities on campus."
—Harlan

the one who is being hazed, you can have people arrested. Do not just accept it as a normal ritual. If you change the culture, tradition will change. If you ever feel that you're being put in an uncomfortable or dangerous situation or that you're being forced to do something that you know isn't right, don't do it. Leave an anonymous message with the dean of students. Leave an anonymous message with the national chapter. You can have your parents leave a confidential message (and then you can say that you never knew about it). Hazing is stupid. It's not necessary. Make sure that you protect yourself and your friends. The biggest problem is that sometimes new members get lost in the group mentality and can't see the real dangers. Alert people who can step in and stop whatever it is that's happening. And yes, this happens all over campus, not just in the Greek community—but hazing in Greek Life is a tradition that doesn't need to continue.

> **For Information on the Realities of Hazing, Read:**
>
> *Wrongs of Passage: Fraternities, Sororities, Hazing, and Binge Drinking* by Hank Nuwer (Indiana University Press, 1999).

Bottom Line

If pledges stopped putting up with hazing, the hazing would stop. One way to stop it is to reporting hazing. You can even email me anonymously and I'll do my best to pass along the word to the right people on campus and in the national organization. Send your note to: harlan@helpme harlan.com, Subject: hazing.

Harlan's Tip Sheet

Greek Life Resources, Websites, and Additional Information

Definitions

- *Greek advisor:* The person on campus who works with the fraternity and sorority leaders to make sure procedures and rules are being followed.
- *Dean of students*: The dean of students oversees the entire campus. If there is a serious problem or concern in a fraternity or sorority, the dean of students will get involved.
- *Interfraternity Council (IFC)*: This is the governing body of the recognized fraternity chapters on campus, made up of representatives from each fraternity. The IFC works to provide programming and leadership opportunities within the Greek community, and also makes sure policies and procedures are being followed.
- *Panhellenic Association*: Every woman who joins a sorority becomes a member of the Panhellenic Association. The association brings sorority members together to work toward common goals for the benefit of the community. A council made up of a representative from each sorority governs the Panhellenic Association.
- *National office*: Most Greek organizations have a national office that oversees each chapter. Contact the national office if you can't find resolutions to your problems within your chapter.

- *Dues and initiation fees*: Fraternities and sororities usually charge a one-time initiation fee and membership fees. Inquire about specific costs before accepting a bid.
- *Philanthropy*: Most chapters organize charitable events to help raise money for an important cause.
- *Executive board*: Each Greek organization has an internal governing board made up of members who run different aspects of the house. Usually there is a president, vice president, secretary, rush chair, social chair, philanthropy chair, and many more chairs.
- *Hazing:* See definition in Tip #38.

Websites (with links to national fraternity and sorority sites)

- Mid-America Greek Council Association (MGCA)
  www.mgca.org
- National Panhellenic Conference
  www.npcwomen.org
- North American Interfraternity Conference
  www.nicindy.org/index.html
- Northeast Greek Leadership Association (NGLA)
  www.ngla.org
- Western Region Greek Association (WRGA)
  www.wrgaonline.org
- Southeast Interfraternity Conference (SEIFC)
  www.seifc.org/
- Southeast Panhellenic Conference (SEPC)
  sepconline.org/

- Stop Hazing Information (by state):
  http://www.stophazing.org/laws.html

Suggested Reading

Wrongs of Passage: Fraternities, Sororities, Hazing, and Binge Drinking by Hank Nuwer (Indiana University Press, 1999).

The Naked Blog: Greek Life: Fraternizing and Sororitizing www.TheNakedRoommate.com

Life Inside the Classroom

Assuming You Wake Up and Go to Class

7

Dear Harlan,

I'm a sophomore in college and stressed over a class. I have to take two years of a foreign language to graduate, and I've taken almost a year and a half of Russian. The end seems so close, but I just don't think I can take it anymore. The class is very difficult and it requires a much larger time commitment than I have been able to offer. Compound that with the fact that I have found myself completely unmotivated to work on Russian, and I have a class in which I do poorly and I feel miserable. There are two weeks of class left in the semester, and I don't know whether or not I should bother to keep going. Even after studying for hours, I failed yet another test, and it doesn't look like it's going to get any better.

It's 4 a.m., and I still can't sleep, because I know I have to wake up and go to this class. I feel terrible, and it's really been hurting my other work, not to mention my general quality of life. Is college really supposed to be like this?

—Rattled by Russian

Dear Rattled,

My original reply was in Russian, but I figured the semester would be over by the time you translated it, so I translated it back to English for you. Listen, man (or woman)—talk to your professor and explain the situation, preferably in English. Tell him or her that you really want to pass and will do whatever it takes. Professors can be surprisingly flexible in these situations. Offer to meet with him or her several times before the end of the semester. Suggest getting an incomplete and doing extra work over the break when you can focus solely on Russian. In the meantime, meet with your academic advisor as soon as possible. I don't know if your professor knows you or not, but the better a professor knows you the less likely you are to fail.

To sum this up for you—go to class, talk to your professors, talk to your advisor, and figure out a way to make this work. Yes, this is what college is about. But no, you don't have to handle this on your own. Unless you're going to be a translator for the United Nations, this class won't break you. Get some sleep and relax.

Tip #39
To Go Or Not to Go

The Tip
You can miss classes once in a while, but you have to be very strategic about it. If you miss a lot of classes, your grades suffer.

The Story
I've learned that college is about figuring out how to make the best possible use of my time. It's not as if I'm sleeping through classes, but sometimes I've found that it's better to miss a lecture if I have to work on a paper or study for something else. The rule is that I'll never miss a lecture around midterms or finals, and I'll never miss a section. The teachers know if I'm there or not because there are usually only about ten or fifteen people in section. In lec-

> **"No matter what time you schedule your first class, you'll find a way to sleep through it."**
> **—junior, DeSales University**

tures, they don't know if I'm there. It also helps that most of my professors post their notes on their websites. One professor refuses to put his PowerPoint presentation online because he feels that it's not fair for students who go to class. There have been a few rare occasions where I've been tired or run-down and missed class, but that generally doesn't hold me back from class.

—freshman, Harvard University

* * *

There's always the chance that you're sitting in bed, blowing off class, and reading this tip. If you are, at least you're doing some reading—be proud. Deciding whether to go to class or not is the hardest choice you'll face in your college career—that and whether or not to secretly borrow clean underwear from your roommate when you run out. The attendance question regularly stares you in the eye—every morning when the alarm goes off (assuming you've even set it). Deciding whether or not to go to class is a new freedom that you have in college; in most cases, you're free of parental supervision, attendance offices, and questioning principals (but some professors do take attendance). If you *choose* to, you can sleep late, watch TV all day, play video games, enjoy a four-hour breakfast at the buffet, go to the gym, go to a party, hang out with your boyfriend or girlfriend, chat online, or just lay in bed imagining all those things that you could be doing—which can be exhausting, leading you to fall asleep again and miss your afternoon classes too.

> "It took me until my last semester to realize that if I went to class nearly every time, the exams were a zillion times easier because I already had a grasp on the material. Now that I'm in grad school and going to every class as expected, I'm finding it a breeze."
> —graduate student, University of Texas

> "Don't get in the habit of skipping classes. As your classes become more difficult, it's more important to go."
> —junior, Manhattan College

The choice to go or not to go is yours, but with every choice comes consequences. In this case, the consequence could be missing essential material, missing a pop quiz with no makeup offered, missing material that will likely be the key to the next exam, losing out on extra credit awarded for simply attending class, getting poor grades, and failing out of school. From time to time you will find yourself unable to make it to class. It happens. Just make sure that you can at least do the following to cover yourself:

> "When picking your classes, pick something you are interested in learning about. If you are not interested in the subject, then you will not want to get up to go to class."
>
> —sophomore, Angelo State University

○ Some professors will award credit just for attending class. Make sure to find out your professor's attendance policy. Ask your professor or teaching assistant if the information is not in your syllabus.

○ Get notes from a friend in your class. The only catch is that you need to actually go to class so that you can make a friend who can share notes with you. And then, when your new friend is out of class, you'll be the one sharing your notes.

○ If you should get sick or miss classes because of reasons beyond your control, you have options. You can drop a class before it counts against you. Talk to your professors and your academic advisor—but be sure to do something. A dropped class doesn't typically count against your grade point average. An F can and will hurt you.

○ If you find that you're consistently missing class because you're nursing a hangover, playing video games, or downloading porn, or that you're still partying in the morning while your class is in session, there's a pretty good chance that you need some professional treatment. That's not normal (see Tip #82).

○ If you find that you're missing so many classes that you forget where your classes are and which days you even have them, ask yourself this question: why in the hell am I here if I'm never going to classes? I might be better off buying a Ferrari with my tuition money.

> "I came to school with a 4.0 GPA and thought that college would be a breeze, just like high school. The first few weeks I went to class religiously and then the party invites started coming. It seemed like the weekend started on a Wednesday and ended on a Tuesday. I was usually too tired to go to my early morning classes and didn't feel like putting much effort into the other ones. It wasn't until the report cards came out that I realized my GPA had plummeted to a 2.5 and I lost my scholarship that I realized I had to do something about it."
> —senior, Northern Michigan University

Bottom Line

Missing a class is the equivalent to paying hundreds of dollars for a ticket to a show and then not going. Unfortunately, you can't scalp tickets to English 101. Besides the price, your grades will suffer.

Tip #40
Nice Professor, Nice Professor

The Tip
Professors are your friends. Don't be afraid to get to know them.

The Story
I started college completely intimidated by my professors. I was afraid to talk to them and even approach them. In high school, the teachers were pushing me, but in college, I had to push myself. I had to be the one to seek out help. In Philosophy 160, I understood most of it, but a few paragraphs confused me. There were about two hundred people in the class. I went to the professor's office hours, and he was in the room with a dog at his feet. I thought that was kind of interesting. He read the paragraph and broke it down to me. He cleared it up in a matter of minutes. I went back to him whenever something was confusing and he was happy to help. All of my professors wanted to help. One professor even invited some students to his house for dinner. His wife made us dinner.

"Make a commitment to visit each professor's office hours at least once a term. My biggest regret from college has been not getting to know my professors—and not just because of letters of recommendation from them. Professors are some of the best people to talk to about the fields you are interested in. They can provide helpful advice on grad school, papers, and college life. I missed out on meeting so many professors."
—senior, UCLA

I was surprised that my professor and I became friends.
—freshman, University of Washington–Seattle

* * *

Professors are often some of the most intimidating members of the college community. Some students tiptoe around them as if walking barefoot on the tile floors in the community bathrooms. (A quick note about community bathroom floors: for God's sake, always wear flip flops!) In reality, professors are some of the kindest, funniest, smartest, warmest, most interesting, and most misunderstood people you'll meet in college.

> "Test dates can be flexible with some professors if you check with them. My professor was totally cool about changing a test date because I was away at a conference. All I had to do was ask."
> —junior, Texas Christian University

The biggest mistake is that students don't get to know their professors. Your professors want you to talk to them. They want to help you. They want to share their passion with you. They choose to teach. They want to be challenged by you. They want to be approached by you. Ask questions. Allow them to get to know you. Unlike high school, not all of them are going to track you down. They might not even know your name—but it's not their fault. In college, you need to be the one to get to know your professors. Approach them. Sure, a few act like they've got a pole stuck up

Scary Facts about Professors

27.8 percent of surveyed freshmen "frequently" or "occasionally" felt intimidated by professors.

—Higher Education Research Institute at UCLA

their professor rear end or they left their personality in the faculty lounge, but most aren't like that. Most won't push you around just because they can.

While researching this tip, professor after professor urged me to encourage students to make it a point to introduce themselves. The better a professor knows you the better your chance of passing a course or getting additional help along the way. Professors can offer you extra help in the way of tutoring, rescheduling exams if you miss one, and giving you an extra point or two for all your effort. They can offer mentoring and support during college and after college. They can offer letters of recommendation for graduate school or for campus jobs or activities. And they can offer a friendship that can last far beyond your college years. The problem is that a lot of students don't want to approach their professors because they are too intimidated or don't want to look stupid when asking a question. But really, these professors are there for YOU. Besides, they need for you to ask questions— even easy ones. If you knew everything, they would have no reason to exist. Give them a purpose. Make an effort to get to know your professors. Don't be shy. Just say, "Hi, I'm blah blah (if that's not your

> ### Who Really Goes to Professors' Office Hours?
>
> 8.7 percent of students never go to office hours
>
> 37.0 percent of students go to office hours one to two times per term
>
> 26.4 percent of students go to office hours one to two times per month
>
> 14.1 percent of students go to office hours once a week
>
> 13.7 percent of students go to office hours more than once a week
>
> —Higher Education Research Institute at UCLA

name, then say your name), and I just wanted to introduce myself to you."

> "Every year just before the first big exam, I have waves of nameless strangers at my door, suddenly trying to figure out what has been going on the first two months of class. At this point, there is little I can do for them, except ask awkward questions ("Did you read the book? Do you have the book? How often have you been to class?"). When someone I have already met comes in, the help comes easier to both of us."
> —college professor in Texas

Quick warning: if you're checking out a professor using RateMyProfessors.com, confirm what you read with real life students on campus, face-to-face. Not all students grade their professors fairly.

Bottom Line

Professors want you to do well, but unless they actually know your name (not just your user email name), and your face (not a .jpeg or .gif), they can't help you do well.

Tip #41
How to Get an A (or almost an A)

The Tip

To get an A, follow these seven steps to academic success, created by me, an average student:

Step 1: Go to class regularly and on time.

Step 2: Do all assigned homework.

Step 3: Take notes.

Step 4: Be in tune with your professor.

Step 5: Take advantage of tutoring.

Step 6: Organize.

Step 7: Have a positive attitude.

The Story

In high school, I was never really able to get good grades. I never understood why. I studied a lot, I did my homework, but somehow I always struggled.

When I got into college, my mentality changed. I decided to completely redo my habits and take on a new form of scholastic work. I decided to come to every single class, write down what the professors would say, and I would study only what I was told to study. And, to this point, after six consecutive trimesters, I am maintaining a 4.0 GPA. I am the vice president of the prestigious Alpha Chi National Honors Society, Iota Illinois Chapter, and I hold lectures and speeches teaching other students just how easy it is to get good

A math professor's guide to making the grade

1) Take all prerequisites before your first collegiate mathematics class. 2) Attend all classes and arrive at least ten minutes early. 3) Buy your textbook early and skim the first chapter. 4) If possible, sit close to the front of the class to reduce any distractions. 5) Find a study partner and try to meet several times a week. 6) Constantly monitor your attitude and study habits. 7) Do not be afraid to ask questions—often high school students think asking questions is a sign of weakness. This is not true in college. 8) Seek help from the Math Lab and/or your professor. 9) Consider taking your math class in a short term where you can focus only on this one course. 10) Keep up on a daily basis and remember, for every hour in class, you should study at least two hours outside the classroom.

grades. I know that if students follow these seven steps, I can ethically guarantee them good grades (A's and B's).

—junior, DeVry University

***

Before telling you how to get an A, appreciate that there are more students than ever before coming into college with A averages. According to the Institute of Higher Education, almost half of all incoming freshman have A averages.

> "When a student gets a *bad* grade, they say, 'The professor gave me a C,' vs. when a student gets a good grade, they say, 'I got an A.'"
> —professional, Otterbein College

This means that getting an A won't be as easy as it was in high school. However, it's possible if you want it badly enough. Here are my tips within the tip for getting an A:

- *Go to classes*. Obviously, you need to be there to listen, learn, and absorb.
- *Sit near the front of the room*. The closer you are, the fewer distractions to pull your focus.
- *Make sure your professor knows who you are*. Introduce yourself to your professor. Do it in class, during office hours, and around campus.
- *Do readings ahead of time*. If you're familiar with the readings, you will naturally absorb so much more of the lecture content in class—and retain it.
- *Study your notes the night after you take them*. Conscientiously review your notes the night after the lecture. Again, the material will stick with you this way.

- *Look over your syllabus before going to class.* The syllabus is the schedule of what's to come. It helps to know when the exams are approaching.
- *Get help.* If you're having trouble in a class, don't go for help the day before the final. Your professor won't be sympathetic. Go as soon as the trouble starts.
- *Go to office hours.* Every professor has office hours set aside for students to come in and get extra help. It's like a free tutoring session.
- *Form study groups.* Find people in class who can challenge you, share notes, and pool resources to help everyone master the material.
- *Ask about extra credit.* If you're not making the grade, ask to do extra work.
- *Question exams when you get them back.* Many professors will change your score if you care enough to bring up a confusing question on a graded exam. It's worth trying.
- *Find out from upperclassmen how a professor grades.* Some professors only give out a few As while others give out many more. It will help you to know how hard you need to work in the class to earn an A.
- *Find old exams.* If it's legal, study off of old exams. You might find a few questions on the new exam that are the same or similar. At the very least, old exams can help you focus on important information.
- *Talk to former students.* Talk to people who have taken the class and ask about the best ways to study and how the professor tests. Many colleges have websites where students list information about professors' procedures and grading styles.

- *Avoid cramming if possible.* You'll retain information longer if you study way ahead of the exam. Cramming might help you pass, but you need to retain information for final exams. (That said, I crammed too much.)
- *Go to exam reviews.* Before exams, many professors or teaching assistants will offer reviews. These are priceless rundowns of the material typically on the exam.
- *Grades can be negotiable.* Fight for a higher grade by all means possible (without breaking any laws or codes of conduct). When the professor says, "If I do this for you, I'll have to do it for everyone," counter with, "If everyone cared, I could understand, but I'm the only one here—the only one who cares enough…"

Bottom Line

The bad news: not everyone can get an A. The good news: most people don't want to do the work it takes to get an A. You can.

Tip #42
How to Just Pass

The Tip
Unlike high school, you actually need to study in college.

The Story
I came to college as a straight-A student, and never really had to study too much in high school. It came as a sur-

prise to me when I got two C's and just two B's my first semester. When I met my boyfriend, I soon came to copy his study habits. Instead of trying to cram it all in the night before, give yourself three solid days to study for your test, and then on the night before, review everything that you've already studied. This will take major pressure off in the hours nearing the exam. This tip has made me face the upcoming exam well ahead of time and not try to avoid it until the last minute. Your grades will reflect the time you put into them—unlike grades in high school!

> **"Check your university's pass/fail policy. It can save your GPA. I took honors religions my first year and got a C in the class. It wasn't even a required course. It wasn't until after the class was over that I was told that I could take two classes pass/fail. I could have saved my GPA."**
> **—junior, Texas Christian University**

—senior, Juniata College

* * *

If you find that you just can't put in the time you need to get the grade you desire, use only the following tips from the previous tip to just pass:

- Go to class.
- Go to the review before the exam.
- Study old exams (if it's legal).
- Find a study group with people more motivated and/or smarter than you are.

If you can go to class and manage to actually stay awake and pay attention some of the time, you should achieve a low C or a solid D (the word "achieve" isn't really worthy of this sentence). Basically, if you go to class and do minimal work, there's a decent chance you'll be able to slide by.

Additional note: for classes that involve essay exams on specific readings, you'll need to read the book or at least have someone explain the book to you. This is why it helps to surround yourself with smart people who are more motivated than you. If you ask them to explain it to you and they respond, "Why the hell should I tell you?" Reply, "If you tell me, then you'll be able to go through the material while explaining it and you'll have a better grasp of it all." If they say, "But I already know it," tell them, "Yeah, but it helps to talk it through. Besides, it's not like I'm going to affect your grade. Just tell me enough to pass." If it's still a problem, try, "I'll get you into a party." It's a win-win situation.

> "It took a while to get used to the fact that I didn't have to raise my hand to go the bathroom. I could just get up and leave when I wanted to leave. The smaller classes made it harder, but no one noticed in the bigger lectures."
> —senior, Northwestern University

Additional additional note: when it comes to the math and accounting classes with number-oriented themes, just going to class and doing nothing else could land you a D or an F. If you're not great with numbers, be aware that you need to do more than go to class. If you're good with numbers, you can still just go to class, review, and pass.

Bottom Line
Minimal work + minimal attendance + minimal effort = minimal grades.

Tip #43
How to Fail

The Tip
Too much partying and no studying can be your downfall. Drinking at college can be a lot of fun, but it can also be your worst enemy.

The Story
I say that I am a college sophomore, which is true, considering that I dropped out of college a year ago, and after three years of attending I was a first-semester sophomore, with a 1.5 GPA. That is a far cry from the 3.65 GPA I graduated high school with. I was all set to go to college, but once I got there, I realized that the easiest places to meet people on campus were parties and bars, and it's much easier to talk to

> **"I lost control, lost my scholarship, and now I'm working my butt off to stay in school."**
> **—sophomore, South Dakota State University**

girls after you've had a couple....Eventually this progressed to going out most nights of the week, sleeping too late to get to half my classes, and being too hungover to go to the other half. Just because no parents are around to stop you from doing things that you probably shouldn't be doing—like drinking—is no reason to dive in headfirst.

—sophomore, College of William & Mary

***

If your major in college is failing, and you succeed, you fail. And that's not good. Ironically, failing takes work. If you want to fail—follow each of the following rules. To pass, just do the opposite:

○ Sleep through your classes (in class or in your bed).

○ Skip class and then don't do the readings.

○ Never buy the books for your classes, making it impossible to do the readings.

○ Avoid your professor when material starts to get confusing for fear of looking stupid or because of pure laziness.

○ Do not go to special review sessions before tests.

○ Refuse to borrow notes when you miss a class.

○ Go to a class drunk, high, or hungover.

○ Attend class and play video games online with people from your study group.

○ Download porn and write online reviews during class (exception: if attending a human sexuality course, this might help you pass).

○ Miss an exam and don't bother to ask for a makeup (although it's rare to get one, you need to at least ask).

○ Show up for an exam and look at someone else's exam for the answers.

○ Show up for an exam and look for the answers on someone else's exam who isn't smart.

○ Show up for an exam and get caught cheating using a wireless device.

○ Listen to your MP3 player or an iPod, or surf the Internet in class while wearing headphones. You might be "in class," but you need to listen to pass.

○ Refer to your teacher as Professor Stupid and the teaching assistant as Professor Stupid's Friend.

○ Date the professor and then start cheating on him or her.

○ Date a professor and then cheat with another professor and have them both find out (a sure way to fail two classes).

If you care to pass and want to pass, you can find a way to pass. Professors want you to pass. Teaching assistants want you to pass. The people who tutor for free want you to pass (yes, there is often free tutoring; ask your RA or advisor). I want you to pass. The guy who just passed by you wants you to pass. The children playing in the park want you to pass. You have to want to fail in order to fail. That said, should you find that you're doing your best and still can't pass, make an appointment with a therapist at the counseling center. The problem might be more than just a "tough course."

Bottom Line
Report Card of a Failing Student
Grades: F F F F F D
GPA: 0.2
Status: Moving Back Home

Tip #44
The Cheat Sheet

The Tip
When it comes to cheating, technology is your friend—and make sure cheat sheets are small enough to eat.

The Story
I've gotten answers via instant messenger, programmed off of my laptop, entered into my calculator, and even handed to me on disk. One time, I heard about a guy on another campus who was failing one course. So he went to the final exam to help the rest of the class. He went into the exam and left

to help the rest of the class. He went into the exam and left about five minutes later. The answers for the test were posted outside the classroom for people to check once they finished. He then text messaged the answers to everyone in the class. And with technology, there isn't hard evidence to convict any of the cheaters. And although I have actually made cheat sheets small enough to be eaten, I've never had to eat them.

—junior, technology school in Michigan

* * *

Sadly, cheating has come a long way in the past ten years (but it's still against the rules and can still get you expelled). The rise of technology has taken dishonesty to a new level of low. Between picture phones snapping up photos of exams, text messaging, instant messenger, scientific calculators, and wireless Internet, cheating has been taken to a whole new high-tech level. And of course, there's the old-fashioned method of looking on someone's paper and copying his or her answers.

If you decide to cheat, you can get thrown out of school, but that's not a huge deterrent for most students. I don't really care if you cheat or not. This tip is more about why people feel the need to cheat in college. Besides having to worry about getting expelled, you're paying thousands upon thousands of dollars to get an education. You pay for it— why not use it? You can get by and pass your classes without cheating. Instead of an A, you can get a B or a C. Not going to classes, cheating to get by, and then graduating is stupid. And if you're someone who is cheating so that you can get a good enough grade to get into a graduate school, that's even dumber, because then all the cheating will only leave you behind, having to cheat to catch up. It's such a cliché (forgive me for this piece-of-crap cliché), but you're really cheating yourself out of an education, out of personal integrity, and out of so much that college is supposed to be.

Some people have a rule that they'll only cheat on courses that don't matter to them, but those courses soon will matter when they get expelled after getting busted. And if you're someone who is taking a class pass/fail and you cheat, you deserve to fail.

> "If you're buying a term paper online, chances are someone else has bought it too. If you both hand it in, it'll be hard to explain it to your professor as one big funny coincidence."
> —senior, Boston University

All that said, if you do cheat, don't be so stupid or lazy that you get caught. Hide, delete, or eat the evidence. Never get 100 percent of the answers correct, especially if you're a solid C- student. And never, never, never copy an old paper or plagiarize someone else's work. There's no way to convince a professor that it's just a weird coincidence. Professors can use technology to see if your writing is original. (It takes less than a second to Google a sentence.) They can also set up devices to survey the class via live video. While your professor looks busy working on her laptop, she's actually watching you via streaming video (not that I've heard of a professor doing this, but it's not a bad idea). People who cheat deserve to be expelled. (For more information, cheaters, you can flip to Tip #62.)

"Scantron exams are your friend. If you encounter an exam that you did not study for, and it is on those Scantron sheets, fear not. Many times professors will pass out approximately four different versions of an exam that makes it seemingly impossible to cheat on. This is not true. The secret to successfully navigating a Scantron exam that you haven't studied for is this: when copying the person next to you, make sure you copy the correct bubble indicating their version of the exam. A lot of times the first or last question will instruct the student to fill in the bubble that corresponds to the exam version. As long as you get this one copied correctly (as well as most of the others) and the person you are copying off of isn't an idiot, you should be okay."

—grad, University of Delaware

Bottom Line

If a professor sees you looking at someone else's test, just tell your professor that you were checking to see who else got the answer right. When you have to see the dean of students, tell him or her the same thing. When the dean throws you out, you can later tell it to your kids when explaining why mommy or daddy was expelled from college.

WARNING: Do Not Skim This Page

The Tip
If you go to class every day, you can do less reading and
more skimming.

The Story
I'll be honest, I don't read the textbook before class.
Sometimes I'll just skim it, but not word for word.
Mostly, I'll read it after the class and then I'll highlight
the points the professor has made. I'll use sticky notes to
highlight. It keeps it cleaner so I don't have to worry
about cleaning the pages. Unless I know a professor will
ask questions about the reading or is giving a quiz, I'll do
the reading after class. It helps to manage my time better.
There just isn't enough time to do all the reading.
Besides, each professor uses the text differently. Some will
test from the book and some will test from class materials.
I've even had professors eliminate entire chapters. Now,
when it comes to buying books, I like to wait until the first
week of class. I want to be sure about what we need and
what we don't need. Some books end up not even being
opened. It's all about the professor.

—sophomore, Lasell College

***

College textbooks are to professors like body soaps are to your new roommates—not all use them the same way. Some never use them.

I'll never forget it—I cried three times when buying my college textbooks for the first time. Once when I saw the price, once when I saw all the pages I had to read, and once when I tried to carry them (the weight of the plastic bag cutting into my hand brought tears to my eyes). To think that you're going to have to read thousands of pages of text over the course of sixteen weeks is insane. There aren't enough hours in the day to read all the pages in the books. Even if you did want to do all the reading, assuming you aren't a speed reader, you couldn't do it all.

> "I don't really have to read the textbooks. The teacher tells us the most important things. If I get confused, that's when I use the textbook. When highlighting, I pick the type that's in bold."
>
> —freshman, University of Georgia

Don't worry, don't panic, don't freak out—a lot of it is just for show. See, your professors need to assign reading—it's part of their job. They know that not everyone will read every page. Unless they test you on it before discussing it, don't worry about reading every word on each page. The text is more of a guide. It's a way to reinforce what was discussed in class and clear up any confusion. Once you get to class, you'll get a feel for the style of your professor and how you'll use the textbooks (this is assuming you actually make it to class).

How to Navigate through All the Text

Read it, skim it, or find a smart friend who has read it or skimmed it.

When it comes to reading for English lit, if the book has been made into a movie, see the movie with a smart friend who has actually read the book. Ask him or her to explain the differences. Smart professors test those questions. If possible, consider getting the book on tape or CD—this way you can "read" while you drive or work out. CliffsNotes (www.cliffsnotes.com) or SparkNotes (www.sparknotes.com) are helpful for offering you plot points and character background info, but they don't always give you the whole picture. Either read the whole thing yourself, or ask the smart friend who has read the book to look over the CliffsNotes or SparkNotes and give you an oral narration. It helps to hear the story. Of course, do the reading if you can do the reading, but if you just can't because you don't have the time, be resourceful. If there are several books to read, have each person in your study group read one and rotate being the "smart" one.

When highlighting textbooks, many used textbooks come with their own highlights. Be careful, some previous users are morons. Even if he or she is not a moron, he or she might have had a different instructor who used the text differently. Or he or she might just be a bad highlighter. Assuming you don't get the book from someone who just finished the same class with the same professor, use a different highlighter color. Once you're in class, you can decide if the highlighting you've inherited will be a good guide.

Bottom Line

Should this book be required text, and should you get tested, this is the part of the book you'd be tested on. The answer to the question is "Sacagawea." If you skimmed this page, you're reading the answer after you got the question wrong. Sorry, I warned you on the top of the page not to skim.

Tip #46
Take Notes Here

The Tip
Sit near the front of the room.

The Story
It seemed obvious, but I was in the last row most of the time. I found myself putting my head down and taking a nap. Other times I would write random notes. Sometimes I would make jokes with my friends. I would stare at a girl a few rows ahead of me. I would watch the clock. In classes where I had my laptop, I would send instant messages or check out the sports scores. I was in class in body, but I was really in other places. I thought I would just absorb material, but I wasn't even listening enough. After midterms, and seeing my shockingly poor grades, I moved up to the front of the room. It's like you become so much more a part of the class. It's harder to get distracted

because the professor is right there looking at the people in the front row. Being close to the action kept me more interested and helped me listen, which helped me to become much better at taking notes.

—junior, University of Southern Indiana

* * *

Seriously, take notes here. Please write in the space below.

This doesn't seem like the most exciting tip, but you're wrong. I'm actually eating fire and walking on shards of glass while writing this one to add some excitement.

Every professor has his or her own teaching style. Come to class with an idea of what will be discussed. Use your syllabus as a guide for taking notes. Come to class with a few pens and loose-leaf paper (this way you can rearrange your notes and add other people's notes). Find a seat close to the action. It helps to see the board to keep you involved. As a rule—anything written on the board or presented in PowerPoint is important. Professors emphasize the most important points by writing them, speaking them, and repeating them. Listen for key phrases that are intended to emphasize key points. If they say it more than once, there's a good chance it will show up on the test.

As you attend more classes, you'll get a better sense of the style of your professor. You'll begin to hear words that emphasize more important parts of the lecture. For example, hearing the words "This is important" is a good sign that it's important. Listen for summaries at the end of class. If you're unsure what's important, ask your professor, "If you were taking notes in your own class, how would you know what's most important?"

When class is finished, review your notes that night. Work through any words that are indecipherable. Highlight key points. Write a summary sentence or two. If you have time, rewrite your notes. It helps so much. Rewriting in your own words gives you an opportunity to process the information and concepts.

Post-exam tip: after the exam, look over the notes and see what was tested and whether the information came from lecture or readings. You can have a better sense of how your professor designs his or her exams.

One more note on notes. You might come across professional note-taking services that sell notes taken in your actual classes. Never rely solely on these notes. If you miss class, use both the professional notes and other students' notes from class.

Bottom Line
If you're not sure which points are the most important to remember, ask your professor. And also, share notes with smart people in class— see how they organize their lecture notes and follow their lead.

Tip #47
Do It in a Group

The Tip
No one is smart enough to always study alone. The group will save you.

The Story
Before coming to college, I never studied with anyone, except maybe once when there was a group project. There wasn't so much pressure or material to cover on high school exams. I would just show up and pass. In college, I had class with a few people from my hall. We would go to class together and then study together. If one of us missed class, we would share notes. What was nice is that one of the people had a friend who knew the professor from the previous year (he was a sophomore). A week before the test, I had to leave town for a week due to a family emergency. Earlier in the month, I had missed classes because I was sick. The group completely saved me. They went to the review and shared the review notes. They even had an old test from a test file. I ended up getting a B and that was better than I could have hoped for. There's no reason to study alone.

> "It was during a group project in the business school that I met my boyfriend and fell in love. The professor told us that it will happen in some of the groups. He was right."
> —senior, Indiana University

—junior, University of Maryland

* * *

If you're looking to pass your classes, pass around notes, and make a pass on someone in your class, find a study group. The study group is one of the most powerful tools for classroom success. It's a way to pool all of your resources—you can share notes when someone misses class, discuss topics that will be covered on the exam, and work through confusing material by listening to friends who have spoken with the professor or teaching assistant. It's also a way to hang out and make studying a good time (or just not a terrible time). Besides getting a better grasp on material, making friends, and getting on the dean's list, you might even find a little bit of lovin'.

Imagine this. It's a long night of studying before your first exam. Everyone is tired and wants to call it a night. You and the object of your affection want to cram a little more in before calling it quits. You decide to grab a late-night snack. Suddenly, that hard calculus problem turns into a titil-lating conversation that's punctuated by a first kiss. As the textbook digs into your side, and the scientific calculator into your thigh, you ignore the pain and focus on that kiss. Not only do you get an A on the exam, you have found a new study buddy that gives you one more reason to make it to class.

Please be aware: there is no guarantee that your study group will lead to crazy love, but it *will* help you do well in class.

How to start a study group: after the first few weeks, people will start to look familiar. A couple weeks before the exam, ask a few people that interest you if they want to get together to study. Find a place to meet (like the library). Don't be afraid to be the one to put it together. Once you get together the first time, it will be easier to do it again. A lot of times, it just happens, but don't be afraid to be the one to make it happen.

"What's great about college is that when you get homework, it's not like you're going home alone. There are a lot of people around who can work together in a group. It sounds bad, but it helps to have everybody do some work and then come together."
—freshman, Harvard University

Bottom Line

Study groups can get you more than just a passing grade; they can create a perfect opportunity to make a friendly pass at someone in class.

Tip #48
Old Exams, Sharing Notes, and Mostly Legal Ways to Pass

The Tip
Old exams, old exams, old exams. Find out who has the best test files.

The Story
I was surprised to find out that my sorority kept a test file. They had old exams from just about every class. What happens is, you take a test, and then you bring it home. (Most professors allow you to keep exams.) The other part that shocked me was that the professors would then use similar test questions,

> "I love my sorority. I also love their test file."
> —freshman, University of Georgia

sometimes the exact questions. It's common knowledge that after a test is completed, students will keep the test. I guess some are just lazy. Once in a while a test that shouldn't have gotten out there got out there, but I never did anything that was unethical or illegal. Some professors will number each test and collect them after the exam to make sure that no takes them home and keeps them on file. It's amazing how a test from ten years ago can show up years later. The test file is a huge resource that helped me, although not on the longer blue book exams.

—sophomore, University of Kansas

* * *

Time is limited, and how to maximize your time while studying is crucial. Because you have a full schedule, you'll need to be smart about studying. At the same time, you don't want to do anything that will get you thrown off campus for cheating.

Old exams are one of the greatest keys to mastering current exams. Many fraternities and sororities, or even local stores, have test files with past exams. Assuming it's legal—and on most campuses it is—these are great guides to how a professor will test you. (I mention that it might not be legal because some professors don't want their old exams to get out.)

There's no better predictor of what will be on a professor's exam than the key points and ideas tested on a previous exam. Oftentimes, test questions are taken right from old exams and put on new ones.

Another huge resource is someone who has recently taken your class. Get in touch with these people. Become friends with them. Ask what they wish they had known before taking the course. Even ask if you can check out their old notes. Ask how the professor grades. Get the inside information and use it to your advantage. Some classes have smaller discussion groups where the teaching assistants give the grades. Some TAs grade more easily than others. Ask, ask, ask the people who were in your seat before you.

When it comes to sharing notes to prepare for exams, some students have a gift for writing at high speed and maintaining remarkable penmanship (some even type notes). Sit in different seats throughout the semester and check out other people's notes. Also, don't be so quick to shun the dorky kid in the front who seems to be best friends with the professor. Usually, he knows what's going on. It's not always *what* you know, but *who* you know and what *they* know. Be smart, be resourceful, and do it legally.

Bottom Line
Old exams are the best study guides available. But as a rule, if an exam is older than you, it might be too old.

Tip #49
The Major Issue: Picking One

The Tip
Don't sweat finding a major right away. And don't worry about changing it should you find out that your heart's not into it.

The Story
I graduated high school and went to a technical college with hopes of becoming a computer programmer. My parents and friends had always told me how well I worked with computers, so I figured it would work well for me as a major. Only after I got there and took classes was I able to realize that my heart wasn't into it. I pushed myself into the major too soon rather than giving myself time to figure out that my heart was into writing. I

> "Whatever major you end up deciding to pursue, it will inevitably change at least once (most likely many more times)!"
> —senior, Governors State University

switched my major and transferred colleges so I could follow my heart.

—junior, Washington State University–Vancouver

* * *

Most students change their majors at least once. You might change it monthly. You might change it in a year. You might have just changed it since reading this previous sentence. What you're thinking you'll end up doing today will most likely not be what you'll end up doing tomorrow. The point? Majors will change.

The best tip is to relax when picking a major. Don't let the world (or your parents) tell you what to be. Try a general direction, take a step, and see how it feels. Once you have an idea of what you enjoy, see how it feels outside the classroom. Get an internship, a part-time job, or do volunteer work to get a taste of it. If you find that it's not what you wanted, great—just change majors. If it is what you like, great—stay with your major. Things to think about when contemplating a *major* change:

- DO NOT let future income be your main motivating factor in choosing a major. If you do what you love and love what you do, you'll make money if that field is important to you.

- DO NOT worry that the field you're choosing is too competitive. Someone has to do it—why not you? If anything, the path you head down will lead to answers that you could have only discovered by going down that road.
- DO NOT buckle to parental pressure. Your life belongs to you. If your parents are forcing you to do something that doesn't feel right, don't do it. You're the one who will have to wake up every morning (or afternoon) and go to work. Not them.
- DO NOT be afraid to change your major. Make sure you seek support on campus when contemplating major change.

> **"It's never too late to realize you have made the wrong decision. I changed majors from engineering to English my junior year. I'm happier, healthier, and thankful. It's hard to make a big decision like that because you have to admit that you made a mistake."**
> **—senior, Binghamton University**

When you figure out what you want your major to be, talk to your academic advisor and put together a plan. Try to graduate in four years, if possible. You might need to take summer classes to help you graduate in four years (see if you can take summer courses at home and transfer the credits). Switching majors can sometimes hold you up. Don't be afraid to change what it is that you want to do. It's only the rest of your life.

> "Choose a major not based on money, but what you love to do. What you do will be a major part of your life. If you love what you're doing, the money you've always wanted will eventually come."
> —senior, University of Arkansas–Pine Bluff

Bottom Line

Most students will change their major at least once. Many more than once. But most do not change it ten to twenty times. That's too many.

Tip #50
Advice on Your Advisor

The Tip
Always make a serious effort to get to know your advisor.

The Story
It was about four weeks into my freshman year of college. I was meeting new friends, staying up all night, and having a blast. But when class time came, I'd drag myself in half asleep and sit around waiting for my next chance to nap. I was interested in my classes, but expected that if I needed to be doing something, my professor would tell me. When fourth-week grades came out, I realized I was doing awful and didn't know what to do. Luckily, one of my professors was also my advisor, and somehow saw in me the potential to be a better student. He took me aside and set up a meeting. We talked about

my personal and professional goals and what I should be doing now to achieve them. It was a day that changed my entire college career. I became a more involved student and realized that my teachers weren't going to come to me—I needed to make the effort. I continued to hang out and have a good time, but also made the classroom a high priority. My advisor turned out to be not only a tremendous asset but a good friend. He's written countless letters of recommendation for me and given me tons of educational and emotional support.

—senior, Gannon University

***

Let me introduce you to your academic or college advisor.

Your academic advisor is the person in the advising office (not a coincidence) who guides you along your college journey. Your advisor is your point man or woman with whom you discuss selecting and registering for classes, selecting a major, switching a major, and dropping classes. Your advisor can be an amazing source of information—he or she will inform you of requirements, procedures, ways to get in classes, and places on campus to find answers when he or she doesn't have them. You can usually speak to

"I didn't find out that it was 'acceptable' to drop classes midsemester until I talked to upperclassmen. My advisor didn't go over dropping courses with me, either. There was a calculus course that I was taking that I was pretty much failing since day one. I didn't know that it was okay to drop a course and pick it up at a later time. Maybe you'll do better when you are less busy or if you have a different professor. If I would have known that, I would not have a bad grade on my transcript."

—junior, Western Illinois University

your advisor face-to-face, via email, or with a call. Navigating the steaming piles of bureaucracy found on many college campuses can be a tough task. It's extremely helpful to have someone in your corner fighting for what's important to you. Take advantage of your advisors.

Beware:

*** Not All Advisors Are Created Equal***

The Good Ones: advisors who listen to you, ask you questions, and allow you to speak. He or she points you in the right direction based on what you say, need, and feel. Good advisors fight for you when you need someone to fight for you. Good advisors get back to you with answers to questions. Good advisors refer you to the people who have answers to your questions if he or she can't answer them. Good advisors do all they can do to guide you during your college journey and make sure that you graduate on time with a degree that fits you. They can even help once you leave campus.

The Bad Ones: advisors who don't listen. They think they know more about you than you know about you. They do what they think is best for you, but ultimately, they don't know you so they can't know what's best for you. If you find yourself with an advisor who doesn't work for you, find an advisor who meshes with your personality and encourages you to be your best. Make sure to check to see that the path your advisor is advising is the best path. Just to be safe, talk to upperclassmen who are doing the things that you want to do. If you find that every advisor on campus is no good, the problem most likely is not the advisors, but you.

Bottom Line

Be advised—not all advisors offer good advice. Make sure to get a second opinion from an upperclassman in your major or a professor to see if you're on the right track.

Tip #51
Pick a Number, Any Number

The Tip

Not getting into a class is not the end of it. Don't let the system beat you down. If people with power know you, they can make exceptions.

The Story

Coming from a smaller high school and going to a larger college was a lot to take in at first. After going through registration, it just seemed like I was one of the masses. Everything had a system that the students plugged into. I remember not getting into a freshman English lit class second semester and dealing with the process of trying to get in. It was like dealing with a utility company at times. It wasn't until I physically went to the class and actually talked with the professor—by the way, something my older brother told me to do—that I received the attention that I hoped for. The professors allowed me to sit in on the class. After about two weeks, she let me in. While there is a system and it's easy to get lost in the system, if you talk to the people—the real people who are making decisions—you don't have to be just another number. That seemed to be what helped most of all.

—sophomore, North Dakota State University

* * *

If your name is actually a number (for example, if your name is 50 Cent—what up, Fiddy), you won't mind being just a number in college (or currency). If your name is not a number or currency, you might not want to be just a social security number, student ID, or other random number when you get to college. And this can happen in big and small colleges.

The difference between high school and college is that in high school, your teachers knew you. They might even have known your family members. Your high school kept track of you during the day. It was hard to slip through the cracks. And if you did, your parents would be notified.

In college, it's easy to float through the system. Education isn't mandatory anymore. Being an individual is much more of an individual choice. You are the one who is now responsible for making sure that you are not just another number, and that takes work on your part. As someone who went to one school with thirty thousand students and another with forty thousand, I know. My first freshman year, I felt like I didn't matter. It wasn't until my second freshman experience, when I put myself out there and paved my path, that I felt like an individual.

It all starts in class. Whether it's a lecture of two hundred students or twenty, you need to be the one to introduce yourself to the professor (and do it before midterms, so if you need help, your professor will know you). Then it continues with finding friends. You need to introduce yourself to new people. You need to get yourself involved. You need to sign up for clubs and activities. You need to show up to play on a sports team. You need to be the one to allow people to get to know you. You can establish who you are, what you do, and where you're going. Unless you let people know who you are, you may be just 54665 (or 54668 or 54675) to everyone. And that can happen at any college.

Sometimes, within the college bureaucracy, you can get lost in the system. Some people just take it and get pushed around. Others take action. Before rolling over and letting the college push you around, make your voice heard. Be an individual by meeting the people who can make exceptions to the rules and regulations. You won't know unless you try.

Bottom Line
At times, you might feel like just another number. When that happens, fight to make your voice heard and don't stop until the people that need to hear are listening.

Tip #52
Time for Time Management

The Tip
Plan for your success and use a planner.

The Story

Using a day planner probably was the single best aid to time management I've found. Whether you use an electronic Palm-style PDA or the old-fashioned paper-and-pencil version, this tool is indispensable for keeping your priorities, deadlines, and other important dates in order. I prefer a nonelectronic planner because it does not crash, it is not likely to be stolen, I don't have to learn a new handwriting style, it doesn't have a battery that will run out (and erase all my data), and it will still work if I drop it or leave it in the sun

> "Time management is all about corner cutting. If I had to do all the readings, I'd never survive. My brother taught me to work in groups, to know what's important to read, and to go to section."
> —freshman, Harvard University

(or freezing cold) all day. The bottom line is that you have to find a system that will work for you. Talk to a friend who uses a planner and try to develop a system of using it that works for you.

—freshman, University of California–Berkeley

* * *

Please take a few seconds to read this one. If you don't have the time, take the time. This will only take about two minutes (I timed this chapter).

> "I got to campus and instantly wanted to get involved with everything. I forgot that I was there primarily for an academic life. Over my college career, I've learned to prioritize what's important."
> —senior, Allegheny College

What I've seen while writing and researching this book is that time management is so much more than allocating a few hours to study. It's really all-encompassing. It's about finding balance. See, the more balance you can achieve, the easier it will be to juggle all the things that you need to do in a day, or a week, or a month. That's why it's so important to take the time to know yourself, so you can better manage yourself, your relationships, and your emotions. Then you can have time to do the things that are important to you. A good part of this book has been about managing life inside the classroom. The second part of this book is about helping you solve all the other problems outside the classroom—dating, relationships, sex, etc.—the issues that take up the most time and energy. If you can manage life inside and outside classes, you will find the time you need to manage your life. Then time management will be less about survival and more about the freedom to make choices. The most important tip for time management: when you need help or have questions, ask those people who can give you the answers you need or point you to the answers you desire. You will save yourself so much time and energy, you won't know what to do with it. While you're here reading, also keep these tools for maximizing your time in mind:

1. Use the first semester to figure out how much you need to study to achieve the grades that you're looking for. Because you're in college to learn, you're better off overstudying than understudying. Getting a low grade your freshman year can haunt you. It's like a weight that pulls your GPA down throughout your college career.

2. Find a routine. Treat college like your job. Sometimes you can have an hour or two-hour break between classes. If you have a break, stay on campus. Do your readings, review your notes, or work on an assignment that's due in the future. The problem is that if you go home, you can get tired or distracted. Find a place on campus where you can do your work. If it's done, you'll have the night free.

3. If you find that you're falling behind, don't panic. Get help immediately. Talk to your professors, a teaching assistant, and veterans of the class. You don't always have to read every page of every single book.

4. If you have to have a job, start with fewer hours and then build from there. You can always add more once you figure out how much time you need to dedicate to your classes. Sometimes when you have a job and a full schedule, it's easier to study because you know when you have to get it done. Being busy can actually help.

5. Get some kind of planner or organizer. Get it out of your head. Figure out your week before starting every week. College doesn't offer as much structure as high school—you need to be the one to structure your time. Write it down and stick to it.

6. If you're having a hard time managing your schedule, find out if there is help on campus. Contact the orientation office and ask. Many colleges offer time-management resources for new students.

> **"Study before you go out at night. Don't say you will get up in the morning to study because you won't!"**
> **—freshman, Southern Illinois**
> **University–Edwardsville**

Bonus tip

Consider attending college near a state that is in a different time zone. Then when you need an extra hour, you can always get it. Just remember, you have to give it back when you cross back over the state line again.

Bottom Line

Save time and have the best time by asking for help every time you need it. If you can take the time to get help, you'll save time and find time.

Tip #53
Wine Tasting, Bowling, and Other Important Electives

The Tip

Take an elective that has nothing to do with your major. Choose something that you've always been vaguely interested in but never had the time or resources to explore. And don't be afraid to take classes at a community college.

The Story

The best elective that I took was actually at a community college. It was costuming for theater class. I took it because it seemed interesting and it was something I'd always been curious about. Taking that class is what led me to major in costume design at Cornish. This same thing happened to my brother. He took astronomy on a whim as an elective at a community college and now he's an astronomy major at the University of Hawaii. If you're not sure what you're interested in doing, go to a community college or just take some classes there. It saves money, and most credits from community colleges transfer.

—junior, Cornish College of the Arts

✳ ✳ ✳

I started playing guitar as part of a group lesson. It was a one-credit class. Every week, we met in one of the residence hall lounges and jammed. It was so cool that I took a classical one-on-one guitar class the next year. There was no extra charge for it. Graduate students taught the course. That's how I learned to play guitar. I didn't know that I'd start writing and playing music as part of my job later in life. I seriously just put out an album (*Fortunate Accidents*, available on iTunes, CDBaby.com, and TheNakedRoommate.com). *The Chlamydia Jive* is both a touching and moving track from the album. It all started with taking a class that looked cool and had absolutely nothing to do with my major (not the chlamydia, the music). I had a couple extra credit hours that would have just been thrown away, so I figured, why not?

My brother took a wine tasting class in college. My good friends took a bowling class. A girlfriend took a self-defense class. There were other electives like aerobics, judo, tae kwon do, archery, ballroom dancing, racquetball, art, acting, pottery, crafts, film appreciation, sex and sexuality, the history of rock and roll, and so many others. Instead of just taking the classes you need to get through your major, take some electives you would never think of taking. If you don't like the class, then drop it before it counts against you. Don't just take them because you think that they'll be easy, though. Take them because they're available. These classes can stick with you for a lifetime.

> "The best classes are those that do not have your best friends from your dorm in them. It was my business and accounting electives that helped change the course of my future."
> —freshman, Mount Union College

I scoured colleges and came up with some classes worth taking; the most popular ones tend to be ballroom dancing and basic swing dancing. Here's one from a college in Wisconsin: class students read selections from *Chew* magazine and debate "The Art of Eating" and "The Primal Cheeseburger." The final project involves tracking a food product to where it all began before it was manufactured. For example, when dealing with ketchup, they track the tomatoes all the way back to the farm. Factors like distance, pesticide use, and whether it was farmed on a corporate or family-owned farm are part of the debate. They even eat food in class. And yes, there really is a wine tasting class and a history of rock and roll class. There has even been a class offered about Oprah Winfrey at the University of Illinois: History 298, Oprah Winfrey, the Tycoon.

Bottom Line

If you have extra credit hours, don't just throw them away. One elective can become the course that changes the entire course of your life. Or, you can try to sell your extra credit hours on eBay (is that legal?).

Harlan's Tip Sheet

Life Inside the Classroom Resources, Websites, and Additional Information

Classroom Vocab

Syllabus: The rundown of the class: required readings, rules, regulations, and procedures, as well as a course outline with important dates for exams and projects.

Teaching assistants (TAs): Sometimes called "teaching fellows" or other names. Typically, graduate students or undergraduates that teach sections or lectures under the supervision of a professor. Go to them for help. These people know things that can help you.

Sections/Labs: In addition to lectures, classes may have sections or labs. These offer a more intimate setting and one-on-one teaching. At larger colleges, these are often taught by TAs.

Semesters/quarters/trimesters: Some schools have semesters (two semesters=one school year), some trimesters (three trimesters=one school year), some quarters (four quarters=one school year)...pretty basic.

Incomplete: The mark you get when you don't satisfy the requirements for a class.

Pass/fail: Some classes are offered as pass/fail. You don't get a letter grade, just a pass or fail.

Auditing: Sitting in on a course, but not for credit or a grade.

Drop/add: The process of dropping courses and adding new ones. Be careful—most schools have a deadline after which you can't withdraw from a course without it showing up on your transcript and affecting your GPA. There may also be different names for this process. Ask upperclassmen.

Waitlist: If a class is full, you can be put on a waitlist. Always approach the professors; sometimes they will make exceptions if you beg to take the class.

Sitting in on a class: If you're waitlisted, ask to sit in on a course. More often than not, a professor will just allow you to officially join the class.

Office hours: Time allocated for students to meet with professors and teaching assistants to get extra help.

Additional Resources

Departmental websites. Visit the website of your department on campus. Often you can find out about new classes being offered, updated procedures, and protocols. Visit regularly.

Free tutoring. Ask your professor, advisors, or resident assistant where and when it's available. When writing papers, there is also usually totally free help for students in a writing center.

Extra office hours. If you can't always make the regular hours, most professors will try to be flexible.

RateMyProfessors.com. Students rate their professors on this site according to easiness, helpfulness, clarity, and rater interest. However, always confirm what you read with a student in person—not all the ratings are fair.

8

Dating and Relationships

Your Higher Education in Lust, Love, and Loss

Dear Harlan,

I am a freshman in college and living in a coed dorm. I met this girl in September that lives down the hall. I have had a slight crush on her since then. Just recently we had a four-hour conversation together, which is the longest I have ever had with anyone. That night I found out she liked a fellow coworker, but she recently gave up that crush because he is under eighteen. I am confused as to what I should do. Should I continue to talk to her or should I tell her my interest?

—Dazed and most definitely confused

Dear Dazed,

My longest conversation with a woman was for just over five hours. It was in high school. It cost $1.99 a minute. She really liked me.

Here's a quick way to clear this up in under a minute of talking time. Walk up to her and say, "I had so much fun the other night. Let's do it again, but next time, let's get something to eat." That's all it takes. Then it would be a date.

The door of opportunity is open. Your chance is here. The time is now. You should continue talking to her and express your interest. If she's interested, great. If not, assume that it's because it's too uncomfortable for her to date someone on the same floor. To not say something would be the greatest risk of all. At least give her a chance to be more than just a friend. She deserves a chance. Just don't wait too long. The more time that passes, the closer to eighteen that underage coworker of hers gets.

Tip #54
The Rules of College Love (or just lust)

The Tip
Relax, chill, and talk to the people you want to date without getting stuck in your head.

The Story

I was way too worried about what girls thought about me and how I could get as many as possible to hook up with me. I'd either say nothing or say the wrong things. It took over my life. Until I relaxed, found a life in college, and stopped trying so hard, relationships eluded me. I was too intense and uptight. Once I relaxed, it became so much more manageable. It took me a few years to figure it out, but now I'm there and much happier.

—junior, University of Illinois–Chicago

* * *

Please note: this tip can get you a date. If you put cologne or perfume on this page and rub it on you, it can be even more effective.

Some of you might plan on hooking up in college. Some of you might plan on dating in college. Some of you might plan on finding your future husband or wife. Whatever you want, here's a quick five-step plan to help you find it all—while sober.

1. *Meet people by putting yourself in as many rooms as possible*. Dating in college works like this—if you're in a room long enough, you will hook up (if you're in a room with alcohol it happens that much faster—not necessarily a good thing). Meet people in the residence halls, in classes, by getting involved (see Chapter 5), and at parties.

2. *Say what you feel*. If saying or doing something is too hard for you, then you need to embrace The Universal Rejection Truth of Dating and Relationships and come out of Rejection Denial. The Universal Rejection

Truth of Dating and Relationships states that not everyone you desire will always desire you. Some will, but not all. It's impossible for everyone you want to want you (sorry). Rejection Denial is a deep, dark, dangerous place where you think that everyone you want should want you, and when someone you want doesn't want you, you think there's a huge problem—but the problem is that you can't embrace The Universal Rejection Truth. Embrace it—celebrate it.

3. *Train for the sport of taking risks.* Training means working to be your personal best, physically and emotionally (e.g., putting on a tight thong and being completcly comfortable with what you see in the mirror). It means surrounding yourself with people who want you to be your best. Training can take months or years. Once trained, you can say what you feel without letting fear stop you from taking risks because you will be equipped to face the possibility of The Universal Rejection Truth of Dating and Relationships. This is the difference between living a life of passion as opposed to one paralyzed by fear.

4. *Take risk after risk after risk.* If the first object of your affection doesn't share your interest, don't let it throw you. Consider him or her a friend and don't let a little rejection stop you—this friend might be interested later or have another friend that could become your perfect match.

5. *Know that you always have options.* If you find that you're in a relationship and it's not working out, move on. Don't let insecurity cause you to hang onto a relationship you know should end. Stay in a bad

relationship too long and you risk ending up getting married to that partner, not out of love, but out of a fear of being on your own and never being able to find anyone else.

> "Don't date just because you think you're supposed to date. There is a lot of pressure when you go to school to get involved with someone. It might seem like finding a relationship or finding someone to be with will help make things better, but it doesn't make it better. Wait until you find someone who can appreciate you for everything that makes up all the parts of you."
> —sophomore, Angelo State University

Bottom Line

Take risk after risk (while sober). If you can't take a risk, then take a look at yourself and figure out why the possibility of facing The Universal Rejection Truth is so scary. Then conduct rejection/risk-taking research on a weekly basis and celebrate R.A.W.—Rejection/Risk Awareness Week on your campus the week of February 7–14. For more information on R.A.W., visit www.rejectionawareness.com.

Tip #55
The College Hookup

The Tip
If you're looking for something noncommitted, ambiguous, and uncomfortable, then the hookup is the perfect love—I mean lust—connection.

The Story
I came to college never having had a serious boyfriend. I met this guy on my floor a week after getting here. We hung out a few times and made out—nothing more. I thought we were together, but he didn't think so. To me, hanging out meant something. Once I joined a sorority, it all became that much more blurred. Just because you take a guy to a dance doesn't mean that you're a couple. It doesn't even matter what happens when you're together. More than once, I thought things were more than they were. As time went on, it became clear that the lack of clarity was the only clear part of it all. The best advice I'd give to myself or to freshmen is to talk about what you want before you get involved with someone. It makes it so much easier. Don't be afraid to be honest. If someone won't hang out with you, then you're better off without him. Unless you are the one to talk about it, no one will talk about it. That's when things kind of get weird. Talk about it and make up your rules as you go along.

—senior, Northeastern University

* * *

The college hookup is the most common of the college relationships (although "hookup" is an insult to the word "relationship"). The hookup is an intimate encounter involving anything from kissing to full sex, void of any commitment. Due to the lack of communication involved with the college hookup, it's often a confusing and ambiguous relationship. The college hookup can fall into one of the following fifteen categories:

The Drunk Hookup:
an alcohol-induced connection

The Friendly Hookup:
friends who go way beyond friendly

The Rebound Hookup:
broken up and looking for some Band-Aid lovin'

The Cheating Hookup:
a hookup with someone other than your exclusive partner (no dignity here—just laziness)

The Desperation Hookup:
looking for anyone—and I mean *anyone*

The Online Hookup:
a high-speed connection where your mouse does all the talking

The Who's Next Hookup:
the love junkie who can't get enough

The Ex Hookup:
reliable, dependable, and oh-so-easy

The I Love You Hookup:
grounded in real love (at least for one of the partners involved)

The Convenience Hookup:

the closest person with a pulse gets some

The First-Week Hookup:

action exclusive to welcome week

The I Just Want to Have Fun Hookup:

it's all good fun until someone falls in love

The Weekend Hookup:

I love you Friday, I love you Saturday, but don't call me Sunday

The Sympathy Hookup:

a charitable donation to someone in need of love (it's always generous to give)

The Repeat Back-Up Hookup:

a go-to guy or girl who is the backup love buddy (aka, the 3 a.m. text message booty call)

The problem with hookups is that once the hookup is hung up, confusion ensues. Because most hookups tend to be with people you don't know that well, communication is strained from the beginning. A few hours ago you were locked in each other's loins; post hookup, you're too afraid to call and say hi. And this is why the hookup becomes the drama of your morning, afternoon, and night. It eats up all of your energy. Seeing the person, thinking about the person, contemplating emailing the person—it eats up so much time and energy. *But it doesn't have to be that way*

> "It's fun to look out of my window in the early morning on the weekends. That's when you see all the people taking the 'walk of shame' in their clothes from the night before. These are the people who hooked up and have to walk home in the morning. It's something worth seeing."
> —junior, Western Illinois University

anymore. All you have to do is talk to your partner before you get too crazy. Figure out which hookup category you're dealing with and then decide if it should continue. If your partner is too busy getting naked to listen, then he or she is not the right

> "I have a lot of girlfriends who have a lot of regrets about past hookups from freshman and sophomore year. If you have regrets, don't dwell on it—just don't do it anymore."
> —junior, University of Vermont

partner—that is, unless you're looking to find confusion, unanswered questions, and needless drama.

Bottom Line
It's a notch below dating and a notch above friendship. It's the hookup and it's the most common, most confusing, and most unstable part of college life. If you're unsure about your hookup, talk about it. If you just can't, hang up the hookup.

Tip #56
Close-Distance Relationships

The Tip
Don't date anyone who lives on your floor in the residence hall.

The Story
We started dating in November of my freshman year. He lived down the hall on the same floor, which is how we met. In the beginning, it was fun because I had someone to date

who lived down the hall. It would be easy to spend the night together. I didn't have to get up early to go home because I was already home. Right before finals week is when it got very frustrating. If I wasn't in class or I wasn't with him, he asked where I was and why I wasn't with him.

> "If I could start all over, I would tell someone not to rush into a relationship. If you rush into something, it may feel too perfect and then, when it ends, it crushes you. I wish someone had told me not to get too involved too fast. I'm someone who got crushed."
> —freshman, Lynn University

And then people were asking about us—and it wasn't fun anymore. We just kind of decided it was too much and we wanted to be friends. Once I broke up with him, I found more friends on the floor and became so much closer with them. I got to see my roommate more and now we're best friends.

—junior, Northern Illinois University

* * *

Messing around with a neighbor (aka "dormcest" or "hall-cest") might seem great when it's all good, but when it goes bad, you want to be as far away as possible. The person who was once your convenient love becomes your inconvenient nightmare neighbor. Don't be so quick to date next door. It can go bad as fast as it begins.

Remember that part about being able to walk down the hall to your room in the morning after shacking up? It's no longer a good thing. And the part about sharing a dining hall and seeing that person at every meal? Meals together will now make you sick. And also, that part about having so many of the same friends you both hung out with? Now that's just too uncomfortable. Then there's seeing who he or she is now dating. Things close by are good until they go good-bye, and most relationships will go bye-bye at some time or another. Think twice before grabbing that person

> "I met my girlfriend in the laundry room. I was sitting on top of the machine waiting for my clothes to dry and she was sitting next to me on her washing machine."
> —freshman, Virginia Tech

close by just because it's convenient. Besides, it's just lazy. There is a lot of love in a lot of places if you're willing to take the risk to find the loving.

That brings me to relationships of convenience. What seems good and easy turns out to be the complete opposite. Things like hooking up with a neighbor down the hall, someone at work, or with your good friend's ex are just bad ideas—especially when it comes to hooking up with an ex. It's convenient, it's easy, and really, it's also lower than low. Sure, it's hard to meet attractive people, but it's also weak to prey on a good friend's ex. Assuming that most relationships don't last

> "Dating your teaching assistant might seem like fun, but the fun ends when you break up and have to see your TA in class. Besides, it's completely against the rules."
> —graduate, Indiana University

forever, when the love fades, you'll be left without your girlfriend or boyfriend and without a close friend.

If you want to find some lovin' that won't leave you jobless, friendless, or afraid to leave your room at night, follow Tip #29 and all of Chapter 5. There are plenty of partners. We each have over one thousand soul mates (many don't live in the same country or speak the same language—yet another reason to take a language of the Orient). Don't choose the easy or lazy route when it comes to finding love. Chances are you'll only be left lonely and full of regret and in hiding from your neighbors.

Bottom Line
Shortcuts to love tend to be the fast route to long-term troubles.

Tip #57
Long-Distance Relationships (LDRs)

The Tip
Don't hang on to a long-distance love just because it's safe and secure.

The Story
When I came to college, I had been seeing a guy for about a year. He was my first serious boyfriend. It was a great relationship in high school. He went to a community college at home while I went away to a new place and experienced a lot of new things. We decided to stay together, even though we are a few hours apart. It worked. We both had the same cell phone plan so we would call each other for free at least once a day. We saw each other every other week. Trust was a never an issue. The relationship was safe—it allowed me to meet more people at college, but still know I had a boyfriend.

Fast-forward to my sophomore year. I ended up meeting a guy in March. At the time, I was having doubts about my high school sweetheart, but stayed together

"While long-distance relationships sound like a challenge, they tend to be a disaster. I ended up being cheated on, despite my girlfriend's constant critiquing of my decision. I always wanted to believe it would work and did a great job convincing myself it was worthwhile. Don't delude yourself—no matter what you had, it won't translate hundreds or even thousands of miles—no amount of IM, cell phone conversations, or planned trips can reverse the fact."
—junior, UCLA

because, again, it was easy and familiar. Meeting this other guy made me realize there are other options that I could be secure with. I'm not the type to cheat, so I decided to end things with my boyfriend before anything happened. My boyfriend was surprised—I told him that if it was meant to be, we would find each other again. Because he was my first boyfriend I needed to see what was out there to better define what I needed in a relationship. We're still good friends.

—junior, Towson University

* * *

I want to be clear at the start of this tip—if you have a relationship that you think is worth hanging on to, don't be so quick to get rid of it just because you're going to college. If you're 100 percent committed to it, there's a chance it could work. But if you're not 100 percent committed, don't even try. And whatever you do, never lie, never cheat, and never pretend—you'll only taint it forever.

> **The Naked Blog:**
> How to Avoid Getting Your Long-Distance Relationship (LDR) Puppy Shot.
> See www.TheNakedRoommate.com.

Long-distance relationships (LDRs) in college have never been so cheap and easy—that is, with free nights and weekends, instant messenger online, email, live streaming video, and weekend visits. But still, the emotional toll of not being hand-in-hand, face-to-face, lips-to-lips makes it too hard for most couples to survive.

The hardest part: long-distance relationships are extremely emotional. They often isolate you from the world. Instead of thinking about college life and how to make a life in a new place, people tend to lean on their old relationships, which keeps them from meeting other people who could become close friends. They can take up too much time, too much energy, and leave you feeling more alone and lost than ever once the relationship ends (and most do). They tend to become a crutch that keeps people from meeting new people and having new experiences. The phone bills, the emotions, the good-byes—it's hard, and for most people, it wears them down. And now, with so many ways to stay in touch via technology, it's that much easier to be in one place physically, and somewhere else emotionally (see Tip #8).

> "I think that probably the one thing that's making my long-distance relationship work is the fact that my boyfriend and I had been good friends even before we started seeing each other. Otherwise, I doubt that it would work. For all of those people out there who are involved in a healthy relationship that is long distance, hang in there. It will only get better."
> —junior, Salisbury State University

If you decide do the long-distance thing, keep the following in mind: you must trust each other, talk about what is bothering you (never let it build up), be completely honest, and make sure you have a life outside of your relationship. If you want to take a break, be honest.

Never, never, never cheat on your partner. Cheating will ruin everything that you've worked so hard to build during the relationship. Should you ever want to get back together, the violation of trust from the past cheating might make it too hard to pick up where you left off.

The best part: if you can survive the distance and make it through all the years apart, you'll be that much stronger to spend years together down the road.

Bottom Line

Long-distance relationships that work are long, hard, emotional, and take A LOT of work. Some can work. Most don't (I'm sorry).

Tip #58
High School Bitter Sweethearts

The Tip

Don't take your high school girlfriend or boyfriend to school. Break up when you leave for college.

The Story

I know it sounds harsh, but take it from someone who goes to an all-girls school. All the girls I knew my freshman year who had boyfriends had lots of problems socially. They would spend a lot of time on the phone with their

> **Quick Note from Harlan:**
>
> In the first edition of this book, some people confused this student tip for my advice. For my take on high school sweethearts, keep reading.

boys and not getting to know their hallmates or classmates, nor doing their work. Also, you don't want to go out, party, or get to know other guys because you'll feel like you're cheating. Whether your boy is still in high school or going to school nearby, dump him at least for your first semester—you'll understand later!

—sophomore, Hollins University

✳ ✳ ✳

The *big* question: what is the best thing to do if you want to experience college life, but you don't want to lose your current love and what might be the true love of your life?

My answer?

Do NOT be so quick to ditch it. Enjoy it while you got it. Until you get to college, until you go to classes, until you figure out what it's like to be in college, don't be so quick to cut all ties. Besides, it's nice to have a close friend to keep you balanced during an unstable time. Figure it out once you get there. Big deal if you miss out on a few weeks of random hooking up. It will still be there if you want to experience it.

Plan on staying together until it doesn't feel right. That said, if you have serious doubts before you go into college, and you know it doesn't feel right, then just end it. If you have doubts when you get to college, then it's not right; take some time and space to figure out what feels right for you. If you have doubts while reading this book, then it's not the right thing, so end it.

> "Don't dump your girlfriend from high school just because you think you're going to college and will find other girls."
>
> —freshman,
> University of Southern Indiana

Here's the best tip: follow your heart. Be honest with your significant other. Respect what he or she has to say (whether you're on the giving or receiving end). And do not cheat. It's tempting to have your high school sweetie in the wings while you date your entire campus, knowing that you always have something or someone to go home to, but cheating is bad. It's not loving, it's not necessary, and it only taints what you once had.

> "My ex-girlfriend and high school sweetheart transferred to my school following our first year at college. We gave it the 'college try' but it didn't work out. 'Relapses' were common, but the committed relationship never worked. Much earlier, we should have resolved to go our separate ways instead of maintaining a friendship. The friendship led to closeness, which developed into romance, which never worked. Cyclical and bad."
> —junior, UC–Davis

Bottom Line

High school relationships don't pack well when taken to college. They're extremely fragile, and many will break. Should you take yours with you, understand that it might break, but don't throw it away before it's broken. Some can survive and last forever.

Tip #59
Imaginary Relationships and Online Dating

The Tip

Don't be afraid to say something to someone you're interested in. The longer you wait the bigger deal it becomes until it becomes too big of a deal to act on.

The Story

If you're interested in meeting someone in your class, don't just sit around imagining what the relationship could be. Find out if it's going to happen. While you're sitting there waiting and daydreaming, some other guy will come along and ask her out. Then all you'll be left with is a fantasy. It happened to me my first semester. There was my dream girl in history class. I just sat there drooling during lecture. When I finally found the courage to talk to her, it was too late. I found out before talking to her that she was dating someone else. I had put so much into our relationship. We had practically been dating (in my head) for the entire semester. I later found out that she had liked me, but it never happened. As I've progressed through my college life, I've become a lot less shy. That's helped me learn to live in reality and make some friends and more.

—senior, Illinois State University

✳ ✳ ✳

No, you're not imagining it. This is two tips in one (no, there's no additional cost).

Imaginary Relationships

When looking for love in college, it's easier and safer to sit and fantasize about what someone might be like to date. Now, with Facebook and MySpace, you have more material to fantasize with than ever before in the history of fantasies. You can imagine the first kiss. Then the first date. Then it's the first night together. Then the first time you say

> "I dated a guy on the Internet long-distance. When I met my boyfriend on campus and we started dating, I had to tell the guy on the Internet what was going on because I could not lie to him. The guy on the Internet went berserk and we stopped speaking to each other."
> —junior, James Madison University

"I love you." Then you're a couple. Then you're visiting each other's home for the weekend. Then you get engaged. Then you get married. Then you have kids. Then you have a family. And yet, you haven't even met the person who is now your husband or wife. Avoid falling into the imaginary relationship world. When you have feelings for someone, just say something. If you can't say something, then turn back to Tip #54. There is always a risk that someone

> "Online dating is convenient. It's easier to turn a relationship on when you want it and off when you don't."
> —senior, Salve Regina University

might not return your feelings. Should that happen, the good news is that it's easy to find another imaginary relationship.

Online Dating

The Number 1 rule of online dating—if you can't date offline, you're not ready to date online. The main problem with online dating is that too many people who are too insecure to date in real life get caught up online. They live in a place I call "realantasy." This is the world of love between fantasy and reality. It appears real because there is someone on the other end interacting with you, but it's hard to know what's real and what is fantasy (that's realantasy). The online world is filled with people who are too afraid or too insecure to experience love in person, but can only experience it through chatting, photos, and phone conversations without ever meeting. Don't fool yourself. Until you can see your partner, touch your partner, and kiss your partner, it's not totally real. If you do go the online route, avoid letting the relationship go months before meeting. Make sure the first date is in a public place, make sure your friends know where you are and who you're meeting (you can even take a friend with), and make sure it's not in a remote location. Also, make sure the person you're seeing knows that your friends and family are aware of what's happening. And really, if you need to keep it a secret, you're not ready to be so involved. It shouldn't be happening. When it comes to online dating, there are thousands of amazing potential partners, but there are also too many bad people out there to give any-one the benefit of the doubt.

Bottom Line

Making love with your mouse might seem safe, but it's not real. And if you're sharing your computer with a roommate, it's not sanitary.

Tip #60
The Friendly Relationship

The Tip
If you're interested in being more than friends, tell that friend, and don't let "no" keep you from still being friends. You never know what might happen later.

The Story
I told her my freshman year that I was interested in being more than friends. She said she didn't see me that way. She just thought of me as a friend. I was upset, but I liked hanging out with her and didn't let it bother me. We stayed friends. I was there when guys came and went. I never tried to make a move. We just hung out. I had a couple relationships along the way. It wasn't until our senior year that we finally got together. It just felt right. She said that if I had never mentioned that I wanted to be more than friends, she might not have looked at me that way. The more I dated around, the more she began to realize that I was the one she should be with. I never let her not wanting me ruin the friendship. If a friend isn't

"We met online and talked for about six months. When it came time to meet her, she was nothing like she described to me. I couldn't get past the fact that she had lied. I'm relieved that she was only a liar and not dangerous. I didn't even tell anyone where I was going or what I was doing when we met."
—senior, University of Florida

interested, don't run from the friendship. It's friends who turn out to be the best relationships. You only risk ruining the friendship if you're someone who isn't all that secure to begin with. Tell if you're interested.

—senior, University of Missouri

* * *

You find yourself hanging out all the time with a friend of the opposite (or same) sex. You're both from the same city. You both hate your roommates. You spend time talking about all your sad past relationships. You eat dinner in the cafeteria together. She lets you nibble on her chicken strip. You let her dip her French fries in your ketchup. You go out to parties together. You drive home together during holiday break. You poke each other on Facebook. You're in each other's Top Eight on MySpace. You are the best of friends, and then one night, at about two in the morning, you look at him or her and think, *What the hell? I think I'm in love.*

The problem with being the friend who wants more is that most friends who want more never let their feelings be known. They secretly want more, but do nothing. No, wait— they complain to all of their friends that they are always the

> **"He told me he liked me as more than friends our sophomore year. I was shocked and rejected him. We stayed friends. Two years later, I fell in love with him. We're now married."**
> —graduate, Northwestern University

friend and never the boyfriend/girlfriend. They hide behind the "friend façade." It's safe, it's easy, and it's secure. And that's the problem. The people who are "just friends" are only friends because they're too afraid to say what they feel. It's all their own doing. And to those "nice guys" and "nice girls" of the world—there's nothing "nice" about keeping your feelings a secret. If your intentions are genuine and you know that you're desirable, you wouldn't be a good friend if you kept your feelings a secret.

The key to avoiding falling into the friend trap is to let a friend know that you have feelings for him or her. The key to not making things weird is to give your friend permission to not share these feelings (this can only happen once you train for the sport of taking risks and are able to face The Universal Rejection Truth of Dating and Relationships). It could take years for that friend to see you as more than a friend. It might never happen. But you need to say something or it is guaranteed to never happen. It's just about sharing feelings and seeing if they are mutual. If they're not, that's cool. Now, the seed is planted. It doesn't have to be weird. It's only weird if you make it that way. So don't make it weird. Move on and be a friend. You'd be surprised how much more attractive you appear once you express your interest and then move on to someone else. The more comfortable you can become with taking risks (see Tip #54) the easier it will be to make your feelings known, and the easier it will be to handle whatever it is your friend does or doesn't feel.

Bottom Line

A true friend would tell a friend, "I'm attracted to you." And that friend would honestly respond with how he or she feels. And then life would go on...o bla di o bla da, life goes on...(it's a Beatles song reference).

Tip #61
Gay/Lesbian/Bisexual Relationships

The Tip

It's very hard to date someone who's not out. If you're gay and want to date, then come out and be who you are.

The Story

I've been out since high school. When I got to college, I started dating someone who was not out at all. It was freshman year. We met at summer camp the year before. I was the first person he came out to, and to this day I'm still one of the few. He went to a local college and none of his friends knew he was bi.

The Naked Blog:
A Very Good Year to Be Gay.
See www.TheNakedRoommate.com.

When it came to our relationship, things would be fine when were alone, but when we went out in public he would become wicked homophobic. Even when we were in places that I felt comfortable and where he knew no one, he would still give me a dirty look or say "not here." I'm not a big PDA person, but I at least like to be close to someone. I like to be myself around my friends, and especially with a boyfriend. After about four months, it was too much. I told him I couldn't do this anymore. I said, "You're not ready for this. I don't want to force you to be someone you're not." He was upset, but understanding.

—sophomore, Wentworth Institute of Technology

The most commonly accepted statistic is that 5 to 10 percent of the population is either gay, lesbian, or bisexual. The actual figure could be higher or lower (there's no way to know for sure), but that's not the point. The point is that a fair amount of people reading this will either be gay, lesbian, bisexual, or transgendered. For a lot of you, college might be your first time dating someone of the same sex in the open or behind closed doors. With this can come some unique challenges. Some campuses have fairly open gay communities and others have more of an underground community. A great way to gauge the climate is to check out the groups and organizations on campus that address sexuality. Typically, these groups have names like LESBIGAY Alliance, the Gay Student Union, or something with gay, lesbian, bisexual, and transgender in its name. Send an email (or Facebook message) to the board members who are involved with these groups and organizations (you should be able to find information for such groups and organizations on your campus website). Ask members about gay-friendly residence halls, hangouts, and hot spots on campus. There might even be a GLBT center on campus. It's also a good idea to contact the dean of students office and to inquire into local resources for the GLBT community.

If you're not sure if you're gay, lesbian, or bisexual, take your time to figure it out. Just know that if you do experiment, from what students have told me, the gay community is pretty much a place where everyone knows everything. Make sure your partner knows if you're out or not. Otherwise, he or she might talk (still, he or she might talk).

If you find that it's too difficult or too uncomfortable on your campus to be yourself, consider relocating to a campus that's friendlier to gays, lesbians, and bisexuals. Otherwise, look to see if there is a gay, lesbian, bisexual, or transgender community on a nearby campus.

Bottom Line

Just be true to yourself. If you don't know yourself, then take the time to figure yourself out. Seek friends and a community where you can find the strength and support to be true to who you know you ought to be.

Tip #62
Cheaters, Users, and Abusers

The Tip

If you think someone might be cheating, there's a good chance that something is happening. Listen to yourself and your friends.

The Story

I didn't suspect anything until a good friend told me that my boyfriend had hit on her. I thought she was just jealous. Then another friend told me something similar. I kind of distanced myself from them. I didn't want to hear anything. A few months later, I noticed that he was getting strange calls on his cell phone. I'd ask him and he'd tell me it was just about studying. When it came to email, he had a separate account and a password that he

> "I was in a relationship that lasted a couple years. We broke up at least four times and got back together every time but the last time. I didn't like the way we argued and screamed and yelled at each other. He would apologize and tell me that he'd change and that he wouldn't be possessive or be jealous...and I would believe him. That's how it was for two years. Finally, I told him I was out and finished. My friends told me that I was in an abusive relationship. It was abusive mentally and they were right."
> —freshman, Loraine Community College

guarded. When I asked him, he made me feel like the worst person in the world. One time, he went out of town and I decided just to double check. I was able to check his voice messages and found out that he was seeing his ex. When I went to the computer, I was able to look at old mail and saw that other girls had been writing sexual messages about their past and future. I was devastated. When I accused him, he accused me of being controlling and jealous. Yeah, right. Luckily, my friends that were trying to protect me took me back. If everyone tells you something is wrong and you think something is off, trust that something is wrong.

—junior, University of Massachusetts–Dartmouth

* * *

Defining the Cheater

Cheaters are selfish and lazy people who don't have the balls, or the ovaries, to say how they feel to someone they supposedly like or love. Instead of being honest, they lie, deceive, cover up, rip out hearts, and scar innocent victims forever. Cheating is NOT about love—it's about being too lazy to be honest with yourself and the people who like or love you. If the world would stop putting up with cheaters and their selfish, destructive, and hurtful ways, cheating might stop. Sadly, too many people who are cheated on don't think they have other options because they don't know how to find a date (see Tip #54 for instructions on how to find a date while sober). Subsequently, these people put up with cheaters and their cheating ways.

National Domestic Abuse Hotline (www.ndvh.org)

Abuse victims can call: 1-800-799-SAFE

To the Cheated On

Don't ignore it. Don't be so quick to excuse it. Think twice before accepting someone's apology. Don't just put up with it. And do not get used to it. No matter what that cheater says, he or she doesn't respect you. Unless that person gets serious help (I mean therapy resulting in major life changes or offers you complete confidence he or she has changed and deserves ONE and only one chance), never take them back. It's easy to promise change, but few are willing to commit to change.

If You're Being Abused

Never justify being physically or emotionally abused. It is *never* your fault and it's *never* acceptable. You might think, *But I love him or her.* If love in your world means being battered, physically or emotionally, then you don't love yourself. You don't need a romantic relationship, you need help. Without your parents so involved in your daily life, you need to be responsible for you. If you're in an abusive relationship, use your resources on your college campus to get out. Talk to counselors on campus. Get support. Do not get used to it. If you do get used to it, when will it stop?

To the Cheaters and Abusers

Rather than cheating and hurting someone who cares for you and ruining that person's life, have some integrity and get out of the relationship. Stop wasting everyone's time. If you're hitting your partner or controlling him or her by saying degrading, demeaning, or negative comments, stop it and look in the mirror. YOU ARE SICK and YOU NEED HELP. It doesn't say much about you if demeaning, controlling, and abusing someone is the only way to get that someone to love you. That's not love. It's control. Help and support are available. Please get it.

WARNING: Facebook and MySpace make it easier for cheaters to get caught. If you suspect someone is cheating, visit their profile page and read the comments. You wouldn't be the first to bust someone this way. You might just find that your S.O. stopped by.

Bottom Line

People who love each other do not hit each other. People who love each other don't cheat on one another. Do not get used to it. Do not excuse it. Do not allow it. There are enough partners who will love and respect you (remember, we each have thousands of soul mates).

Tip #63
I Have No Life Other Than My Relationship

The Tip
Do not make someone your world. You'll feel confused and empty, and you'll end up searching for yourself.

The Story
I entered my freshman year of college with an optimistic and even naïve mind-set. I thought that everyone out there did not have the capability to hurt anyone, let alone me. I met this amazing, talented, caring, and loving individual who took my heart the minute I saw him. I knew that by the end of the semester I was going to have to talk to him. After weeks of contemplating how I was going to approach him, I finally did it. We instantly clicked.

Weeks after our encounter, we were official. He and I were together all the time. We were one. Every weekend and every chance we had to spend with each other, we did. Things moved incredibly fast and soon we were so involved with each other that it seemed as though he was my present, my future, and my world. I was so in love with him that I forgot who I was and what I stood for. Sometimes, things came up that I did not particularly agree with or was uncomfortable with, but I was so scared to lose him that I shut them out and forgot about them. I got lost in his presence and

> "Don't let relationships hold you back from the things you want to do on campus."
> —senior, Misercordia College

warmth. I never thought that this person would be the one to give me my first heartbreak. I cared for him so much that I was willing to take any aches and pain to spare him.

He broke up with me. He did not feel the same way about me anymore. It took me months to discover myself again. It took me months to realize that you should *never* make someone your world; they should be a part of *your* world. If someone cares for you enough, they will respect you and want you for every inch of soul that you are. Be true to yourself, take care of yourself, and *do not* put somebody's well-being over yours, because the world is not as caring as you may think.

—sophomore, Eastern Illinois University

* * *

There comes a time in many students' relationships when they realize that they have no life other than their relationship. One day, you park your Winnebago of Love and realize that you're in the middle of nowhere, friends are gone, college is gone, and life isn't about you, but instead who you're with. Welcome to the land of "I have no life other than my relationship!" Population: 2.

It can happen without you ever even realizing it. It starts when you fall in love. No better place to be than with the love of your life, right? The things that used to occupy your time aren't as interesting or as important as the person you're with. It's better than spending time with friends. It's better than spending time with yourself. It's better than spending time with strangers you could be meeting in clubs, activities, or organizations. There really doesn't seem to be anything or anyone else in the world that makes you as happy. And then…

- Friends and family get hurt and pissed off. And it's true, most relationships don't last as long as most friendships. Even if you think it's going to last, it's not likely to last. And it's friends and family who will help you when it ends.

- You become so dependent on this one person for your happiness that you end up putting up with things that you should never put up with. You don't think you have options and start feeling trapped. Having isolated yourself from the world, you are left with little or no life outside of your relationship. With no outside life, you tend to hang onto crappy relationships that should be trashed.

- It's hard to grow, make friends, and find new experiences when your only experience is that relationship. So many people I've talked to wish they hadn't made their relationship their whole life. It just takes up so much time. And there are so many other things that you can be doing. You can still have a relationship, but find balance.

- You become so isolated and so alone that your relationship becomes a crutch that you need to lean on in order to find balance. Eventually, the crutch gives way and you fall hard.

Bottom Line

Don't abandon yourself, your family, or your friends. Should you get dumped, you'll be left with no one. Should you not get dumped, you'll be too afraid to dump your partner. That's when things go from bad, to the rest of your life—until you cheat, get divorced, or get so badly hurt your significant other is arrested.

Tip #64
I Got Dumped and No Longer Have a Relationship

The Tip
Always believe that the worst is over and things can only get better with the friends you have around you.

The Story
I broke up with my boyfriend of three years and it was a messy ending. I came into college just beginning this relationship and I regret the last three years of college because I had limited myself to just one person. I had friends from all over calling me, coming over, and taking care of me. Never underestimate that your friends will always be there and the old ones will never stop caring. It's not easy breaking up with someone in college, especially someone you were serious with. However, you will get through it and make new friends.

—junior, Texas A&M University

* * *

There's breaking up with a first love, then there is sitting naked in a bathtub filled with angry bees while covered with honey. No, this isn't a kinky fantasy; it's an analogy that illustrates how much each of these situations can sting.

It's so unbelievably painful to lose love, especially your first love. It's the first person you've loved and who has loved you so completely. It's deep, it's excruciating, it's intense, but it does pass over time. Here's a guide to help you survive:

Phase I: Get Upset

Cry and get emotional. Avoid detaching yourself or hooking up with the first person who shows you some attention. Allow yourself to get upset—do it alone or do it in a place where there are mirrors. I always like to do my crying in a mirror. I think it helps to see the raw emotion, plus it's a little more dramatic. It's a bonding experience with yourself.

Phase II: Know That You're Still Desirable

Too many times people panic and think, *No one else will love me.* This is why so many people run into rebound relationships. That thinking is wrong, wrong, wrong. (Not a typo; yes I wrote it three times. It's really that wrong.) Breaking up is all part of the dating process. Most couples break up. Sure, some will get married, but then about half of

> "When my girlfriend of two years broke up with me, I went through at least two months of depression and then a period of about three or four months where I was doing stupid things because I really didn't know who I was. Finally, I found what I thought to be my true self."
> —junior, Rutgers University

those people will end up breaking up (it's called divorce). Breaking up can be brutal, but it's part of the process. It's better to be free and available to be with someone who appreciates all you have to offer than to be with someone who isn't sure what he or she wants!

Phase III: Surround Yourself with Friends and Stay Busy

Friends are great because they'll tell you all the things you need to hear. Things like: you're better than him or her, it's her/his loss, he/she never treated you well, I never liked him/her anyway, you're hot. It's all true. Listen and don't go running back to your ex. If you don't have a ton of friends, tell these things to yourself and stay busy.

Phase IV: Take a Break from Dating

This can be for as long as you need. But give yourself time to heal. I like to use the Wite-Out example. Unless you allow the Wite-Out to dry on the paper, writing over it will just cause a smudge and uncover what is still underneath. Wait until you heal before getting back out there.

Phase V: Avoid Running Right Back to an Ex

So many people break up and then run back to an ex. If you're running back to an ex out of loneliness and insecurity, you're running toward trouble. If you're running back because the relationship is the healthiest thing in the world for you and the space apart provided clarity, then proceed with caution.

Phase VI: Get Back Out There

When you do get back out into the world, you will be so much smarter. Learn from your past relationship. Trust that it will only get better.

> "I'll never forget the night he called me and the tone of his voice and the words that came out of his mouth. He said, 'I'm not sure if I'm in love with you anymore. I don't know if I want to be with you anymore.' I was shocked, hurt, and devastated. He was the person who said he would be with me forever and couldn't live without me forever. It was like he was taking a knife and stabbing me in the heart. It was like all the memories and future dreams were passing before me. Of course, I cried for a couple weeks, thinking about it every day. I'm still trying to get over it. I still hear his words and it still hurts."
>
> —junior, High Point University

Bottom Line

Sitting naked with bees in honey can sting, similar to a bad breakup. But it all gets better over time (assuming you're not allergic to bees).

Harlan's Tip Sheet

Dating Resources, Websites, and Additional Information

Definitions

- Realantasy: A combination of fantasy and reality most commonly found in online relationships and imaginary classroom relationships.
- The Universal Rejection Truth: The unavoidable truth that not everyone you desire will always desire you. Millions will, but many others will not.
- Rejection Denial: A deep, dark, dangerous place where you think that everyone you like should like you. When someone you like doesn't like you, there's a big problem. But the problem is that you never give people permission to not like you.
- Self-Rejection: Never taking a risk because you assume the results will end in your being rejected. You reject yourself before giving anyone else an opportunity to do it.
- Rejection by Circumstance: Someone doesn't return your interest because of a circumstance. Oftentimes, the circumstance has nothing to do with you. But for those in a state of self-rejection, they assume the circumstance is undoubtedly about them.
- Raw Rejection: Someone doesn't return your interest because of you—the way you look, your culture, your religion, all the things that make up who you

are. When changing is possible, it often means compromising your character.

- Training for the sport of risks/rejection: Working to be your personal best so that you can overcome self-rejection, rejection by circumstance, and raw rejection. Once you train, you can find a date while sober because taking risks are no longer so risky.

- Rejection Awareness Week™ (R.A.W.): Feb 7–14. An annual event celebrating the risk that leads to love. Founded in February 2003, R.A.W. is a time to expose the unspoken truth about dating and relationships— that relationship rejection is unavoidable, normal, and a natural part of the dating process. This international holiday is celebrated by taking the risk that leads to love. If you can't take the risk, then take a look in the mirror and figure out what you need to do so taking a risk isn't so risky. The greatest risk is never taking one.

- The International Risk-Taking Project (I.R.P.): A worldwide project encouraging individuals to put themselves in the path of opportunity in the name of risk-taking research. You can find more information at www.rejectionawareness.com.

Websites

National Sexual Assault Hotline
1-800-656-HOPE
http://www.rainn.org/
National Domestic Violence Hotline
1-800-799-SAFE (7233)
http://www.ndvh.org/

Gay, Lesbian, Bisexual, Transgender Issues
http://www.outproud.org
Dating Websites:
Pick two websites and give it at least a year
(match.com, Yahoo! Personals, etc.)

Best Relationship Advice (Yes, I'm Biased)

Visit www.helpmeharlan.com, www.TheNakedRoom
mate.com, or send an email to harlan@helpme
harlan.com.

Sex

9

Having It, Not Having It, Hearing Other People Having It

Dear Harlan,

I always told myself that I would wait to have sex, but last week, in the heat of the moment, I kind of lost my virginity and now I regret it. My problem is that he still wants to see me, but I'm stuck on this guy who lives a floor below me and who I hooked up with once last month. We didn't talk much after that, but now I see him everywhere. He's always smiling at me. I really like him and want to start something more. What should I do to make him notice me again? Should I just forget about the guy I lost my virginity to? I need help.

—Extremely Confused

Dear Extremely Confused,

You can always have sex with the guy you now like

—that will get him to notice you (for at least a minute). And NO—I'm not serious…

You "kind of" made a mistake losing your virginity, and now you kind of have to fix it. But before doing anything, figure out why it happened. Think about what you're using sex for. If it's to get guys' attention, it's a weak technique. Slow down and be careful.

Now, regarding your situation—talk to the guy you slept with, just in case you and the sex actually meant something to him, and assure him that he didn't do anything wrong. Let him know that it just doesn't feel right to be a couple. As for the guy a floor below you, it seems that you already have his attention. Start with a conversation and keep your clothes on, so as to not get his attention using sex. You might not be a virgin anymore, but you can still "kind of" wait to have sex with another guy. Another thing to keep in mind—be careful when using sex as a way to get attention. Things like bad reputations, sexually transmitted diseases, and children (that you'll give birth to) can end up following you around for years. And then, when you do find someone whom you want to date for more than a night, the past might become an issue.

Tip #65
Deciding to Do It

The Tip
Make sure the first time is with someone comfortable.

The Story
When I got to college, I was a virgin. I had dated, but never felt ready. I had kept my virginity. When I came to college, it was easier to have sex. People talked about it as if it wasn't a big deal. Hearing all the conversations made it matter less and less. I ended up losing it my freshman year to a guy that I was kind of dating. It wasn't great, but he made it comfortable. He was also a virgin. We talked a lot. He was surprisingly sensitive. The most important thing is to make sure that it's with someone comfortable. It wasn't physically all that great and it was much more comforting to be able to talk about everything. I could not have imagined doing it with some hookup from a party. I know a lot of friends who lost it to someone who they barely knew. That, I would have regretted.

> "My friend was a virgin for eighteen years and he said to her, 'You look like you listen to rock music,' and then she lost it."
>
> —freshman, University of Nevada–Las Vegas

—junior, University of Montana

* * *

If you've already done it, please don't skip this tip. In fact, I'm going to give back your virginity just for visiting this tip. I can do that. It's part of being an advice columnist and author. So, for all you virgins and nonvirgins, it's safe to assume that some of you are planning on having sex in college. Considering that over 80 percent of students graduating from college have done it, many of you who are planning not to do it might decide to do it. Just in case you choose to, keep reading…

When deciding to have sex, keep the following virgin questionnaire in mind. If possible, copy this checklist and keep it close to you when making your decision. You have my permission to reproduce it and keep it in your pocket. If you don't have pockets, keep it in your sock. If you're not wearing socks, then stash it in your underwear. If you're not wearing underwear, then it's probably too late…

○ *Will you be filled with regret when it's over?*

○ *Can you communicate with your partner before, during, and after?*

○ *Do you have contraception (including condoms)?*

○ *Have you asked your partner about herpes, genital warts, and other sexual souvenirs (that would be, asking them if they have them, not just asking them questions about them)?*

○ *Do you want to give this person something so special? And no, you can't get it back once it's given. If anyone says that, the person is trying to get you in bed again.*

○ *Have you talked about what would happen if the woman got pregnant?*

○ *Are you doing it because you want to or because you're feeling pressure?*

○ *Are you sober?*

○ *Does this decision work with your religion?*

○ *Will be awkward to see the person the next day?*

○ *Is it happening in a comfortable place (not while your roommate sleeps)?*

○ *Does it feel 100 percent right?*

○ *Do you know the person's first and last name? Can you spell them? Can you pronounce them?*

Besides the whole sexually transmitted disease (also called sexually transmitted infections) and pregnancy scare factors, there is the emotional factor. Sex is intense and it can bring on a flood of emotions. Unless you're sure it's right, and unless you're with someone who makes you comfortable, it's not right.

Bottom Line

When in doubt, don't do it. If you do, practice safer sex. FYI: Some STDs/STIs can be transmitted even when a condom is used.

Tip #66
Deciding Not to Do It

The Tip
If you can't talk about sex with the person you're going to sleep with, then you obviously aren't mature enough to have it.

The Story
I met my boyfriend at college. We started going out about one week into school and seemed to be really compatible. We talked about everything, including sex. I told him that I didn't want to ruin my chance at life by getting some disease or becoming pregnant, because honestly, I'm just too selfish right now to have a whole other human being depending on me. We talked it out, and still do, and he completely respects my decision. Talking about it even made him respect me more, and made him feel like I really trusted him and felt comfortable enough to share that sort of thing with him. If anything, talking about waiting has brought us closer together.

—freshman, Redlands College

Visit the Naked Virgin forum at www.TheNakedRoommate.com.

* * *

According the National Institute of Virginity, a virgin walks by you every 3.5 minutes. Actually, I made up that statistic and the Institute, but the point is that virgins are all around you. They're everywhere. It's just that not everyone flaunts it. A truthful stat reports that more and more teens are waiting longer to have sex.

Some wait for religious reasons. Some don't want to risk getting pregnant. Some aren't emotionally ready. Some just haven't found the right partner worthy of the honor. And then there are the reluctant virgins—those who want it, but can't get it. But really, if you want sex badly enough, you can find someone who is desperate enough, lonely enough, intoxicated enough, or affordable enough (not recommended). Choosing to have sex is easy. Waiting until it's right—that's the challenge. Virgins make a choice. It's not a curse—it's a gift.

If you're a virgin, hang on to it for a while. Whatever you do, avoid losing it by accident, while drinking, due to pressure, or out of fear of losing someone. Many virgin men and women have confided in me—some people don't always want to date a virgin, but still, there are a lot of people who find it extremely attractive. There are so many people who will be so excited to *not* make love to you, *not* have to worry about pregnancy scares, *not* have to worry about STDs/STIs, *not* have to deal with contraception, and *not* have to deal with all the emotions that go along with having sex!

One more thing worth mentioning—just because someone isn't interested in dating a virgin doesn't mean that they're sex-crazed and looking to use you. There are some people who want to have a sexual relationship before marriage. It's a choice, just like not having sex is a choice. Respect their choices and be sure to remind them that not having sex with you is their loss. Besides, being a virgin doesn't mean that you're not sexual.

Bottom Line
All virgins are virgins by choice. Don't be so quick to give it away. It's not a bad thing to hold on to for a while.

Tip #67
Doing It Way Too Much

The Tip
It's easy to have sex once you start. Pace yourself.

The Story
I started off as a virgin in college. It wasn't for religious reasons; I just didn't find the right person to be with. I lost my virginity the first month in college. Once it was gone, it became so much easier to have sex. There wasn't the pressure of, "Wait, hold on, oh my god, I'm a virgin. Ahhhh." What happened to me next is the bad part. I kind of started being too promiscuous. I'd go out, party, and come home with some different partner. No, I never got an STD that I know of or anything like that, but I was with some people that I would have never been with normally. I lost control. It seemed like fun at the time, but

I wish that I had, let's say, been more selective. It's hard when you see the people you slept with freshman year on campus like at the library or at a game. I'm not proud of the past.

—senior, University of Oklahoma

* * *

If you've been trying to read this tip, but keep getting distracted because you keep having sex, then you're probably doing it too much.

For some students, sex is used as a way to escape reality; for others it's a way to feel connected. With no curfews, no parents, and no one other than yourself to watch over you, the decision is yours to make.

Be aware—the most common problem with new students is that sex is sometimes used as a crutch to make it through the whole transition. Look at it like this—a new student on a new campus is naturally uncomfortable. One way to feel connected for ten minutes, or five minutes, or less than a minute (depending who you're with) is to have sex. It's a quick fix, a fast connection, and a way to feel like you're not alone.

Fast sex (or random sex) is often just a temporary distraction from a bigger problem. It's an ego boost, it's a drug,

> "It's just expected now; you go to a party, you hang out, and then something sexual will happen."
> —senior, Alfred University

it's an escape, it's a way to feel comfortable in an uncomfortable place. The problem is that when it's over, you can end up hurt, pregnant, with an STD/STI, with a bad reputation, in a dangerous relationship, or confused—

wondering if someone likes you for you or only for the sex, and leaving you feeling even more uncomfortable and alone.

Besides using sex as a crutch, there's also the "he/she's too easy" phenomenon. This is when a guy or a girl has sex, enjoys the sex, but is then disappointed because the sex was so easily offered by his or her partner. It's a post-coital loss of respect. In retrospect, the partner wishes the sex had been denied for longer. The longer the wait the better the couple can get to know each other. The better they know each other the more meaning behind the sex. There's

> "Just because a girl has sex doesn't mean that she's a slut."
> —junior, Angelo State University

really nothing to be gained from having sex too soon (other than STDs/STIs and possibly children—see tips to follow).

Having sex too soon is best described by using the analogy of building a new house—until the walls are up, the roof is shingled, the plumbing is in place, the electricity is flowing, and the carpets are installed, entering the house can be dangerous. Should you go into someone's "house" too soon or invite someone inside yours, always demand a hard hat is worn. You never know what you're getting into or who was there last.

Bottom Line

Too much of anything isn't good—sex included. (Yeah, hard to believe. I know.)

Tip #68
The One-Night Stand

The Tip

Make sure sex is consensual. "No" means no. That goes for the person saying it and the person being told it.

The Story

When a guy is getting into a random hookup, he needs to make sure it's consensual. I have a good female friend on another campus who was intoxicated and was with a guy who wasn't intoxicated. They had sex. She says that she never consented to it. She pressed charges because she thought that he took advantage. Guys are in a vulnerable position when engaging in a one-night stand. I'm extremely careful. I won't do anything with any woman unless she says it's all right. It's just not worth it.

—freshman, Earlham College

* * *

The scene: It's a hot night. You're at a party. The music is playing. You've had a long week. Midterms were hell. You just broke up with your boyfriend/girlfriend. You've had a couple drinks. You're looking to relax and blow

---

Be Prepared for a Sex Emergency

Consider carrying two condoms with you just in case one breaks or tears while it's being put on. Both men and women are equally responsible for preventing STDs/STIs and using contraceptives, and both should carry condoms.

—The BACCHUS Network, www.smartersex.org

off some steam. You then find yourself kissing someone you never imagined kissing. You think, *I've never done this before, it's college, I'm looking for some love, and someone to hook up with*....Things get intense. The heat is now blazing. You can either end the night by getting his/her number, or you can just go home together and do it.

> "As a rule, we'll only stop our friends from taking someone back to their place if they're in a relationship or if the person is totally unattractive. Beer goggles can do that."
> —senior,
> University of Nevada–Las Vegas

What you do is up to you. It's one night—one night that can cause weeks, months, or years of aggravation and problems.

Reasons to avoid the one-night stands:

- Condoms are not always effective in protecting you from the elements. It's hard to know where or with whom your partner has been. It's even harder to trust him or her to tell you the truth.
- Sex makes some people crazy—they have a one-night stand and then want to spend the rest of their life with you. Can you say stalker?
- Someone might be in a relationship, or living with someone who might not take kindly to you having sex with his or her partner.
- It's hard to know if you've gotten someone pregnant; this is especially true if you don't know your partner's name.
- It's uncomfortable to see your one-night stand around campus days, weeks, months, and even years after the sex happens. People who have seen each other naked can never look at each other the same way again.

- If drugs or alcohol are involved, you don't know for sure if the sex is consensual. Rape is a horrible thing.
- You might change your mind and your partner might not be willing to listen—this is when things get dangerous.

* * *

If a one-night stand happens (and it does happen for some people), be smart about it. Make sure it's what you want. Make sure both of you understand that it's a one-night thing. Make sure that you use protection and that you ask your partner about his or her sexual history.

Bottom Line
You might be asking, "If the hook-up sex happens during the day, is it still considered a one-night stand?" The answer is, technically, it's a one-day stand. But you can still call it a one-night stand to help others understand.

Tip #69
Pimps, Hos, and Reputations

The Tip
News travels fast, especially on a smaller campus.

The Story
When someone does something with someone, other people on campus will know about it. The smaller the campus the

faster the news travels. It can be as bad as high school. A guy will know if you're a girl who sleeps around or doesn't sleep around. What you do becomes public knowledge. I'm a pretty good girl when it comes to what I do, but the one time I did hook up and went a little too far, I heard about it from people who barely knew either of us. Everyone loves to talk about who did what with who. What you do will totally follow you around. On a bigger campus, that's not so true. It's easier to get lost in the crowd, but it's not true on a smaller college campus—not at all.

—junior, DePauw University

***

Reputations are like really bad gas—they can stick to you and follow you for a very long time.

The smaller the campus the more the reputation sticks to you. When it comes to what happens in the bedroom (or at the library, or in the laundry room, or wherever you find yourself in an intimate moment), news travels fast. People talk. They talk a lot. And now, with Facebook, MySpace, and cell phones, news travels even faster. You might as well put the story of your affair in the campus newspaper (no explicit photos, please).

> "Never sleep with more than one person in a fraternity or sorority. Everyone will know what you did."
> —senior, Ohio State University

You might not realize it, but when you sleep with someone, there's a good chance other people will find out. When you sleep with someone and then sleep with their friend, there's an even better chance that someone will find out (especially it you're sleeping with them both at the same time and in the same bed). If you sleep with someone and then sleep with their friend and then sleep with two more of their friends, everyone will know. Then you will either be known as easy, a manwhore, a manbo, a slut, or some other expression that isn't all that endearing. And then, when you do find yourself wanting to have a serious relationship, the person whom you want to take you seriously won't. And even if he or she does want to be with you, the fact that you've slept with their friends makes it close to impossible. It takes years to change reputations. Be extremely careful when making them.

Should you make a habit of sleeping around, bring a change of clothes with you so that you don't have to take your walk of shame in your evening wear. There's nothing more obvious than a woman in a miniskirt and sequined top or guy in an all-black outfit walking the streets at nine in the morning on an eighty-degree day.

Bottom Line
Quick note: it's hard to deny sleeping around if you've slept with most of the people on campus.

Tip #70
Sexual Souvenirs
*Note: STDs and STIs are the same thing.

The Tip
Be careful. Girls—make sure you get yearly pap smears!

The Story

I am a very good student with morals that are unfound in today's society, but that doesn't really help you out when you start drinking. I was (and am) a virgin (no vaginal intercourse) and went on spring break to have a little fun.

> "When living in the dorm with a common bathroom, remember that certain STDs travel through water and live on porcelain. My roommate freshman year caught pubic lice from the bathroom toilet. She wasn't sexually active and realized what had happened after a red and raw rash broke out."
>
> —senior, Manhattan College

Little did I know that having any kind of sexual contact can lead to HPV (human papilloma virus) and a whole lot of other problems. I still have not had actual intercourse, but I'm faced with a not-so-fun situation. A year after my spring break, I had an abnormal pap smear and had the LEEP procedure to have the abnormal cells removed that came back as severe dysplasia. While the cells were removed, for the rest of my life I have to worry about it either coming back and causing cervical cancer or causing other kinds of cancer that could be life-threatening or prevent me from having kids. I also have to tell future partners that I have HPV (the virus that cause genital warts). They say that 80 percent of the sexually active population has the virus that causes this, so it is pretty hard to stay away from if you're sexually active. My tip is to only have intimate contact with people that you know well, and girls should definitely get a Pap smear every single year, whether you are "sexually active" or not. That is the only way to detect if you have any problems from the virus. I had very little and non-risky sexual contact and ended up with these problems, which I would not want anyone to have to go through. Prevention is the key!

—sophomore, Miami University (Ohio)

* * *

Some people come home with a souvenir shot glass from college. Some people come home with a T-shirt bearing a school mascot. Some people come home with herpes, genital warts, and chlamydia. If your hobby is collecting STDs/STIs, college is THE PLACE to do your collecting. The challenge—you don't always know who has them and who doesn't have them. People don't wear signs or T-shirts saying, "Hi,

> "There are days when I am grateful for my herpes. I have to risk rejection when I tell a potential partner, but it weeds out the jerks and lets me save my time and heart for someone who actually deserves it."
>
> —junior, American University

I've Got Herpes." (Visit my website to get your sex souvenir T-shirt.) The STD/STI truth is that—brace yourself—one in five college-age people have at least one (and some say the percentages are even higher).

According to the U.S. Centers for Disease Control and Prevention, 45 million people in the United States ages twelve and older (or one out of five of the total adolescent and adult population), are infected with herpes simplex virus-2. Health experts estimate that there are more cases of genital HPV infection than of any other STD/STI in the United States.

Beyond the whole physical side of STDs/STIs, there's the emotional part of it. With many of these STDs/STIs, once you get them, they stay with you for the rest of your life and they change your life. You have to tell your future partners. As for how you get these

things, while condoms are effective, they don't always protect you. So, if you plan on rubbing yourself against someone else, cover up and be sure to get their sexual history.

Should you end up with a sexual souvenir, get treated quickly. And yes, there is treatment available to help control outbreaks. While STDs/STIs like HPV and herpes don't ever go away, they can be managed. Another huge problem is that some STDs/STIs do not show symptoms or do not show up in tests. Unless a man shows symptoms of HPV, it's not possible to know if he has it. Chlamydia can have no symptoms in 50 to 75 percent of cases, although it can show up in tests. If gone untreated, it can lead to pelvic inflammatory disease, which can lead to sterility. Herpes is another one that is hard to see—especially during viral shedding prior to an outbreak. As for HIV, college-

age people are the most at-risk group, especially women. So if you are sexually active, get tested and screened at your campus health center at least once a year. You might also want to look into the new HPV vaccine (HPV can be a precursor to cervical cancer). Most campuses offer testing (including pap smears—for women, not men) that are low-cost (a great holiday gift). If your health center doesn't have screening on campus, the health center can direct you to another center off campus.

The following is a list of sexually transmitted diseases available on your college campus (and yes, quantities are unlimited). Should you find yourself with a sore, an itch, or a bump that can't be explained, the following can help point you in the right direction—the direction of the health center.

Bottom Line
If you want to find a sexually transmitted disease, college is the most convenient place in the world to find what you want. Get tested before getting into bed. With the new HIV tests, all it takes is a mouth swab—no needles.

Some STDs/STIs you might get to meet
Chlamydial Infection

This infection is now the most common of all bacterial STDs/STIs, with an estimated four to eight million new cases occurring each year. Chlamydia can be transmitted during vaginal, anal, or oral sex. It's often referred to as a "silent" STD/STI because symptoms can be mild or absent. In both men and women, chlamydia may cause an abnormal genital discharge and burning with urination. In women, untreated chlamydia may lead to pelvic inflammatory disease (PID), one of the most common causes of ectopic pregnancy and infertility in women. Many people with chlamydia, however, have few or no symptoms of infection. Once diagnosed, a person can be treated with an antibiotic.

"A buddy at another college got diagnosed with chlamydia. He didn't know it, but his girlfriend got diagnosed. They gave him some horse pills just to be safe."
—junior, Western New England

Genital Herpes

Nationwide, at least 45 million people ages twelve and older (or one out of five adolescents and adults) have genital HSV infection. The incurable viral herpes infections are caused by herpes simplex virus (HSV). The major symptoms of herpes infection are painful blisters or open sores in the genital area. These may be preceded by a tingling or burning sensation in the legs, buttocks, or genital region. The herpes sores usually disappear within two to three weeks, but the virus remains in the body for life and the lesions may recur from time to time. Severe or frequently recurrent genital herpes is treated with one of several antiviral drugs that are available by prescription. These drugs help control the symptoms but do not eliminate the herpes virus from the body. Suppressive antiviral therapy can be used to prevent occurrences and perhaps transmission. Women who acquire genital herpes during pregnancy can transmit the virus to their babies. Untreated HSV infection in newborns can result in mental retardation and death.

> **"After college, people tell you things they don't tell you in college—like who has herpes and who gave it to whom."**
> —professional, University of Vermont

Genital HPV Infection

Approximately 20 million people are currently infected with HPV. At least 50 percent of sexually active men and women acquire genital HPV infection at some point in their lives. Genital HPV Infection is an STD/STI caused by human papilloma virus. Some of these viruses are called high-risk types, and may cause abnormal Pap smears. They may also lead to cancer of the cervix, vulva, anus, or penis.

Genital warts (also called venereal warts or condylomata acuminata) are caused by human papilloma virus, a virus related to the virus that causes common skin warts. Genital warts usually first appear as small, hard painless bumps in the vaginal area, on the penis, or around the anus. If untreated, they may grow and develop a fleshy, cauliflower-like appearance. In addition to genital warts, certain high-risk types of HPV cause cervical cancer and other genital cancers. Genital warts are treated with a topical drug (applied to the skin), by freezing, or if they recur, with injections of a type of interferon. If the warts are very large, they can be removed by surgery.

> "One of the girls I know just got genital warts. She was sleeping with this kid who was pretty active. She was scared to confront him. She didn't want to accuse him, but she wanted to inform him in case he didn't know so he wouldn't give it to someone else."
> —junior, Western New England

HIV Infection and AIDS

AIDS (acquired immunodeficiency syndrome) was first reported in the United States in 1981. It is caused by the human immunodeficiency virus (HIV), which destroys the body's ability to fight off infection. An estimated nine hundred thousand people in the United States are currently infected with HIV. People who have AIDS are very susceptible to many life-threatening diseases, called opportunistic infections, and to certain forms of cancer. Transmission of the virus primarily occurs during sexual activity and by sharing needles used to inject intravenous drugs. If you have any questions about HIV infection or AIDS, you can call the AIDS Hotline confidential toll-free number: 1-800-342-AIDS.

Gonorrhea

Approximately 700,000 cases of gonorrhea are reported to the U.S. Centers for Disease Control and Prevention (CDC) each year in this country. The most common symptoms of gonorrhea are a discharge from the vagina or penis and painful or difficult urination. The most common and serious complications occur in women, and, as with chlamydial infection, these complications include PID, ectopic pregnancy, and infertility. Historically, penicillin has been used to treat gonorrhea, but in the last decade four types of antibiotic resistance have emerged. New antibiotics or combinations of drugs must be used to treat these resistant strains.

Syphilis

The incidence of syphilis has increased and decreased dramatically in recent years, with more than 32,000 cases in 2002. The first symptoms of syphilis may go undetected because they are very mild and disappear spontaneously. The initial symptom is a chancre; it is a painless open sore that usually appears on the penis or around or in the vagina. It can also occur near the mouth, anus, or on the hands. If untreated,

"A pretty promiscuous buddy of mine came to my room and asked me about a rash he had in his genital area. He asked me if he should get it checked out or if taking a shower would be enough. I told him to run to the health center. I think it turned out to be syphilis."
—senior, Lasell College

syphilis may go on to more advanced stages, including a transient rash and, eventually, serious involvement of the heart and central nervous system. The full course of the disease can take years. Penicillin remains the most effective drug to treat people with syphilis.

Other STDs/STIs

Other diseases that may be sexually transmitted include trichomoniasis, bacterial vaginosis, cytomegalovirus infections, scabies, and pubic lice. STDs/STIs in pregnant women are associated with a number of adverse outcomes, including spontaneous abortion and infection in the newborn. Low birth weight and prematurity appear to be associated with STDs/STIs, including chlamydial infection and trichomoniasis. Congenital or perinatal infection (infection that occurs around the time of birth) occurs in 30 to 70 percent of infants born to infected mothers, and complications may include pneumonia, eye infections, and permanent neurologic damage.

Most condoms are made from latex rubber. Others are made from lamb intestines and are often called lambskins. Some condoms are made from polyurethane. If you aren't allergic to latex, you should use latex condoms because they are best at preventing pregnancy and they also protect best against AIDS, herpes, and other sexually transmitted diseases (STDs). Condoms shouldn't be used with Vaseline or other brands of petroleum jelly, lotions, or oils. But they can be used with lubricants that don't have oil, such as K-Y jelly.

The Baaad News About Lambskin Condoms

Lambskin (or natural membrane) condoms, while effective for contraception, should not be used for disease protection because the naturally occurring pores in lambskin are large enough to allow some viruses to pass through.

—FDA

Tip #71
The U of Birth Control

The Tip
Free condoms are all over the place. Never pay for a condom again.

The Story
I can't remember the last time I paid for a condom. I get my condoms all over campus. The people in the health office are great. They have a wide selection. I've also picked up free condoms at campus health fairs. They are all shapes, sizes, and flavors. I've even grabbed some glow in the dark ones. It's better than a store. Stock up on free condoms. Buying them can run you about ten bucks a pack or more. I'm a poor college student. Stock up. If you don't see them in the health center, ask. They're available. I went to a party at my friend's school and a guy dressed up as a condom man was walking around the bar handing out free condoms. I never leave home without one. If you don't use a condom, you're just dumb. There's no reason not to.

> "I overheard my dad tell my brother, 'Don't be a fool—wrap your tool!'"
> —senior, Alfred College

—junior, Western Kentucky University

* * *

Some people graduate with honors, some with a new job, and some with a new child. Few people expect to leave with a new member of the family—but it happens.

If this isn't your plan, then plan accordingly when you're having sex.

Birth Control in College

There couldn't be an easier place or time to find birth control. Most college campuses offer many accessible and affordable birth control options. This includes both prescription and over-the-counter choices through the health center. In addition, such services as pelvic exams, pap smears, STD/STI testing, and counseling are also available. If your campus health center doesn't offer these services or cannot prescribe birth control, they can typically offer you a referral to resources off campus. If they won't offer you a referral, talk to your family physician, a local Planned Parenthood, or look up "family planning" in your local phone book. To help in your birth control education, I've listed the following birth control options from the FDA's website. The first one (no sex) is my addition to their list. The rest you may or may not know...

> **Sex Fact**
>
> 76.1 percent of college students who had sexual intercourse during the past three months used a condom or birth control pills during their last sexual intercourse.
>
> —The BACCHUS Network, "Tell It Like It Is—National Collegiate Alcohol Awareness Week"

No Sex

Description: no vaginal intercourse

Failure Rate (pregnancies expected per 100 women per year): 0

Protection from STDs/STIs: 100 percent (this includes no oral or anal sex)

Method of Use: Keep your pants on.

Male Condom, Latex/Polyurethane (Nonprescription)

Description: A sheath placed over the erect penis blocking the passage of sperm.

Failure Rate (pregnancies expected per 100 women per year): 11

Some Risks: Irritation and allergic reactions (less likely with polyurethane)

Protection from STDs/STIs: Except for abstinence, latex condoms are the best protection against STDs/STIs, including herpes and HIV.

Method of Use: Apply immediately before intercourse; use only once and discard. Polyurethane condoms are available for those with latex sensitivity.

Note: Condoms made from lambskin are available for those with latex sensitivity, although latex condoms are best at preventing pregnancy and protecting against AIDS, herpes, and other sexually transmitted diseases.

Female Condom (Nonprescription)

Description: A lubricated polyurethane sheath shaped similarly to the male condom. The closed end has a flexible ring that is inserted into the vagina.

Failure Rate (number of pregnancies expected per 100 women per year): 21

Some Risks: Irritation and allergic reactions

Protection from STDs/STIs: May give some protection; not as effective as latex condom

Method of Use: Apply immediately before intercourse; use only once and discard.

Diaphragm With Spermicide (Prescription)

Description: A dome-shaped rubber disk with a flexible rim that covers the cervix so that sperm cannot reach the uterus. A spermicide is applied to the diaphragm before insertion.

Failure Rate (pregnancies expected per 100 women per year): 17

Some Risks: Irritation and allergic reactions, urinary tract infections, risk of Toxic Shock Syndrome (TSS)—a rare but serious infection—when kept in place longer than recommended

Protection from STDs/STIs: None

Method of Use: Insert before intercourse and leave in place at least six hours after; can be left in place for twenty-four hours, with additional spermicide for repeated intercourse.

Spermicide Alone (Nonprescription)

Description: A foam, cream, jelly, film, suppository, or tablet that contains nonoxynol-9, a sperm-killing chemical.

Failure Rate (pregnancies expected per 100 women per year): 20–50 (studies have shown varying failure rates)

Some Risks: Irritation and allergic reactions, urinary tract infections

Protection from STDs/STIs: None

Method of Use: Instructions vary; check labeling. Insert between five and ninety minutes before intercourse and usually leave in place at least six to eight hours after.

Oral Contraceptives—Combined Pill (Prescription)

Description: A pill that suppresses ovulation by the combined actions of the hormones estrogen and progestin.

Failure Rate (pregnancies expected per 100 women per year): 1–2

Some Risks: Dizziness; nausea; changes in menstruation, mood, and weight; rarely, cardiovascular disease, including high blood pressure, blood clots, heart attack, and strokes

Protection from STDs/STIs: None, except some protection against pelvic inflammatory disease

Method of Use: Must be taken on daily schedule, regardless of frequency of intercourse.

Oral Contraceptives—Progestin-Only Minipill (Prescription)

Description: A pill containing only the hormone progestin that reduces and thickens cervical mucus to prevent the sperm from reaching the egg.

Failure Rate (pregnancies expected per 100 women per year): 2

Some Risks: Irregular bleeding, weight gain, breast tenderness, less protection against ectopic pregnancy

Protection from STDs/STIs: None

Method of Use: Must be taken on daily schedule, regardless of frequency of intercourse.

Patch—Ortho Evra (Prescription)

Description: Skin patch worn on the lower abdomen, buttocks, or upper body that releases the hormones progestin and estrogen into the bloodstream.

Failure Rate (pregnancies expected per 100 women per year): 1 (appears to be less effective in women weighing more than 198 pounds)

Some Risks: Similar to oral contraceptives—combined pill

Protection from STDs/STIs: None

Method of Use: Apply a new patch once a week for three weeks. Patch is not worn during the fourth week, and the woman has a menstrual period.

Vaginal Contraceptive Ring—Nuvaring (Prescription)

Description: A flexible ring about two inches in diameter that is inserted into the vagina and releases the hormones progestin and estrogen.

Failure Rate (pregnancies expected per 100 women per year): 1

Some Risks: Vaginal discharge, vaginitis, irritation. Similar to oral contraceptives—combined pill

Protection from STDs/STIs: None

Method of Use: Inserted by the woman; remains in the vagina for three weeks, then is removed for one week. If ring is expelled and remains out for more than three hours, another birth control method must be used until ring has been used continuously for seven days.

Post-Coital Contraceptives—Preven And Plan B (Prescription)

Description: Pills containing either progestin alone or progestin plus estrogen

Failure Rate (pregnancies expected per 100 women per year): Almost 80 percent reduction in risk of pregnancy for a single act of unprotected sex

Some Risks: Nausea, vomiting, abdominal pain, fatigue, headache

Protection from STDs/STIs: None

Method of Use: Oral pill; must be taken within seventy-two hours of having unprotected intercourse.

Injection—Depo-Provera (Prescription)

Description: An injectable progestin that inhibits ovulation, prevents sperm from reaching the egg, and prevents the fertilized egg from implanting in the uterus.

Failure Rate (pregnancies expected per 100 women per year): less than 1

Some Risks: Irregular bleeding, weight gain, breast tenderness, headaches

Protection from STDs/STIs: None

Method of Use: The woman receives one injection every three months.

Injection—Lunelle (Prescription)

Description: An injectable form of progestin and estrogen

Failure Rate (pregnancies expected per 100 women per year): less than 1

Some Risks: Changes in menstrual cycle, weight gain. Similar to oral contraceptives—combined

Protection from STDs/STIs: None

Method of Use: The woman receives one injection per month.

IUD—Intrauterine Device (Prescription)

Description: A T-shaped device inserted into the uterus by a health professional.

Failure Rate (pregnancies expected per 100 women per year): less than 1

Some Risks: Cramps, bleeding, pelvic inflammatory disease, infertility, perforation of uterus

Protection from STDs/STIs: None

Method of Use: After insertion by physician, can remain for one to ten years, depending on type.

*Consult your doctor for additional birth control options.

> "I get my pills at the health center. My doctor at home gave me a prescription and I fill it at school, but my friend got examined by the nurse and then got her prescription. It's so inexpensive, too. If your college doesn't offer them (some don't) then you can try a local clinic. My friend goes to Planned Parenthood."
> —junior, Northwestern University

Bottom Line

If you're sexually active and not looking to start a family, stay in control of your birth control. Otherwise, you might end up with a child, or two, or three. And there's not a lot of space in dorm rooms for cribs.

The Tip
If you think you might be pregnant, get help immediately.

The Story
It was January of my junior year; I had just come off of the pill in December. I was gaining too much weight from it. I was on my last pack. I didn't quite know when my cycle was because I had been on the pill for years. I was with my boyfriend one night. We were doing what we do. It ends up, the condom slipped off, but we didn't realize that until it was *all* over. When my boyfriend was looking for the condom after we finished, he couldn't find it anywhere. That freaked the hell out of us. We were looking everywhere. When I went to urinate the next day, I found it. It had slipped off and was inside of me. That next morning, I called my aunt who is a nurse. She has dealt with this sort of thing before. She guided me to seek help. I took a couple of pills that were prescribed for me. I told my boyfriend what happened. He was supportive. The next week was nerve-racking. I wasn't sure if it worked. I had some cramping and wasn't feeling so great, but I didn't get pregnant. Every time after that, we checked to make sure that the condom was still

> "The condom broke and it was too late. The next morning we went to the health center and she took the morning after pill. The next few days were horrible."
>
> —senior, Indiana University

on. And we're still checking to this day! I don't want to be that 10 percent...

—junior, Florida International University

* * *

A condom breaks, a pill is forgotten, a drunken night ends and you realize, um, yeah, okay, we've got a big problem... If you think that you're pregnant, don't just sit there and panic. Contact your health center, doctor, or family physician and pick up an over-the-counter pregnancy test. If it's been within 120 hours of unprotected intercourse, ask your doctor or emergency room about emergency contraception. Help is all around you. Here is some helpful information on emergency contraception from the FDA:

- Emergency contraception, or emergency birth control, is used to keep a woman from getting pregnant when she has had unprotected vaginal intercourse. "Unprotected" can mean that no method of birth control was used. It can also mean that a birth control method was used but did not work—like a condom breaking. Other things can happen as well that put a woman at risk for getting pregnant. A woman may have forgotten to take her birth control pills. Emergency contraception should never be used as a regular method of birth control.

- Emergency contraception keeps a woman from getting pregnant by stopping: ovulation (stopping the ovaries from releasing eggs that can be fertilized), fertilization (stopping the egg from being fertilized by the sperm), or implantation (stopping a fertilized egg from attaching itself to the wall of the uterus).

- There are two types of emergency contraception available to women in the United States: emergency contraceptive pills (ECPs), and intrauterine devices (IUDs). In most states, you need to see a health care provider to get either type of emergency contraception. The health care provider may take your medical history and do a urine pregnancy test, and will talk with you about which type of emergency contraception is best for you. You should never take ECPs that belong to another family member or friend. It is very important to first talk with a health care provider.

If the scare is real, and you're pregnant, don't rush any decisions. Some people have babies while in college, some choose not to. Talk to all the people around you. Make sure that you have a strong support system. Talk your parents (if possible), someone in the counseling office, a sibling, an extremely trusted friend, a spiritual leader, a therapist, or a family planning counselor. Then, move forward. And if you're a woman reading this tip, contact the dad. He's part of this, too.

Bottom Line
If you have a pregnancy scare, don't freak out. Get help (then freak out).

Harlan's Tip Sheet

Sex on Campus Resources, Websites, and Additional Info

Campus Health Center

Doctors are standing (and sitting) by. Most college health services offer free or extremely inexpensive screenings for sexually transmitted diseases, contraceptive consultation, and pregnancy counseling—start at your health center and counseling center. The people on campus will be able to direct you to local resources.

National Resources

National Herpes Resource Center and Hotline
919-361-8488 (9 AM to 7 PM Eastern Time, Monday through Friday) http://www.ashastd.org/hrc/index.html
National STD and AIDS Hotline
1-800-227-8922 or 1-800-342-2437 (24 hours a day, 7 days a week)
National Institute of Allergy and Infectious Diseases
http://www.niaid.nih.gov
National Library of Medicine—MEDLINEplus
1-800-338-7657
http://medlineplus.gov
Centers for Disease Control and Prevention
1-888-232-3228
http://www.cdc.gov

The Alan Gutmacher Institute Website:
http://www.agi-usa.org/
The BACCHUS Peer Education Network
http://www.smartersex.org
HPV Confidential
http://www.hpvconfidential.com
The American College of Obstetricians and Gynecologists
202-863-2518
http://www.acog.org
The National Women's Health Information Center (NWHIC)
800-994-WOMAN (9662)
http://www.4woman.gov/
Emergency Contraception Hotline
888-668-2528
http://ec.princeton.edu
Planned Parenthood Federation of America
800-230-7526, 800-669-0156 (to order materials)
http://www.plannedparenthood.org/
Sex Addicts Anonymous:
http://www.saa-recovery.org

Drinking on Campus

10

Tapping the Keg of Truth

Dear Harlan,

I'm a nineteen-year-old college freshman. I have several very good friends that I've known for a long time, some since middle school. Even now, we seem to get along most of the time, but there is one thing that always sets me aside from them: I don't drink.

I don't criticize them for drinking. I just don't join in. When I become legal, I will drink socially, but I don't see a point in drinking just to get drunk. Lately, two of them, whom I consider my best friends, have been excluding me. When I ask them why, they tell me that they feel bad that I'm not drinking and they are. How do I let them know that I'm not judging them?

I've thought about just giving in and getting drunk with them, but alcoholism runs in my family and I want to be the exception to that disease. I realize that by drinking every once in a while, I will not become an alcoholic, but I think there are better ways to spend my nights than drinking and spending the whole next day hungover. Am I just being too conservative?

—Sober

Dear Sober,

Too conservative would be walking into their rooms when they drink and grabbing their beer, then pouring it on them while screaming at the top of your lungs, "Too drunk to get an umbrellaaaaa?!"

Your friends' excluding you just sucks for them—not only do they lose a friend, but also a designated driver. The colder the winter the more they'll miss you and your sobriety.

Thank them for their concern, but tell them that it makes you more concerned to be excluded. Remind them that you don't care if they get drunk, and they shouldn't care if you don't. If anything, they have someone to drive them around, watch their back, and bail them out should they do something stupid. You're a great friend to have.

Make sure they also know that you honestly don't mind hanging out and drinking something non-alcoholic. Should they still exclude you, don't worry, you'll find other friends. Not everyone drinks on campus (or gets so drunk that other people who aren't drunk are a problem). If you find they're just too insecure and stupid, use your free time to get involved with clubs, activities, sports, organizations, religion, or anything to help you meet people.

It's sad that this is what's happening, but friends can grow apart. Don't become a drunk just to keep your friends.

Tip #73
Drinking on Campus

The Tip
If you can't handle drinking and going to school then you're not responsible enough to do both. Accept the fact that you're not and pick one.

The Story
My future is really important to me. I wanted to party, but I also wanted to go to class. The further I went into my major, the more I realized that college is the most important thing to me. I've had friends that have had really low GPAs and quit because they partied too much. My one friend was only sober two days a week. She had to move back home

Time to Party, Or Not
Hours per week spent partying:
None: 23.4 percent
Less than 1 hour: 11.6 percent
1–2 Hours: 15.9 percent
3–5 Hours: 23.0 percent
6–10 Hours: 15.7 percent
11–15 Hours: 5.5 percent
16–20 Hours: 2.4 percent
21–30 Hours: 2.5 percent

- Most students have not driven a car after drinking.
- Most students have not let alcohol use negatively affect their academics.
- Most students do not drink to excess.
- Most students drink one time a week or less.
- Most students have found a way to make sure friendships, health, education, and their future are not put at risk due to drinking.

—The BACCHUS Network, "Tell It Like It Is—National Collegiate Alcohol Awareness Week"

to Wisconsin. Most of us are mature enough and figured it out—that you have to do your homework and go to classes to stay here. Your job is to go to classes. There are mornings when I wish I didn't have to go to school but I need to. I just can't live my life drinking. We'll be in the library in our going-out clothes, and I don't go out unless my homework is done. I go to all my classes, even if I'm hungover. If you're going to do it, then you have suffer the consequences.

Our rules for drinking:
- No skirts at parties—you can get violated too easily.
- Tequila makes us psycho—my friend got into a bar fight after drinking tequila.
- No drunken dials—it always leads to a call to an ex and making an ass out of yourself, so we take away the cell phones.
- No friends with benefits—you hook up after drinking and then have sex. We try to keep that rule, but sometimes we break it.

—junior, University of Nevada–Las Vegas

* * *

If you're using this book as a beer coaster, you might have a drinking problem...

Alcohol has a reputation for being available and abundant on college campuses. In fact, alcohol has become such an issue that many college campuses are now considered dry campuses, meaning there is *no* alcohol allowed on the college soil (no watering the trees with beer). This is all part of an ongoing effort to curb college drinking.

Some students drink, but not as many drink as you might think. Freshmen have this illusion that most college students get drunk all the time. Then, they come to college and start drinking to fit in. But most students don't get drunk. It's reported that 69 percent of college students have zero to five drinks per week. Considering that the National Institute on Alcohol Abuse and Alcoholism lists up to two drinks per day for men and one drink per day for women as a safe amount to drink, zero to five drinks per week is not a lot of drinking. Some college students drink a lot— most college students don't drink a lot. How much you decide to drink or not drink is up to you (assuming you're of age).

> ### What Is Defined as a Drink:
>
> One beer – 12-ounce beer
>
> One glass of wine – 5 ounces of wine
>
> One shot of alcohol – 1.25 ounces of 80 proof distilled spirits
>
> (a 20-ounce beer is 1.75 drinks)

Reasons Why New Students Drink

- *It's a Group Thing.* Drinking is typically pretty social and it's easy to hang out with people who are drinking. The way you are included is if you drink.

- *It's a Social Crutch.* A lot of people have a hard time talking to strangers while sober. Get people drinking and suddenly they are no longer afraid to take risks by talking.
- *It's an Emotional Crutch.* Going to college is a huge change, and big changes are naturally uncomfortable. Put people in an uncomfortable situation and give them the chance to drink and they'll drink. But they don't need to drink to accomplish these same things.
- *It's an Addiction Thing.* Social drinking can become antisocial drinking, which can become an addiction. Students with a family history need to be extra careful (yes, alcoholism has been proven to run in families).

- More than half of the respondents (54.2 percent) never drank beer in high school
- Slightly less than half of the respondents (47.1 percent) never drank wine or liquor in high school

Bottom Line

Not as many people drink as you might think. If you know the reasons why students drink, then it's easier to avoid drinking. Mostly it's to get comfortable, to fit in, and to hook up—all those things can be done without drinking.

Tip #74
Slow Down, Don't Drink Too Fast

The Tip

If you are not an experienced drinker, go slowly and figure out your limits.

The Story

I was not much of the partying type in high school. I was what you'd call inexperienced. I went to a party my first week of school and made the mistake of consuming a lot of alcohol on an empty stomach. I had whatever my friends were having. We had fun for a while, until things started spinning. About two hours into the night, I was on my hands and knees puking my guts out. I didn't quite make it into the bathroom, but no one saw me spill it. I was sick. I was the opposite of holding my liquor. I didn't know how much or how fast I could drink. My friends from my floor and a buddy from high school were there to make sure that I got home. This was the night before I had the worst hangover of my life. As for the hangover—water, drink lots of water. Never again did I partake in the

"Do not eat the fruit out of the punch bowl at frat parties. When I got to college, the first week we were invited to a frat party. Not being a big drinker, I was basically watching everyone get wasted. I noticed all this fruit floating in the punch and started eating it. I had no idea that all the fruit absorbed the alcohol and that they had also soaked some of the fruit in the alcohol beforehand! Needless to say I don't remember much after that."
—junior, Wake Forest University

brew without first eating the food.

—junior, Eastern Connecticut State University

* * *

Should you decide to drink, pace yourself and know what the hell you're drinking.

A common recipe for party punch is a combination of grain alcohol, water, and sugary fruit punch mix. Grain alcohol is about 190 proof, or 95 percent pure alcohol. For the most part, it's odorless, tasteless, and potent. Because it doesn't have a lot of taste, it's extremely dangerous when consumed—even in small quantities. Someone who doesn't weigh much and doesn't eat much doesn't need to drink much to get wasted, and get sick. It happens all the time. *Do not drink the punch*. If you do decide to accept some concoction that someone hands to you, then just hold it. Let it spill or pour some of it down a sink. If you do drink it (bad idea), don't drink much. Drinking too much too fast will make you sick and create serious problems.

The other problem is that it's hard to say how much is too much. Factors like gender (the same amount of alcohol will always affect a woman more then a man), body

Sobering Stats

Assault: More than 696,000 students between the ages of 18 and 24 are assaulted by another student who has been drinking.

Injury: 599,000 students between the ages of 18 and 24 are unintentionally injured under the influence of alcohol.

Death: 1,700 college students between the ages of 18 and 24 die each year from alcohol-related unintentional injuries, including motor vehicle crashes.

—According to the NIDA

weight, full/empty stomach, medications or other drugs, an individual's mood, what someone drinks, one's tolerance (the amount it takes to feel the effects of alcohol), and how fast someone drinks all contribute. Even if you know what you're drinking, you might not know how you'll react to it.

Another problem with so many new students is that they're also new drinkers. According to the Higher Education Research Institute at UCLA, more than half of all new college students never drank in high school. This is the truth. They don't know their limits. And they start figuring out their limits during the most important and unstable time in college.

It's those first couple months of college that are so important to your college career. The first eight to twelve weeks are when you're supposed to get comfortable and figure out how to do well. But the first eight to twelve weeks of college are also the time when people seem to party the most. It's a free-for-all where everyone's looking to find friends, hook up, and get comfortable. So, you can see the problem. Drinking too much too soon can mess you up. You can oversleep, sleep around (and that can consume your thoughts), and sleep through classes (if you even make it to classes). And a crappy GPA your first semester can end up burying you. So, if you choose to drink, pace yourself.

> "The key to any social situation where drinking is involved is to know your limit."
> —junior, Indiana Purdue–Fort Wayne

Bottom Line
Go slowly, don't feel like you have to drink, and don't drink the punch!

Tip #75
Not Everyone Is Drinking

The Tip
A lot of people drink, but that doesn't mean you have to.

The Story
My first semester I was determined not to drink, and I didn't. I was worried about what my sorority sisters would think, but they were cool with that. You learn to hold an empty beer can after a while—the problem is when someone takes it from you and wants to get you a new one. I just tell them that I'm taking a break…like for the rest of the night. I still don't drink and none of my friends seem to care. A lot of my friends do things that I don't feel comfortable doing, and I don't say anything to them. I don't feel like I'm missing out on any part of college life. My boyfriend respects that I don't drink. There are a lot of things to do besides get drunk. It just doesn't interest me.
—junior, Western Illinois University

* * *

Some people look like they're drinking, but really, it's all just a big illusion. That guy holding the beer? It's filled with Mountain Dew. That guy pouring drinks from the keg? He's totally sober and trying to hook up. That girl with the mixed drink? It's cranberry and water. Not as many people as you think are drinking the alcohol. But sure, some are.

If you don't want to drink, then don't drink. If you don't want to tell people that you don't drink, just hold a drink and disguise it. You can pour out the beer and fill the container with something that looks like what you're supposed to be drinking (ginger ale looks like beer, coke looks like rum and coke, grape juice looks like cheap wine). If the problem is holding something, then you can hold a cup with 7UP and a lime. If you want to hold something and don't have a cup, you can just hold yourself. If you don't want to hold yourself then you can hold a small pet, like a ferret, guinea pig, or mouse (all great for making conversation).

> "I see the weight they've put on due to their alcoholic binges. Alcohol is a sure way to gain the infamous freshman 15."
> —freshman, University of Florida

If someone gives you a hard time about drinking, think to yourself, *Man, this person is such an insecure loser*, and smile at him or her. Then say that you just don't drink. If that's not enough then say you have a medical condition or you're on antibiotics. If that still doesn't work, let him or her know that you don't drink because you tend to vomit uncontrollably in the person's room who pressures you to drink (that should do it). The point is that if you're underage or uninterested, you have a choice.

Too often, people only make friends with people who drink and don't feel like they have a choice. But if you can design a world in college where you have options (a few groups of friends, for instance), you can have the power to say what you feel and do what you want to do without feeling pressured or trapped.

Like with drugs (see Chapter 11), if you tend to make friends who drink all the time, chances are you'll begin to drink sooner or later. It just seems to happen that way. People tend to become like their friends.

Bottom Line

To recap: if you don't want to drink, hold a cup, hold yourself, or hold a small pet. You really don't have to hold alcohol.

Tip #76
The Social Lubricant

The Tip
It's easier to hook up and do stupid things when you're drinking.

The Story

During spring break of my senior year, I went Cancun with some friends. We usually would go with a group of guys, but this time it was just the girls. When we are with guys, they kind of protect us. This time it was different. When we went to bars everyone was all over us. It was "free drinks for girls all night." I was already questioning my current relationship and whether it was still something I wanted to continue. I was going to graduate and we were going to be living far apart. My friends met up with a group of guys. The one I met knew I had a boyfriend, but was pretty persistent. He made a move on me at the bar. My friends tried to stop him, but I didn't. We made out that night. The next day I felt *so* guilty. My boyfriend found out. He asked me if I had ever cheated. I told him I didn't mean to do it. When I'm drinking, I tend to do things I wouldn't normally do.

> **"Every time we drink we hook up, but we can't seem to talk when we're sober."**
> —advice seeker, Help Me, Harlan!

> **"If you can't call someone you've hooked up with twenty-four to forty-eight hours after you've exchanged bodily fluids, because you're afraid of being annoying, it should never have happened."**
> —an occasional drinker

One more thing people do when drinking—some of my friends are drunk dialers. These are people who call the people they haven't talked to in a while. They will literally go through their cell phones and delete numbers if they go out drinking so they're not tempted to call them when drunk. After a few drinks, it's easier to call an ex-boyfriend or someone you're interested in. Bad idea.

—graduate student, College of Wooster

*** *** ***

As I mentioned earlier in Tip #54—if you put a group of people in a room together long enough, they will start to hook up. Put people in a room, lock the door, and in a few months people will be making love. It happens on *The Real World* all the time. Now, if you put alcohol in the room, it all happens much faster—not a good thing. Here's why:

Most people can't talk to someone they like while sober because they're too afraid of taking a risk for fear of rejection. When people drink, they suddenly find the courage to do things and say things they wouldn't say or do when sober. It's easier to take risks after drinking because the more you drink, the less you remember who you are, and the less you worry about taking risks. People call it being "less inhibited," but I call it being less aware and not as afraid of rejection (to take risks sober, see Tip #54).

The problem with the drunken relationship is that when two people can only connect after drinking, once sober it can leave one or both feeling awkward, uncomfortable, confused, shy, paranoid, and afraid of making mistakes. That's when partners start getting controlling, jealous, and insecure. Assuming most of your life is lived while sober, you'll probably want to be comfortable with someone that way. That's why it's so much better to connect with someone while sober, assuming you want the connection to last longer than one night (even if you don't, you still have to worry about if what you're doing is consensual).

Now, if you find that you can't find the courage to approach someone while sober, and instead you're drinking or doing a shot to find your courage, turn to Tip #54 and look into training for the sport of taking risks. You can also read more about this on my website. Drunk love typically turns into a sobering and sad reality with bad morning breath.

If you can't do it sober, then you shouldn't do it at all. A relationship that's built on drunken hookups is a relationship built on a sloppy foundation that can fall apart at any moment. If you can't do it, say it, or feel it when sober, then it's not good.

Bottom Line
Drunk people say and do stupid things. Sober people say and do stupid things too, but drunk people say and do more stupid things and are too drunk to be aware of how stupid they appear.

Tip #77
~~Safer~~ Unsafe Sex and Alcohol

The Tip
Don't be so drunk that you bring home a random guy, don't use protection, and then freak out when you realize what happened.

The Story
We had had a party at our house. I drank way too much with my sorority sisters, to the point that I was blacking out.

I then went to a bar with some close friends. I proceeded to drink even more. I don't remember anything, just snapshots of the night. You think you're taking in everything you see, but in reality, you're only taking in ten minutes of the night. While waiting for my friends outside, I bumped into some random guy. We started making out. I brought him home. We ended up having sex. My friends thought it was funny. Once you're not a virgin, your friends are not going to stop you. A few hours later, I just kind of snapped out of it and then freaked out. I kicked him out. I had some alone time where I just bawled. We didn't use a condom and I was freaking out. I went to the health center and got emergency contraception. The next day, everyone wanted to know what happened. I denied that it happened because I was so embarrassed. More than anything, I'm disappointed with myself. I let one night of intoxication almost ruin me.

—junior, Alfred University

* * *

If you're going to do it, then don't do it drunk. When you're drunk, you get sloppy and then you often mishandle the equipment. Let me explain…

It's a night where you meet that someone "special" (this would be the kind of special that you feel after that drink you had right before getting the spins). You and the object of your affection find a cozy place to get more comfortable. You are in a deep kiss, bodies pressing, arms exploring, and hearts beating. You think to yourself, *Mmmm, this is oh-so-good, but*....This is the BUT that tells you that you have no clue who your partner has been with or what your partner may or may not have in his or her pants. I'm talking about herpes, genital warts, chlamydia, syphilis, gonorrhea, HIV...the list goes on and on. The action is too hot to stop and have your partner fill out a sexual resumé. Plus, you're too drunk to really care and it all feels "Mmmm, oh-so-good." You let it go. And you also let the rest of your clothing go. Now you're wearing nothing but each other's hands. Things start moving, churning, yearning, and grinding. You decide that the moment is right to have sex. While you're drunk, you're not too drunk to remember to use a condom (assuming there is a condom in the area). But being so drunk, you and your partner fumble with the condom. First it goes on wrong, then it goes on right (but it could have sperm on it now). You forget to pinch the top of the condom to allow a reservoir for the ejaculate. While you're protected, you're not really all that protected. Besides, a condom can't protect you from some STDs/STIs. The sex happens, the sex ends, and the problems begin. One minute you're screaming, "Ohhh GOD," the next day you're screaming, "Help me, Harlan!" (No, I'm not the one in the bed, I'm the one people write to with their problems in the morning.)

According to the National Institute on Alcohol Abuse and Alcoholism, four hundred thousand students between the ages of eighteen and twenty-four have had unprotected sex and more than one hundred thousand students between the ages of eighteen and twenty-four report having been too intoxicated to know if they consented to having sex. Those statistics are sobering (I know, I also hate it when people use that analogy when talking about alcohol, but it's true). This doesn't even factor in those who use protection and use it incorrectly, or use it correctly and still find themselves dealing with STDs/STIs. And emotionally, it's all so draining. When things go bad, you end up putting so much time and so much energy into these issues. Talk about time mismanagement. Save yourself the trouble and do it sober.

Bottom Line
When you drink it's easy to fumble a condom, go too far, or just get messy, leading you to possible sexual souvenirs or pregnancy scares.

Tip #78
Sexual Assault and Alcohol

The Tip
Watch out when you go drinking; you never know who is watching and what they may put in your drink.

The Story
The first night I actually got to go out and drink, I thought I knew the guys I was with, but I didn't. One of the guys put something in my drink. Usually, you can't taste roofies or other date rape drugs—I sure didn't. I didn't remember the night—my friends told me the next day how I acted and who I left with. But I do remember the next morning.

I woke up and I knew what had happened. I went to class and couldn't concentrate—all I could do was cry. I am so thankful to have friends that would listen. If it ever happens to you, most colleges have student health centers and they really helped me out.

—freshman, University of Tennessee

* * *

Women (and some men) often write to me or tell me after a speaking event that they are survivors of sexual assault. They then tell me how much it hurts to keep the secret inside. And then they tell me how much shame they feel from putting themselves in a position to be assaulted. They think it's their fault. They think that they did something to bring it on. To this day, it still upsets me to think about it. Please know:

> No victim of rape, whether sober or drunk, is ever at fault. Never, never, never. It's not your fault! Please don't feel ashamed.

Sad Fact:

More than 97,000 students between the ages of 18 and 25 are victims of alcohol-related sexual assault or date rape.

—National Institute on Drug and Alcohol Abuse

The National College Women Sexual Victimization Study estimated that between 1 in 4 and 1 in 5 college women experience completed or attempted rape during their college years.

For more info on sexual assault, see Tip #101.

The ugly reality is that approximately one in four to one in five college women will be the victim of attempted rape or rape by the time they graduate. Most survivors know their attacker.

When people drink, they become less inhibited. They become bad listeners. They become aggressive, and far more dangerous. And they don't always take no for an answer. Sadly, you can't give anyone the benefit of the doubt when that person has been drinking. It's one night that can change your life forever.

Please be careful. Watch out for your friends. Watch out for yourself. If you're drinking, never drink from an open beverage that you have not prepared and had your eye on the entire night. Hang on to your drinks, even if you go the bathroom (a great time for someone to slip roofies in drinks). I've had several people tell me stories about this during my research for this book.

As for going home with hookups, one girl on a campus I visited told me the rule that she and her friends follow— no one goes home with anyone who has been drinking. They live by it. For the men and women who are aggressors—if you're with someone who is not sober enough to consent to sex, it's not consensual sex. If someone says no, listen. If you don't, it's called rape. It doesn't matter what *you* call it.

For those who are victims of sexual assault—get help immediately. Most college campuses have a support system in place. You can always call your local police or you can go directly to the emergency room after the assault. Tell the nurse and doctor what happened. They can collect evidence that you can decide to use later. And again, please never think it's your fault. It's not. More than seventy thousand students between the ages of eighteen and twenty-four are victims of alcohol-related sexual assault or date rape. And that stat only reflects reported incidents—who knows what the real numbers are. Just knowing that it happens can help keep it from happening.

Bottom Line
There's a 100 percent chance that someone reading this will be (or has already been) a victim of sexual assault. Please, know that you're never alone, and please get help.

Tip #79
Don't Be So Stupid That You Accidentally Kill Yourself

The Tip
If you drink, at least make sure there is someone sober around.

The Story
My freshman year in college, a bunch of us went out to a party sometime in the first couple of weeks. This one guy, who was one of our friends, was drunk out of his mind—just belligerent. He was screaming at everyone and being really ignorant. Everyone got mad at him. A couple of us were designated drivers. He didn't want to leave the party and

freaked out when we drove him home and got back to the dorms. He was screaming at everyone, and throwing punches. We took him back up to his room. He went inside and closed the door. We thought he'd be fine. A half hour later, someone was on my floor talking about how he was in the hallway screaming again, but went back into his room and passed out. When I heard this, I went to see if he was all right. I opened the door and saw him lying on his back with vomit all over his mouth. He had thrown up and had passed out. It was all in his mouth and he was definitely not breathing. I started screaming for anyone to come and get help. I then stuck my hand in his mouth and was pulling out the vomit. It was so disgusting. I turned him over onto his stomach and was retching while trying to clear it all away. He then came to and started choking. The paramedics arrived and took him to the hospital where he had his stomach pumped. When he was well enough to leave, they arrested him. The judge near our school is hard when it comes on underage drinking. He had to spend the night in jail to sober up. We bailed him out the next morning. He was so embarrassed. Since then have I never seen him that drunk again.

—senior, Valparaiso University

* * *

I had a roommate my junior year of college who almost died. You've never heard about him unless you're related to him. Not many people have. Unless you die, incidents like this don't make the headlines. Happily, he survived.

It all started after a party one Friday night. He had consumed just enough alcohol to make him vomit in the middle of the night and throw up blood. He didn't think much of it because this had happened to him once before. As the day progressed, he looked worse and worse and worse. When we saw him in the afternoon, he looked green. He said that he wanted to take a nap and sleep it off. My friend and I didn't think that was a good idea. That's when we told him, either we drive you to the hospital or we call an ambulance. At first he resisted, but then he backed down and was taken to the hospital. Upon arrival, he started to pass out. He was then rushed into the emergency room for an emergency surgery. It turns out that he had ruptured his esophagus when he vomited and had been hemorrhaging through the night and day. He almost died. Luckily, he made it through surgery and was back at school a few days later. His parents were very appreciative. They bought me a shirt from the Gap to thank me. He survived, and I got a new shirt—a happy ending for everyone.

> "The first week of school I found out that my friend was diabetic. He played soccer with me and was always monitoring his insulin levels during practice. One night, he drank heavily and wasn't paying attention to his insulin level at all. When I got back home, I found out that he was passed out in the middle of the hallway and I called the paramedics. When they got there we informed them that he was diabetic. They asked what his insulin level should be—for some reason I remembered what it was supposed to be. They used the information to save his life."
>
> —sophomore, Carthage College

Do whatever you want to do, but be smart about being stupid. Don't accidentally kill yourself or stand by quietly while a friend kills himself or herself. If you're vomiting and you see blood, go to the doctor. If you're feeling sick beyond sick—get help. If you see that your friend is unconscious, call the paramedics. They can tell you what to look for to see if it's a true emergency. Just call them. Take care of yourself and then take care of the people around you. If you see that your friend is drunk and wants to drive home, stop him or her. If your friend won't listen, call the police and anonymously report them. If your friend is mixing drugs and alcohol, stop him or her. If you see that your friend is drunk and drinking a fifth of vodka from a beer bong, stop him or her. When a friend is too drunk and starts being stupid, you need to be the smart one, or your friend might end up the dead one or the one in the emergency room. If a friend won't listen to you, enlist other friends, parents, professionals, and even the police. Don't stop until the friend stops.

Bottom Line
If you're going to be stupid, don't be so stupid that you accidentally kill yourself or me or someone reading this. If your friends are going to be stupid, don't let them be so stupid they accidentally kill themselves.

Tip #80
Drinking and Driving

The Tip
Even one or two beers can screw you up and follow you around. It can also cost you a lot of money. I've seen this happen to many people.

The Story

A couple of friends and I went to a bar. They were having dinner. It was five miles from my school. I drove there with two twenty-one-year-olds. I had three beers in a little over an hour. So, you know, they all had the same beer. I thought I was fine to drive. So, I got in the car and was driving back home. To get to Elon, you have to cross over a railroad track. Of course, there was a train. To my left was a municipal building and there was a side road. It didn't seem like a good idea to cut through a police station after drinking a couple of beers, but I did. Of course, there were two police officers standing in front of the building. One motioned for me to stop. He said, "Are you lost, son?" I said, "No, sir, I'm just cutting through." Then he asked if I'd been drinking. Then I said, "Yes, sir." I didn't think I could lie. He asked if I was twenty-one years old. I told him I was twenty. Before I knew it I was out of the car and he had me by the arm guiding me into the police station. He unlocked the door and put me inside. My heart was beating out of my chest. He sat me down and gave me a Breathalyzer. The first time, I blew .03. I did it again ten minutes later and it was the same exact thing. Since I was drinking and I was underage, he could have taken my license and put me in jail. We would have never been caught had we not tried to take a shortcut. Since I was cooperating, he didn't arrest me, but he gave me a DUI (the same charge that would have gotten me arrested). Two years later, it still hasn't been resolved. It cost me about $1,000 for a lawyer, and I've been to court eight times. Now I'm twenty-one years old, I have a job, and I still have this unresolved issue that shows up everywhere I go. The employer did a report for an internship—have you ever pled guilty or been convicted of a misdemeanor—I thought that I wasn't convicted. A couple weeks later I was called and this was discussed. I need to disclose it. You never want this to happen again—it never goes away.

—sophomore, Elon College

∗ ∗ ∗

I hate that people do this. It sucks to have to share the road with them. If there were a drunk driving lane, it would make it so much easier for the people who don't feel like putting their lives on the line when running to the store or driving home from a date—but there isn't. We all share the same roads.

I know—it's so much easier not to bother asking the person driving you how much they've had to drink. I know—it's only a few blocks. I know—it seems so much easier to assume it will all be fine. But it's not easier, because should you run a stop sign, hit someone, get hit, swerve into oncoming traffic, brake too late, react too slowly, hit some ice, run into a tree, or just be lucky enough to only get pulled over and arrested, it will be hell. That's what can happen in a few blocks. A few blocks and a lifetime filled with regret.

The truth is that most college students do not drive under the influence of alcohol—to be exact, a recent survey indicates that 67.5 percent have not. There really isn't any reason to drive drunk. Between buses, taxicabs, campus shuttle services, walking, and sober friends who can do the driving, there's no reason to drive drunk. Besides the safety issues, a felony charge for drinking and driving can follow you around for the rest of your life. Drinking and driving is one of those things that you wish you could go back in time and never let yourself do. Assuming you're not reading this while awaiting trial for DUI, this is your chance to not get into a situation where you know you'll be filled with terrible regret and possibly do time in prison. I meant it when I mentioned it on the tip before—if you're in a situation where someone drives drunk, don't just look the other way. Call the police and report them. Wait a few minutes and then drive by your friend pulled over on the road to see if there's anything you can do to help. A true friend will not ignore drunk driving.

And really, you can still get where you want to go without driving. A lot of campuses have free driving services that pick up students and drop them off—no questions asked. The idea is to provide a safe place to live and go to classes.

Bottom Line
Before driving drunk, think about the people you could possibly kill on the road and their grieving families (that could include your grieving family), then think about jail time if you survive. It's so much easier to walk or to call for a ride.

Tip #81
Still Hungover...

The Tip
Drink water and rehydrate. It's cheap and it works.

The Story

As an expert in the art of the hangover, I'd say don't drink more just to drink more. Switch to water before the room spins. If not, you'll fall over the edge and pay for it the next day. Me, I have the worst hangovers. It's a sandwich of nausea. I can't eat. I barely keep my head up. It hits me in the morning or afternoon, depending on when I wake. Coffee doesn't work. The caffeine makes me urinate and lose liquid. The secret is hydration. I've found sports drinks to be helpful. I've tried protein shakes, but the consistency makes me gag. The best attempt to cure the hangover is sleep and water. Actually, that would be water and then sleep. I drink a glass of water before I go to bed. If I'm sick when I wake up, I drink another glass of water and then keep sleeping. I try to eat. If I'm not too sick, I'll stay up. The better advice is to not drink so much that you get a hangover in the first place. Drinking bad, very bad.

> **"I never found a hangover cure. I was miserable. I drank tons of water."**
> —grad, Northwestern University

—senior, University of Southern California

* * *

A hangover is the headache, nausea, and aftereffect of drinking too much beer or liquor.

When it comes to curing the college hangover, a lot of people will tell you a lot of different things. Everyone has a "magic cure." There are even entire websites that share ways to move beyond the pain that comes after the party—from treatment with Borscht (beet juice) to a tuna hoagie to dill pickles to hot chamomile to cold milk. Whatever concoction you try is a waste of time, because time (again, not be confused with the spice thyme) is the only magic cure that will help your hangover. Should you drink and find yourself feeling not so great when the buzz becomes a banging headache, drink some water (to help dehydration) and watch the clock. That said, if you're feeling lower than low and not getting any better, don't hesitate to call your doctor or take a trip to the emergency room.

If you get really desperate and start frantically searching for one of those miracle cures for your hangover, make sure that you read the fine print on the page. On two websites that claim to cure hangovers, the fine print (below) says it all (but really, most people are too drunk to focus on the fine print).

THESE STATEMENTS HAVE NOT BEEN EVALUATED BY THE FOOD AND DRUG ADMINISTRATION. THIS PRODUCT IS NOT INTENDED TO DIAGNOSE, TREAT, CURE, OR PREVENT ANY DISEASE.

If you're reading this, thinking, *Listen, the only way to cure a hangover is to drink some more alcohol*, you should put down your cocktail and jump over to Tip #82. You, my friend, are someone who is in serious need of some help.

Bottom Line
Drink too much and you'll pay and pray later (when people are sick, they tend to turn to a higher power for healing).

Tip #82
You Might Be an Alcoholic If...

The Tip
It's hard to know how bad your drinking problem is because there are so many times where everyone is drinking. Listen to your friends. They see what you're doing when you're too drunk to remember.

The Story
I have friends who I think have drinking problems. They seriously drink every night. They can go for hours. On a home game weekend, they're pretty much wasted or close to it for two days straight. They think it's not a problem because there are other people who are drunk with them. It's not like they're sitting in a room alone taking shots. I've mentioned something to them and then they say I'm the one with the problem. They think because they pass all of their classes, there isn't any problem, but it's possible to pass classes and still have an addiction. One of them has even told me that alcoholism runs in his family. The problem I've seen is that college is filled with so many people who drink and party regularly that it's a part of life for them, and it's hard to tell when it's really a problem. Other than passing their classes, they're unreliable, irresponsible, they get in fights, and have a different girl every week. They drink all night to get wasted and miss at least a class a week. They say it's normal. I call it being in denial.

—senior, University of Georgia

***

If you are reading this particular tip while sipping a beer after promising yourself that you are done drinking, you might have a problem. If you're reading this in the morning while craving alcohol, you might have a problem (that means no vodka in your morning coffee). If you're reading while drinking several alcoholic beverages because your tolerance has increased, you might have a problem. If you find that you drink more than you plan on drinking, can't seem to control yourself, drink to relieve symptoms of nausea, sweating, shakiness, and anxiety, then you have a problem. If you find yourself falling into any of the above categories while reading this tip, you might be alcohol dependent.

Alcohol Abuse and Dependence:

31 percent of college students met criteria for a diagnosis of alcohol abuse and 6 percent for a diagnosis of alcohol dependence in the past 12 months, according to questionnaire-based self-reports about their drinking —Knight et al.

You can deny it all you want, but denial is a sure sign that you're in trouble. If your friends think there's a problem, there's a good chance they're right. So, if you do have a problem, and can admit you have a problem, you can do one of two things. You keep drinking, or you can get help.

As for figuring out when you or someone you know has a problem, answering the following four questions can help you find out:

○ Have you ever felt you should cut down on your drinking?

○ Have people annoyed you by criticizing your drinking?

○ Have you ever felt bad or guilty about your drinking?

○ Have you ever had a drink first thing in the morning to steady your nerves or to get rid of a hangover?

One "yes" = possible alcohol problem.

More than one "yes" = highly likely that a problem exists.

If you want to get help, there is so much available. Most colleges have alcohol treatment counselors. If your campus doesn't have a counselor, the counselors in the health center can refer you. The best part about being an alcoholic is that there is so much help and support available to help control your alcoholism. There is counseling. There are support groups. There is even medication.

And in case you didn't know, alcoholism runs in families. If you have family that has a history, you might be a part of family history about to repeat itself.

Bottom Line

College offers lots of opportunities. Unfortunately, one is to become an alcoholic.

Harlan's Tip Sheet

Drinking on Campus Resources, Websites, and Additional Info

Resources On or Near Campus
Campus Health Center
Alcohol counselors on campus
Local hospital

Resources and Websites
Alcoholics Anonymous
http://www.alcoholics-anonymous.org/
Al-Anon/Alateen
Call 888-4AL-ANON, Monday through Friday, 8 a.m.
to 6 p.m. ET for meeting information.
http://www.al-anon-alateen.org/
National Sexual Assault
Hotline Phone: 1-800-656-HOPE
http://www.rainn.org/
Domestic Abuse Hotline
National Domestic Violence Hotline at 1-800-799-
SAFE (7233)
http://www.ndvh.org/
The BACCHUS Network:
http://www.bacchusgamma.org
http://www.smartersex.org
http://www.friendsdrivesober.org

Centers for Disease Control and Prevention:
www.cdc.gov
Higher Education Center for Alcohol and Other Drug Prevention:
www.edc.org/hec
National Institutes on Alcohol Abuse and Alcoholism:
www.collegedrinkingprevention.gov
Substance Abuse of Mental Health Services Administration:
www.samhsa.gov

Drugs on Campus

11

The Smoking, Snorting, and Pill-Popping Truth

Dear Harlan,

In November, my friends and I were heading back to campus at 1:30 in the morning after a night out. We were pulled over. We were immediately taken out of the car and searched. Unfortunately, I had a joint in my pocket and was whisked away to the police department.

I'm not two months into my one-year probation, but my parole officer informed me that my arrest might not clear my record by the time I apply for a job. It is sad that my future may be affected by such a meaningless and harmless crime, but it can happen to anyone. Word to the wise: if you are in a car and you have drugs, you are in danger. You do not have any rights, because a determined cop will always find what you have in your pocket.

—F. Justice

Dear F. Justice,

I appreciate the word to the wise, but I don't think the wise would have joints in their pockets. It should be a word to the really high people who get stupid and forget things…

This isn't about a determined cop. It's about a careless guy (you) packing a joint, taking a risk, and getting busted. This doesn't just happen in cars; it happens at parties, on the way to parties, in residence halls—all over. Getting arrested is the ultimate in coming down. Thanks for the note.

Tip #83
About Drugs on Campus

The Tip
If your closest friends smoke pot, chances are you'll cave in and smoke, too.

The Story
I'm not a smoker or a drinker—never have been one. I had a roommate I knew from high school. She was so against smoking pot when she got to college. I think in high school she was even in

organizations against smoking tobacco. So this girl from high school, she met someone at orientation who smoked pot. She was like, "I'll never be in the room with her." She vowed to never smoke. The next year, I moved out. She then moved in with her friend from orientation (the one who smokes). That's when we started drifting apart. Last I heard she started smoking pot, too. I was shocked when I found out. I didn't think she would smoke. I was just shocked. I know her whole family. I'm sure they have no idea. That's all I know. I really don't talk to her anymore.

—junior, Florida Gulf Coast University

＊＊＊

When I visit college campuses to speak, I ask students about drugs on campus. It's not the first question I ask (that would be weird, especially if my follow-up question were, "Just curious, where can I find some?").

The students typically fall into two categories—those students who haven't seen any drugs on campus, and those who see it on occasion. It's not like anyone is forcing anyone to do it, but it's around if you're looking. Generally, pot is the most common drug. Then there's ecstasy. Now cocaine is popping up a lot. No one will force you to use, but people might invite you. Whether you accept the invitation or hang with people who

"It is a creed amongst smokers that pot should be shared and enjoyed amongst others; it is a very communal thing. Some may say that marijuana is harmful, some may say that it is harmless, but I say it is beneficial, although I think that moderation is important."
—recent graduate, Rutgers University

use drugs is your call, but if you hang out with them, there's a great chance you'll end up using, too. And if you think that you'll never use, even if you hang out with people who do, you're probably wrong.

The typical drug story is: you go to college vowing never to do drugs. Then you have a roommate or some new friends or a friend from high school who start partying a little bit. Let's say it's smoking marijuana. You don't agree with it. You don't like it. You are still never going to do it. No one pressures you, but the more you hang out with your friend and the people who are using, the less it starts to bother you. It might be a month, a year, maybe two years or three years—over time, you become desensitized. Like sitting in the middle of the manure factory, the smell and lifestyle choices become the norm. And then, one day, you decide to try it. It's not a big deal. You like it. Then you try it again. You then become a recreational user. Another year goes by and you've started to wake and bake (smoking up in the morning) and progressed to trying harder drugs. Sometimes, you just end up dating someone who does harder drugs and then pulls you into the experiences. Some people can manage their lives and stay in control, but even if you think you're in control of your drug use, you open yourself up to getting arrested, getting hurt, or getting expelled—risks that can mess up your life (it's not pretty having to check the "have you ever been convicted of a felony?" box yes).

> "I've seen pot and cocaine at parties; I would never do any of the hard stuff."
>
> —senior, MIT

Bottom Line

Drugs are around. You can choose to do drugs or not to be around drugs. If you find that drugs choose to be around you, then you're probably on drugs because drugs can't really make choices.

Tip #84
How to Avoid Them

The Tip
If you stay away from the people who do drugs, drugs will not be a problem.

The Story
No one has ever forced me to get high or roll (take ecstasy). My friends ask me if I want a bong hit and I'll just say, "Nah." They're just like, "Cool, more for me." When my friends party, and not all of them do, I'll sometimes hang out. When the bong, pipe, joint, or apparatus they've designed comes by me, I'll wave it off or just pass it along. I don't feel like I need to get high because it's there. I just don't like it. I also have a job where drug testing is done and I'm not about to let that get me in trouble. Sometimes I'll have a beer or two if I'm hanging out. In my college career, I've never seen anyone I've been around forced to do drugs. Everyone I've ever seen is an extremely eager and willing participant. If someone wants to avoid drugs they just have to pass it along or say

no. Most of the people offering it end up too high to care what anyone else does or doesn't do.

—senior, University of Southern California

* * *

Drugs can typically be found in Columbia, Jamaica, and the shoebox in the closet under the dirty clothes of the guy who sells it on campus to make a few extra bucks. Once in a while, you might stumble across them. If you want to find them, you can ask around, and people will tell you where they're hiding. But you have to make an effort.

If you're someone who doesn't want to do drugs, then avoid asking people where you can find drugs and avoid hanging out with friends who do drugs. If that's just not possible, then at least avoid your friends while they're using drugs, because if you hang around people who do drugs all the time, you'll most likely end up doing them too. It's like going to the national buffalo wing tournament—it's hard not to sample some of the wings when that's all anyone is eating. And really, even if you don't end up using, then you'll end up being in places where a lot of people are using. You might end up at a party in a dorm room or in a car where someone is using. You could end up in a situation where people are possessing or trafficking drugs. Then if the party gets busted, and if you're near the drugs, your life goes to hell. The best way to avoid drugs is to avoid the people who do them or sell them.

Drug Fact:

Once you sell drugs, even if it's 0.1 ounce of marijuana to a friend, you will forever be a drug dealer.

—anonymous

The first few months of college are filled with drug temptation—bonding over a bong or shared joint could seem alluring. It's tempting to want to party with people who invite you. It's hard to say no, especially when you don't have a lot of friends on campus. But if you start hanging out with these kind of people, this is what you'll do together. Getting wasted will become the centerpiece of activity. If you don't want to use, but you still want to be friends with these people, then meet up with them after they're done partying. And make sure they're going to a place where drugs won't be the main attraction (and that you're not in the car or close by if the cops show up).

Bottom Line
Avoid drugs by avoiding the people who do drugs, and avoid traveling to the countries where they grow drugs (a summer internship at a Columbian cocaine farm—extremely bad idea).

Tip #85
Why Not to Do Drugs

The Tip
Drugs take up too much time—there's finding them, doing them, talking about them, and then recovering from them the next day.

The Story

I don't have the time to waste by doing drugs. I don't have the time to get high and then to come down. I don't have time to worry about random drug testing. I don't get enough out of it to make it worth it. I'd rather be sober. I'm trying to get a decent GPA, plus I'm also working twenty hours a week to help pay for school, and I'm in a relationship that's better than any drug I've tried. I only see him a few times a week. He's not a real "drug." I've been finding that my friends who are into drugs really waste a lot of their time doing them, talking about them, and then worrying about what they did while on them. I'm as happy as my drug friends—even happier, I think. It's never interested me. From what I've seen, drugs are for boring people who don't have much else to do. There are so many other things I'd rather do with my time. Maybe that's just me.

> **"My girlfriend dumped me because of my obsessive pot smoking habit and the fact that I pawned off some of her old CDs for pot."**
> —senior, University of Portland

—junior, New York University

* * *

The two most honest reasons why I never got into drugs in college:

Smoking pot makes you hungry and it makes you eat a lot of carbs late at night. As an overweight kid my first two years of high school (I was 5 feet 2 inches tall and 192 pounds in high school), I hated being heavy. It would always put me in a terrible mood. My pants got tight and then I was miserable. Pot might have zero calories, but everything consumed after you smoke is packed with flavor. Getting high makes you eat. Usually it's eating late at night and you get tired and go to sleep. The more you eat late at night, the easier it is to pack on the pounds.

The other reason I never got into drugs was a fear of dying. Seriously, I was afraid I'd try cocaine and die the first time. I thought I might get some bad ecstasy and possibly freak out and die (I've had friends who have had some bad trips from bad pills). The big problem with dying from experimenting (it happens) is that it puts my parents in an awkward position. They then have to explain that Harlan was only experimenting when he overdosed. They'd have to tell friends and family, "It was his first time, really it was." Of course, no one would believe that I was just experimenting. They'd think I was a junkie. My parents would then have to keep explaining to everyone that I was honestly just experimenting— clearly a tough sell that no parent should have to deal with. Besides, I like living. And really, the world is messed up enough without having to do drugs.

> **"I never smelled pot before— it smelled like burnt oranges."**
> —college student in Florida

The other reason not to do drugs is that there are better things to do. If life is so horrible for you that you feel like you need to escape, then get some help. Because one day, when you do stop doing drugs to escape from the life that you find to be so hellish, you'll still need help. College campuses have free counseling and unbelievable support services. But again, it's your decision, not mine.

Just know what you're getting into if you decide to get into drugs.

Bottom Line
(no pun intended...okay, maybe a little)
I've never done a line because there's always a chance of dying the first time. And sure, you can die crossing the street, but it's much more dangerous crossing the street high on the way to visit your drug dealer.

Tip #86
Just Don't Accidentally Die

The Tip
Drugs are bad, mmmkay?

The Story
In November, I visited a good friend of mine. There were five of us crammed into his tiny apartment. I bought three ecstasy pills to share between my three friends and myself. Since I am very small, a half a pill can get me really high. (P.S.—this was not my first time tripping on E, this would be my fourth). So, the drug takes its effect, and I'm loving it. I am feeling so happy, so loving, so wanting to tell everybody how much I loved them. Everything was going so well. I "peaked" (when the drug is most intense) and I crashed very gradually. My friend asked if I wanted to take a hit of pot on a bong while I was crashing. Sure, why

not? I took a huge hit and immediately I started to feel odd. My head was swimming and my body felt shaky. I went into the bathroom and lay on the floor, completely fixated on a small piece of lint on the bathtub. I was staring and concentrating so hard, I started drooling. My friend asked me what was wrong, but his voice was an echo. And it kept on happening, over and over. I would slip out of reality, hear echoes, see really crazy stuff, and then be fine. I thought I could control myself and the hallucinations, but in the end, I started screaming for my friend and I was convinced I was going to die. I wanted to jump out the four-story window in the room. I had never been so scared in my life that I was not going to come off an E trip alive. Finally, the pot wore off and I was fine. Everybody sounded normal, everything was okay, and I felt better. The next day I drove all the

> "Ever wonder why six people come pouring out of the bathroom, wide-eyed and giddy while you are waiting to take a leak? Most of the time, it's because the bathroom becomes the playing field for blowing lines. It's no big deal, right? What happens when someone does too many lines and it becomes their last? Or what about the holder of an eight ball before it gets cut up? Federal prison? Death? What makes it worth it? I see cocaine all the time."
>
> —junior, **Frostburg State University**

way back to my old college (about two hours) and slept for a good twelve hours. I have not been the same since that trip. I would get high (off pot) and get the same loopy "fading in and out" feeling. It has gotten better, but recently, I took a sleeping pill my doctor prescribed, and I started hallucinating badly. I don't know what brought it on, but I'm sure it has something to do with my nasty experience.

—college student, campus unknown

It would really be bad to do drugs and accidentally die (understatement of the book). The best idea is not to do them. But if you're going to do something stupid, again, don't be so stupid that you accidentally kill yourself doing it. I've seen a girl pass out at a fraternity party. I've seen a friend think that he was having a heart attack and go to the emergency room (he didn't really, he just freaked himself out and got scared). I've seen a guy almost fall into an empty swimming pool because he was too high to see that there wasn't any water in the pool. I heard about bad ecstasy trips where it was a near-death experience. Then there was the guy who shroomed and then came home, sprayed the fire extinguisher in the hall, and grabbed a girl's breasts (then he was arrested). There was the ex of a friend who did another line of cocaine and was found dead. Every year, students accidentally die from drug-related incidents. And sadly, it will happen again this year.

> "My ex-boyfriend kept blacking out from doing drugs. He did everything. He shroomed. He smoked weed. He did coke. You name it, he was on it."
> —junior, University of Nevada–Las Vegas

Of course, you shouldn't do drugs. But should you do, keep the following in mind:

- Know where the stuff you're doing is from. It's hard to be sure that what you're doing isn't going to kill you. At least don't be the first to do it. Wait for other people and see how they react. Then decide whether or not to partake.

- Don't leave home while doing it. If you're going to be doing something stupid, make sure that you're in a place where you won't get arrested. Don't drive. Don't be a public nuisance. Don't do things to draw attention to yourself.
- Do it in a "safe" place. A safe place is with people you know. Surrounding yourself with strangers is just stupid, especially if you're doing something for the first time. It's hard to know how your body will react. It's also hard to know how others around you will react. Drugs alter judgment and reasoning. Strangers who you think are safe people can turn out to be dangerous.
- Make sure you have friends with you. If something unexpected should happen, you need friends to make sure you're taken care of.
- Don't mix alcohol and drugs. It's hard to know how your body will react to drugs alone. Add alcohol and you can go on a crazy trip, or just end up dead. It happens. Avoid drinking and drug use.
- If you're freaking out, seek medical attention. Some people just think that it will all pass. But that's dumb. If you or your friend is in a bad way, then get some medical attention. The object is not to die.
- If busted, get a lawyer and talk to your parents. No one wants to deal with the expense of an attorney and the hassle of parents, but if you make the wrong moves this can haunt you for the rest of your life. Laws vary from state to state and the right representation can help you make the best of a terrible situation.

Bottom Line

Be smart about being stupid. The obvious choice is to avoid drugs. But I can't tell you what to do or what not to do. It's your call. Please, just don't accidentally die.

Drugs in College

The following is a list of drugs and what they can do to you. One thing worth mentioning—it's a fact that on rare occasions doing cocaine for the first time can kill you. It's rare, but it happens. The combo meal of cocaine and alcohol is bad—very bad, perhaps even lethal. And yes, meth can kill you. Now that list…

Marijuana

Other Names: pot, herb, weed, grass, boom, Mary Jane, gangster, chronic. There are more than two hundred slang terms for marijuana. Hashish ("hash" for short) and hash oil are stronger forms of marijuana.

Method Administered: Smoked, ingested.

Health Effects and Risks: cough; frequent respiratory infections; impaired memory and learning; increased heart rate; euphoria; slowed thinking and reaction time; confusion; impaired balance and coordination; anxiety; panic attacks; tolerance; addiction. Recent research findings also indicate that long-term use of marijuana produces changes in the brain similar to those seen after long-term use of other major illicit drugs. People who smoke marijuana often develop the same kinds of breathing problems that cigarette smokers have, like coughing and wheezing. They tend to have more chest colds than nonusers. They are also at greater risk of getting lung infections like pneumonia.

Cocaine

Other Names: blow, bump, C, candy, Charlie, coke, crack, flake, rock, snow, toot.

Method Administered: injected, smoked, snorted

Health Effects and Risks: increased heart rate, blood pressure, and metabolism; feelings of exhilaration; energy; increased mental alertness; feelings of restlessness, irritability, and anxiety; increased temperature; rapid or irregular heartbeat; reduced appetite; weight loss; heart and respiratory failure; chest and abdominal pain; nausea; strokes; seizures; headaches; malnutrition. In rare instances, sudden death can occur on the first use of cocaine or unexpectedly thereafter. However, there is no way to determine who is prone to sudden death. Once having tried highly addictive cocaine, an individual cannot predict or control the extent to which he or she will continue to use the drug. An appreciable tolerance to the high may be developed, and many addicts report that they seek but fail to achieve as much pleasure as they did from their first exposure. High doses of cocaine and/or prolonged use can trigger paranoia. Prolonged cocaine snorting can result in ulceration of the mucous membrane of the nose and can damage the nasal septum enough to cause it to collapse. Cocaine-related deaths are often a result of cardiac arrest or seizures followed by respiratory arrest.

Added danger: cocaethylene. When people mix cocaine and alcohol, they are compounding the danger each drug poses and unknowingly forming a chemical experiment within their bodies. NIDA-funded researches have found that the human liver combines cocaine and alcohol and manufactures a third substance, cocaethylene, that intensifies cocaine's euphoric effects while possibly increasing the risk of sudden death.

MDMA (methylenedioxy-methamphetamine)

Other Names: Adam, clarity, ecstasy, Eve, lover's speed, peace, STP, X, XTC.

Method Delivered: swallowed.

Health Effects and Risks: mild hallucinogenic effects; increased tactile sensitivity; empathic feelings; confusion; depression; sleep problems; drug craving; severe anxiety; impaired memory and learning; hyperthermia; cardiac and liver toxicity; renal failure; increased heart rate and blood pressure; muscle tension; involuntary teeth clenching; nausea; blurred vision; faintness; chills; sweating. In high doses, MDMA can interfere with the body's ability to regulate temperature. This can lead to a sharp increase in body temperature (hyperthermia), resulting in liver, kidney, and cardiovascular system failure. Other drugs chemically similar to MDMA are sometimes sold as ecstasy. These drugs can be neurotoxic or create additional health risks to the user. Ecstasy tablets may contain other substances in addition to MDMA. The combination of MDMA with one or more of these drugs may be inherently dangerous. Users might also combine them with substances such as marijuana and alcohol, putting themselves at further physical risk.

Methamphetamine

Other Names: Desoxyn, chalk, crank, crystal meth, fire, glass, go fast, ice, meth.

Method Delivered: injected, swallowed, smoked, snorted.

Health Effects and Risks: in the short term, meth causes mind and mood changes such as anxiety, euphoria, and depression. Long-term effects can include chronic fatigue, paranoid or delusional thinking, and permanent psychological damage. Meth may be as addictive as crack and more powerful. An overdose of meth can result in heart failure. Long-term physical effects such as liver, kidney, and lung damage may also kill you.

LSD

Other Names: lysergic acid diethylamide, acid, blotter, boomers, cubes, microdot, yellow sunshines.

Method Delivered: swallowed, absorbed through mouth tissues.

Health Effects and Risks: altered states of perception and feeling; nausea; increased body temperature, heart rate, and blood pressure; loss of appetite; sleeplessness; numbness; weakness; tremors; chronic mental disorders; persisting perception disorder (flashbacks). Effects of LSD are unpredictable. They depend on the amount taken; the user's personality, mood, and expectations; and the surroundings in which the drug is used. Usually, the user feels the first effects of the drug thirty to ninety minutes after taking it. The physical effects include dilated pupils, higher body temperature, increased heart rate and blood pressure, sweating, loss of appetite, sleeplessness, dry mouth, and tremors.

Rohypnol

Other Names: forget-me pill, Mexican Valium, R2, Roche, roofies, roofinol, rope, rophies.

Method Delivered: swallowed, snorted.

Health Effects and Risks: visual and gastrointestinal disturbances; urinary retention; memory loss for the time under the drug's effects.

GHB—Gamma-Hydroxybutyrate

Other Names: G, Georgia home boy, grievous bodily harm, liquid ecstasy.

Method Delivered: swallowed.

Health Effects and Risks: drowsiness; nausea/vomiting; headache; loss of consciousness; loss of reflexes; seizures; coma; death.

Ketalar

Other Names: SV, cat Valiums, K, Special K, vitamin K.

Method Delivered: injected, snorted, smoked.

Health Effects and Risks: increased heart rate and blood pressure; impaired motor function/memory loss; numbness; nausea/vomiting. For ketamine at high doses: delirium; depression; respiratory depression and arrest.

Psilocybin

Other Names: magic mushroom, purple passion, shrooms.

Method Delivered: swallowed.

Health Effects and Risks: nervousness, paranoia; if eating wrong kind of mushroom, death.

Codeine

Other Names: Empirin with codeine, Fiorinal with codeine, Robitussin A-C, Tylenol with codeine, Captain Cody, Cody, schoolboy, (with glutethimide) doors and fours, loads, pancakes and syrup.

Method Delivered: injected, swallowed.

Health Effects and Risks: pain relief; euphoria; drowsiness; nausea; constipation; confusion; sedation; respiratory depression and arrest; tolerance; addiction; unconsciousness; coma; death.

Amphetamine

Other Names: bennies, black beauties, crosses, hearts, LA turnaround, speed, truck drivers, uppers.

Method Administered: injected, swallowed, smoked, snorted.

Health Effects and Risks: increased heart rate, blood pressure, and metabolism; feelings of exhilaration; energy; increased mental alertness; rapid or irregular heartbeat; reduced appetite; weight loss; heart failure; nervousness; insomnia; rapid breathing/tremors; loss of coordination; irritability; anxiousness; restlessness; delirium; panic; paranoia; impulsive behavior; aggressiveness; tolerance; addiction; psychosis.

The Tip
Smoking in college isn't as exciting as in high school. It's no longer forbidden. It's not as cool. You don't need to smoke to stand out.

The Story
I smoked from seventh grade all through high school. In high school it was like the rebel thing to sit around and smoke cigarettes—but when I got college, it all just wasn't fun anymore. The thrill was gone. I no longer had to steal cigarettes from my mom. I could buy them. Once I got to college, I just stopped smoking. It got really disgusting. I started to smell like it; my roommates didn't like it. Cigarettes became a nuisance. We used to have a smoke bubble to encase the smokers on campus. We got rid of it. The ceiling was discolored and the windows were tinted yellow. I was just repulsed. Besides losing the thrill, I've noticed that a lot of guys are disgusted by it, too. It's not so glamorous. In the words of a close guy friend of mine, "She can be the hottest girl, but once she lights up, I turn around and walk away."

—sophomore, Wilkes University

* * *

To help with research for this tip, I went into a busy bar near my place (a bar where people can smoke). I wanted to see what it was like to actually kiss an ashtray. So, one busy Saturday night during a playoff game, I looked for an ashtray to kiss. I started with small talk, and when the time was right, I made my move.

As expected, it was really disgusting.

While it's proven that cigarette smoking causes cancer and other serious health risks, it also makes you stink like an ashtray, and costs you a lot of money to support your habit—I can't believe cigarettes cost about $4 a pack. Three packs a week is over $600 a year. Save your money and buy a plasma TV at the end of your sophomore year! Smokers are all over campus. If you're not planning on smoking, be prepared to see people lighting up around you. Then don't start—not even socially when you're drinking.

The social smoker is an interesting phenomenon. One of my good friends started off as a social smoker. He'd only smoke when drinking. Ten years later he's still smoking. He smokes in the morning, when he takes a break at work, after he eats dinner, and on the toilet (he says it helps him go). Basically, it's whenever he's awake. It's the social smokers who become regular smokers. It's not like people start smoking and say, "From now on, I'm going to smoke every day for the next twenty years." It's a gradual process.

The best way to avoid it is to not start. It's tempting to want to stand around and bond, and it gives you something to hold (for more things to hold, see Tip #75). But the smoke only lasts about five minutes. Then it's over.

If you should find that you are smoking and can't quit, see if your campus has a group to help smokers quit. Also, check into tobacco replacement systems via your campus health center. They have cheap drugs to help you kick the habit. If you want to quit, you can do it. But if you don't start, then you won't have to quit.

Bottom Line

Just appreciate that the casual smoker becomes the regular smoker. Instead of smoking, don't start. Please note: you can still stand around with the smokers and breathe secondhand smoke. They're cool with that.

Harlan's Tip Sheet

Drugs on Campus Resources, Websites, and Additional Info

Hotlines and Websites

Alcohol/Drug Abuse Referral Hotline:
    800-ALCOHOL (800-252-6465).
    24-hour hotline provides referrals to treatment facilities.
National Clearinghouse for Alcohol and Drug Information:
    800-729-6686
    http://www.ncadi.samhsa.gov

National Council on Alcoholism & Drug Dependence (NCADD).
800-NCA-CALL (800-622-2255)
Provides information on counseling services for alcohol or drug abuse.
http://www.ncadd.org

U.S. Dept. of Health and Human Services National Drug and Alcohol Treatment and Referral Routing Service: 800-662-4357
Get confidential information on and referrals for drug or alcohol abuse.

National Hotline Cocaine Information and Help:
800-COCAINE (800-262-2463).

National Institute on Drug Abuse
http://www.drugabuse.gov

Ecstasy and other club drugs:
Call the Do It Now Foundation:
480-736-0599
or find them online at
http://www.doitnow.org/pages/nowhome2.html.

The National Youth Anti-Drug Media Campaign
http://www.freevibe.com
Hotline: 800-788-2800

Drug Free America—information and a diary of people who have lost loved ones to drugs.
http://drugfreeamerica.com

The BACCHUS Network
http://www.bacchusgamma.org
http://www.tobaccofreeu.org

Crystal Meth Anonymous
http://www.crystalmeth.org

Money, Laundry, and Cheap Eats

12

Assuming You Have Enough Money to Eat and Do Laundry

Hey Harlan!
How hard is it to make it financially at an out-of-state college without my parents' support? Is this possible?

Short on Cash

Hey Short on Cash!
Here's something to make you smile:

According to the College Board, "About 29 percent of students attending four-year colleges pay less than $4,000 for tuition and fees per year." The less money your parents have to support you, the more need-based assistance that's available.

The college of your dreams—in state or out of state—might be more possible than you think. Get in touch. Pick up the phone and get connected with the financial aid counselors at the schools that interest you. Speak with an advisor. Explain your situation. See if the advisor on the other end can give you a general idea of the type of aid available. Ask about academic and need-based assistance. There are grants, loans, scholarships, and work-study programs that can help you pay for college. You won't be able to get exact figures, but you could get a rough idea. Then apply and see what happens.

The next step is to get familiar with scholarships. Become familiar now and continue to apply as you go through college (use the free online scholarship searches). Once in school, you'll come across even more scholarships through the department of your major, service organizations, religious organizations, parents' place of work, professional organizations, national fraternities, and national sororities. If your financial aid counselor can't show you the money—keep looking. It's there. And should you want to take out loans, you can always do it that way. It would be nice to have your parents' support, but if you don't, you can still get to where you want to go.

Tip #88
Loans, Grants, Scholarships, and Loose Change

The Tip
There's money out there if you go after it.

The Story
I have found in my experiences that people are always willing to give money outside of the resources available in the financial aid office. I went to a professional website for occupational therapists and read about scholarships available. I had to write an essay about why I wanted to be an OT and why I should receive the scholarship. So, I wrote the letter, sent in my transcript, got a letter of recommendation, and sent it in. A few months later, I got a check for $1,000 for books and expenses. I didn't think that I was going to get jack. I thought thousands of people would send in letters. If more people took the time to write the essay, get a copy of their transcript, and send it in, they would get a lot of money. They said the most you can get is $1,000 and the least is $250. I would have gotten something just for doing the work. These foundations raise money and set it aside for scholarships. It's the same in a lot of fields. I didn't hear about this through my advisor— I just searched on a scholarship website. Also, Fastweb.com is the best one I've seen. When a grant or scholarship comes up they email me a notice. It doesn't get much easier than that. I used it in undergrad and I use it

now. It's as easy as writing an essay and then it's boom, bang, you send it out. The money is so there.

—graduate student, Touro College

* * *

The average cost of tuition at a private school is $27,677, and it's $12,841 (in-state tuition) for a public school. If you're paying in loose change, that would be 276,770 dimes or 128,410 dimes.

When it comes down to the actual cost of tuition, most students don't pay full price. What you pay varies from campus to campus. Most students get some kind of financial aid. Aid is money in the form of student loans, grants, scholarships, and jobs that can help cut costs. Visit your financial advising office and connect with a financial aid counselor to guide you along the process (see the next tip). In the meantime, here's a brief overview to get you familiar with each part of financial aid. If you already know, skip to the final paragraph, or keep reading (it's fast).

Grants and Scholarships

This is money that doesn't have to be repaid and that you don't have to work to get. Grants come from federal and state governments and from the particular college you're attending. Scholarships are usually awarded based on achievement inside and outside the classroom. Use the free online scholarship searches to see what's available (see chapter Tip Sheet for URLs). Also, inquire about available scholarships within the college by talking to professors and advisors in your department. If you're in a fraternity or sorority, look into scholarships awarded through the national office. Scholarships can also be available through churches and religious organizations, your parents' place of work, within community organizations, via athletics, academic excellence, and being the right application at the right time. Unbelievably, millions of dollars for scholarships go unawarded every year. You can change that.

Loans

The federal government offers and sponsors loans—most are low-interest loans awarded based on student's financial need. Because the government subsidizes loans, there is no interest charged until the student graduates. But then it's payback time. DO NOT take more than you need. The new digital surround sound stereo system, forty-two inch plasma TVs, and designer clothes are phenomenal now, but when the stuff is outdated and out of style, the loan payments will begin.

Work-Study

Work-study programs are part-time jobs that are offered as part of the financial aid packages. It's money students work to earn to help with extra expenses like books, fees, and other costs (like food). It's also a way for student workers to gain experience and help serve the community and campus. If you see someone at the campus info desk studying or napping when not dispensing info, there's a good chance he or she is part of work-study program.

When paying for college, the best tip is to talk to upper-classmen and your financial aid counselor—see the next tip. It's the people who have been through the process and know the process who can share lessons learned. Use the people around you. Each college has its own way of navigating the system. Do not be afraid to ask!

Bottom Line
Look for money during all four years. Talk to people who have been there. And if anyone tells you to take out a bigger loan so that you can buy a plasma TV, assume that the person is just dumb, or working on commission at an electronics store.

Tip #89
Your Financial Aid Advisor: Money, Money, Money, Monnnnneeey

The Tip
Find an advisor that you feel comfortable with and trust, and stay with that advisor the whole four years. Take the advisor's card and build a relationship. It will make future visits so much easier.

The Story
It's so annoying to have to meet with a new advisor each time you go and explain your story from the beginning. This means having to start over every time. When I got to school, I found an advisor who got to know me and my family's financial situation. I met with other advisors when he wasn't available, and it wasn't comfortable at all. I learned to call ahead and to make an appointment with

him. Even if I had to wait a day or two for my answer, I'd wait. He helped us find as many loans as possible and looked over my parents' financial documents every year to help us get as many government loans as available. My grades weren't good enough for scholarships, but he was familiar with them. Make sure that your advisor is someone you like and someone with whom you have a positive rapport. Really, it makes it so much better. Going to the same person made something totally foreign to me easier to understand. Having a great relationship has even helped me after graduation. Whenever I have questions on loan statements, I call him and fax over what's confusing and he's still there for me.

Another tip that I'd love to go back and tell myself is to apply for loans early because the sooner you get your financial aid forms in the more money that is available. That's something that not a lot of people told me.

—senior, University of Delaware

* * *

It's like having your own personal money advisor in your corner—a coach to help you beat, or at least navigate, the system. There is money out there—you just have to go after it and know the people who can show you were to get it.

Before even setting foot on campus, contact your college's financial aid office and get hooked up with an advisor (no, not like the hookup in Tip #55). An advisor should be happy to talk to you.

> FAFSA FORMS: The government forms that you need to fill out in order to apply for financial aid (www.fafsa.ed.gov).

They encourage calls. Their job is to help you pay for college. Between Stafford Loans, Perkins Loans, Pell Grants, filling out those FAFSA forms (the only thing worse is filling out the forms while getting your teeth pulled), making deadlines, and sorting through your financial aid package, it helps to have an expert in your corner who has seen it all before. And when your parents have questions, if they're the ones handling the paperwork, you can get the answers. That's what the advisor is paid to do.

If you're unhappy with your financial aid award package, see if they can reconsider your award. Many times, what you're initially offered is largely part of a computer formula. Each situation is unique. There could be additional grants or scholarships available. Walk into the office, be polite, smile, and plead your case to the director (crying can help). A conversation can get you hundreds, if not thousands, of dollars more in free money. It's happened to my friends.

The biggest obstacle in getting the most financial aid is that most students don't care enough to make the added effort. Use your financial aid advisor. And like I mentioned in the previous tip, use the people who have just been through the system as your second, third, and fourth advisors. It was through a friend that a close friend of mine heard about a

---

Loan Resources and Info

Sallie Mae
(www.salliemae.com)

Fastweb (www.fastweb.com)

Citiassist (studentloan.com)

FAFSA (www.fafsa.ed.gov)

The College Board
(collegeboard.com)

And never pay for a scholarship search service—check out the free services online.

---

scholarship offered through a country club. She was given thousands of dollars each year. There is money all over the place—ask around. Do not be shy. You might just win the college lottery!

Bottom Line
Take advantage of your financial aid office and find an advisor who can get to know you as an individual. Should this tip help you save money, please consider buying several hundred copies of this book with your saved cash.

Tip #90
Part-Time Jobs, Big-Time Benefits

The Tip
By becoming a Resident Assistant (RA), you can get free housing and/or food and a stipend! Not to mention help students on campus.

The Story
I became a summer RA after my freshman year so I could attend summer school and get free housing and food to boot! I met so many people, gained leadership experience, and got to stay near my boyfriend, too! Parents love the idea of having their child be an RA because it shows that you are responsible and it takes

"Work a lot over the summers and save money. Once you are at school it goes so quickly!"
—senior, SUNY Cortland

a huge financial burden off of the student and their family. As an RA, I met a diverse group of student leaders and I also became a knowledgeable person about the campus. Being an RA isn't for everyone, though. You have to be willing to enforce and follow all the rules, which can put a damper on the whole college experience!

—sophomore, University of Texas

* * *

I had few part-time jobs in college. I sold T-shirts to freshmen during orientation, going from room to room (it was kind of illegal to sell T-shirts, but people needed clothes, right?). I worked in the campus newspaper advertising office for a few months. I got paid commission and was given an "A" parking pass (it was so beautiful it made me want to cry). I also worked on the campus newspaper (that's how I started writing my advice column). I had a friend who made a ridiculous amount of money working as a computer lab student worker. My ex worked as a paid research lab assistant. A quiet friend worked in the library. A buddy of mine was a server at a sorority—second-best job to being a sorority houseboy.

"Work-study programs are by far the best. My freshman year, I approached a dean about getting a job in her office. Working for her has given me contacts in the administration and faculty that I never would have had otherwise. Great work-study jobs are always available, you just have to be motivated enough to look for them."
—sophomore, Wells College

One suggestion—if you need to get a job to help pay for college, then try to find a job that can help you figure out what you want to do with your life. If you're interested in going to medical school, get a job in the campus hospital or health center. If you're interested in going into the restaurant business, get a job working as part of campus food service. If you want to go to law school, work in the law school or at a local law firm. If you want to go into psychology, find a job helping a professor in the lab. The best-case scenario is that you'll love what you do and find contacts who can help you get into grad school or get a job. The other best-case scenario is that you'll find out that you just don't love doing what you thought you wanted to do—and then you can do something else.

As for work-study jobs, these come highly recommended. These are jobs that the school makes available for students as part of their financial aid packages. Typically, they're jobs on campus that range from working in an academic office, working in a residence hall, and shelving books in the library, to putting brochures together in the admissions office. They can pay anywhere from minimum wage on up, but generally are pretty decent. I know one girl who was paid $8 an hour to make copies and answer phones. If you get a job in a department within your major, you can make money, make contacts, and build relationships that can help you when it comes to letters of recommendation and jobs. Ask upperclassmen what the cushiest jobs are. Working with the sports teams has huge benefits. If you're looking to make good money and have a flexible schedule, waiting tables is the best. I used to wait tables at home during breaks—I'd make about $100 on a good day.

"Wait tables—quick cash, cheap food, lots of laundry quarters. I waited tables at Red Lobster. I was easily making $400 a week (and sometimes more). It is a lot of work—I will not lie about that—but the cash does come in handy. When I was working, I received a 50 percent discount on my meals. When I was off the clock, I had a 25 percent discount (and it included other restaurants that were owned by the same company). I was able to pay for school and still have money left over, and I had so many quarters I was able to trade some out for cash from friends! Restaurants are always looking for servers and I have really had no problems with scheduling around my classes."
—junior, University of Dallas

Bottom Line

If someone offers you a job where they tell you the benefit is having keys to all the buildings on campus, the job probably comes with a broom, mop, and a shirt that reads, "Campus Custodial Services." But you would get to know campus...

Tip #91
The Credit Card and the $600 Candy Bar

The Tip
Getting a credit card is so easy on campus. When you get one, don't skip town when the bills arrive. You'll pay for that free gift later.

The Story

I went to college and innocently signed up for a credit card. I was hungry and they were giving away food. It had a credit limit under $500, so I knew I wouldn't get into too much trouble with it—so I thought. I used the card a few times and then just kind of forgot about it. I left town for summer break and skipped out on the bills. I didn't think to have them forwarded. A collection agency tracked me down during the summer at home. My dad answered the phone and freaked out. They ended up bailing me out. It cost over $600 and my credit history is a mess. I don't even know if I can rent an apartment now.

> "After receiving three cards in the mail, I figured that I would just use them for books and other school-related expenses. What I didn't realize was that when your books are about $500 a semester, there is no way that you can pay that off right away. To make a long story short, three years and several thousands of dollars in debt later, I'm still paying for that English 101 book."
>
> —junior, Northern Michigan University

—junior, Savannah College of Art and Design

* * *

While walking around campus, you'll find friendly people in the most populated areas handing out things like candy, T-shirts, footballs, mugs, stuffed animals, bottled water, and other random crap that people tend to take and then put in a closet or throw away. These friendly folks aren't on campus giving you something for free. They want you and they want you badly. It's kind of sexy. But they're not interested in your love or body, they just want to give you credit—that is, a credit card and a candy bar. And all you need is a pulse, a mailing address, and a signature to get one.

Credit cards don't make people go into debt; people who use credit cards and don't have money will go into debt. The credit cards often get a bad rap because college students who don't have money tend to go into credit card debt. When it comes to credit cards, it's only bad if you use it and can't afford to pay it immediately. That's where people run into problems.

> "My parents charge everything. They figured that they should put tuition charges on their credit card. They've gotten thousands of miles because of me."
> —senior, Indiana University

As a rule, get your credit card and only charge what you have money for at that moment. Transfer the money (you can do it online) that day. Use your credit card to establish credit, in case of emergencies, and to get mileage awards or whatever reward you sign up for. This doesn't justify opening ten lines of credit, but one or two credit cards is enough. Make sure there are no annual fees. Look for incentives. I qualified for free airfare to Europe or the equivalent in cash after using mine for four years. And be careful with online purchases. They can add up sooo fast. Whatever you do, if you do carry a balance make sure you pay the minimum. If you can't afford the minimum, contact the credit card company and make arrangements. Don't just ignore them.

> "The Internet, a credit card, and college don't mix. E-commerce bills run up fast. Make sure you have a way to check your account before they send a statement to school."
> —sophomore, Juniata College

Beware: it's easy to get carried away if you're not careful. Check out the little mock charge demo I put together to show you how quickly things can add up and get out of control (the following example is based on a credit card with a 17.5 percent interest rate and a 2 percent monthly minimum).

One Semester:

Spring Break $1500 + Books $225 + Food/Restaurants $125 + Clothing $150

Total Balance: $2000

Minimum Payment 2 Percent: $40

Interest: $1,600

Time to Pay: 7.5 years

> "It all started with one credit card. I think they gave me a miniature football or a T-shirt. I received the card and put it in my drawer. The first time I used it was to buy a pair of shoes. I knew I had the money in the bank and promised myself that I would pay the bill immediately. That was the beginning of the end. I started to use it for meals, for groceries, for spring break, airfares, clothing, and books. When I maxed out the first card I moved on to the second and third card in my drawer. I went wild. My balance was over $8,000 and I had a 17.9 percent interest rate."
> —debt-free graduate, Mesa State College

Bottom Line

Credit cards can be used to open doors (no, this isn't a metaphor—I mean if you lock yourself out of your place you can unlock your door).

Tip #92
Bad Checks, Bad Credit, and Bad Ideas...

The Tip
When you can't pay the minimums, make arrangements with creditors.

The Story
I used my four credit cards and got in too deep. Three years later and thousands of dollars in debt, I couldn't make the minimum payments and pay rent, the cell phone bill, and the utility bills. I was working, but it was no longer enough to cover it all. I'd been late on bills before for the credit cards and as a result my interest rates were jacked up. I called to try to have it lowered, but no luck. I was transferring one balance to the other one, paying with those instant credit checks. It got to be too much, so I just stopped paying. I shut down. The accounts were suspended and then the companies started calling and calling. I eventually told my parents what was happening and they helped me out. I'm now working to pay off my bills and trying to figure out how I can fix the damage. They say it can take seven years to repair credit. Had I at least called and made payment arrangements, the companies wouldn't have been so aggressive.

—senior, College of Charleston

* * *

For every action, there is a reaction. If you skip classes, you risk failing out of school. Have unprotected sex, and you risk getting a sexually transmitted infection/disease. Write bad checks, and you risk establishing a terrible credit history that can follow you around for years and years and haunt you when you least expect it.

Now, you might be thinking that it's not a big deal to blow off a payment here and there. But it becomes a big deal when you want to take advantage of the zero percent interest financing for that new car only to find out that you don't qualify because your credit rating from college is a disaster. It doesn't seem like a big deal now, but it will when you fill out an application to rent a place and the landlord runs a credit report that comes up "NO WAY IN HELL" and refuses to rent to you (and no, NO WAY IN HELL is not an actual credit rating). Messing up your credit doesn't seem like a big deal until you try to buy a home and can't secure a mortgage because your lender ran a credit report and your credit rating

How Your Credit Score Works:

Credit scoring is a system creditors use to help determine whether to give you credit. Information about you and your credit experiences, such as your bill-paying history, the number and type of accounts you have, late payments, collection actions, outstanding debt, and the age of your accounts is collected from your credit application and your credit report. Using a statistical program, creditors compare this information to the credit performance of consumers with similar profiles. A credit scoring system awards points for each factor that helps predict who is most likely to repay a debt. A total number of points—a credit score helps predict how creditworthy you are; that is, how likely it is that you will repay a loan and make the payments when due.

—Federal Trade Commission Website

http://www.ftc.gov

was abysmal. It's fun to pass bad checks, not pay bills, and pay late, but once you start living life beyond college, your terrible payment habits will become a huge problem. And by the way, passing bad checks is a crime.

In case you're not familiar with how credit works, lenders, landlords, and other credit card companies look at your credit rating to determine how much of a risk you are to do business with. The worse your history is the higher you are as a risk. Things like paying bills late, not paying bills at all, opening too many lines of credit, overdrawing your checking account, and having a history of companies reporting you to one of the three big credit bureaus reduce your credit rating. The lower the rating the worse your chances are of being someone people want to do business with (see the sidebar on the previous page for the FTC explanation of your credit score).

> **"Don't write bum checks. I would write bad checks for food and groceries when I got to college. I didn't care. My credit is pretty much screwed. I shouldn't have done that."**
> —sophomore,
> Eastern New Mexico University

For free credit reports visit www.freecreditreport.com (from Experian)

Do it the right way and save yourself all of the aggravation. If not for yourself, then do it for your future. You'll thank yourself tomorrow for being responsible today.

Bottom Line

It can take seven seconds to write a bad check— it takes seven years to repair your credit. (Note: actually time to write check can vary.)

Tip #93
Checking Out the College Checking Account

The Tip
Set a budget, use cash, and don't abuse the ATM/debit card.

The Story
I had an idea what college would cost, but I was way off. I would use my ATM debit card to handle costs that came up. I had it on an auto-billing service where there was an automatic deduction. I also used it for an organization that didn't run the charges until after I thought the money was already gone. It was impossible to figure out where the money was going to and where it was coming from. I ended up getting overdrawn and paying over a hundred dollars of fees from all the times it happened. I had to close the account and start over. I now have an ATM card that is just an ATM card. I can now track where and when the money moves. It also helps me to know what I'm spending. I do have a credit card, but I only use it for emergencies or when I need to purchase something over the phone. When I do, I transfer the money right away. The credit card and the bank are hooked up online, so it's easy to transfer money.

> "I paid for my book with my debit card and I was overdrawn by $90. Overdrawn fees are a bitch."
> —junior, University of Southern Indiana

—senior, San Diego State University

* * *

> **"Get overdraft protection in case it happens—and it can happen to responsible people like me."**
> —senior, Northwestern University

This seems like kind of a boring tip, but it's an important one. If it will help, play some music for atmosphere. That song, "Money Money Money, Monnnnneeey" will work, or something by 50 Cent is close enough (his name is currency). I was an idiot when it came to my checking account in college. I never wrote it all down. It was after bouncing a check and dealing with the wrath of my parents and paying ridiculous fees that I started paying more attention. It took me years to straighten myself out. Take the time to do things the right way now and you won't have to spend hours dealing with "idiot you" years down the line. I'm being vulnerable here. Please, don't be like me. Set up your finances and be responsible—it will help you throughout your entire life. Here's the plan to do it right.

When you get to school, or even during a summer visit, establish an account at a local branch. Ask about student accounts. You want to avoid fees. This includes ATM fees, minimum balance fees,

> **"Only take money out once a week. Take out an amount you know you'll need to get by easily with, but don't use an ATM for the rest of the week. You can't lose what you don't have on you to lose."**
> —sophomore, York University

checking fees, and teller fees. They add up fast. Get checks that come with carbons (it helps to know who you wrote checks to in case you don't record your checks in a ledger). Appreciate that banks are competitive and want college students as account holders. Don't be afraid to negotiate to get the best plan. Also, make sure that you have overdraft protection (in case you get overdrawn you won't have all the ridiculous fees). And make sure you know how many ATM transactions you can perform a month without being charged. Check to make sure that there isn't an additional fee for transactions with a live teller—some banks charge teller fees (which I could understand if they were fortune tellers, too).

> "I'm overdrawn all the time. My bank charges me $32 each time. I recently received a note from them that said I was overdrawn at least ten times in a year. That means that I lost $320 and God knows what happened to my credit future."
> —fifth-year senior, UCLA

As for these debit/credit cards, they are the devil. They are too much work to keep track of. It's hard to know when the transaction goes through and when the money leaves your account. If you want to charge something, get a credit card separate from your checking account and make sure you only buy things that you can pay for immediately (unless you have so much money that you will never overdraw the account). If you can use your card and get mileage or some kind of bonus, there's nothing wrong with that. Just pay the balance immediately. If you're afraid of losing control, get a credit card with a small credit line or a credit card where you load cash on it. They now have these cards that work like gift certificates. You put on a certain amount and then once you run out of money, you have to recharge the card with cash. One more suggestion—include the names of your parents on the account. It helps so that they can transfer money into the account (and bail you out if you lose control).

Bottom Line

Look for the lowest fee checking account (like free, if possible) with online access. Avoid those debit/credit cards; it's too hard to keep track of when they take the money out of your account and it's too easy to get overdrawn—and that can be sad (see the depression tip ahead).

Tip #94
Sorry, This Book Is Now "Used"

The Tip

Utilize the Internet—sites like Half.com and Amazon.com. They have the same books as the campus bookstore, and often for at least a third of the price. Plus, you can actually get money back when you sell your books.

The Story

Most college bookstores have a monopoly on the market (especially private college bookstores). They overcharge massively. For example, I bought a British history textbook that was $70 new in the bookstore, but was on Amazon.com used for $6. Then I resold it for $22 (I printed a prepaid shipping label off the computer). The student bookstore was buying it back for $10. Also, make sure the book you're buying is the same edition that the professor

"The only way I get books now is through the Internet."
—student, University of Delaware

is using. That's the part of buying used books online that you have to be the most careful about.

—senior, Franklin College

* * *

A sadistic professor once made me buy a book on Russia for $50. I didn't even open it. When I went to sell it back, they offered to give me $5. I offered them a dirty look. I kept the book and used it as a doorstop—it was a nice doorstop. I hope you don't use this as a doorstop. Actually, I don't mind. If you're not reading it, at least it can be useful while it's not being read. Hmm…now I'm kind of hoping you'll use it as a doorstop.

> "Try to find upperclassmen who had the same class and get books from them."
> —student, Manhattan College

When it comes to buying books, the best suggestion is to buy used. Now you might think, *Harlan, I don't buy anything used*. But this time, it's different. It's not like underwear, socks, or shoes. It's not a status symbol to have a new book—just a symbol that you throw away money. The average used book is dramatically less expensive than the new book and it has the same exact words (minus the doodles in the cover). The only difference is that you might deal with a little wear and tear. Some books have minimal wear and maximum savings. When coming across used books that have already been highlighted, they're still good books. Just use a different color highlighter to represent your

> "Don't buy books until you need them. Go to the library and check out textbooks. I rarely buy books."
> —senior, Emerson College

highlights. Do not depend on someone else's highlights. The owner of your previously owned book might have failed out or have been an artist who highlighted based on emotions, not the lecture notes.

When the semester ends, chances are you'll want to sell back your book. Most campus bookstores run the traditional, "We buy back your book and you feel as if you've been robbed in broad daylight" buyback options. Even the economics professors marvel at how the price of a textbook can drop 80 percent in three months. Before running to a bookstore, consider selling your books online, to a local bookstore, or through a campus book network. There are now these mini networks popping up where students who finish a course list their books to sell to students beginning the course. Ask an upperclassman or your RA about your options. Make sure that the used book you're buying isn't a foreign version of the book (ask the seller if buying online).

"Make sure if you shop online that you're getting the right edition of the book. I know a lot of people who thought they got a deal, but found that they were stuck with an old edition. Do not overlook the edition."
—junior, Earlham College

One more book tip: when it comes to non-academic books (like in English class), call your college library and then your local community library. There's a chance it might be in circulation so you won't have to buy it.

Bottom Line

Used books still have the same information inside. It's the information on the outside that tends to be different—namely, the huge price difference.

Tip #95
Cheap Strategies for Eating (or barely eating)

The Tip

If there is a Save-A-Lot or other similar discount grocery store around, go to it!

The Story

Ahh, you're finally in college. But the food is terrible, so what do you do? Find one of your close buds that has a car and drive to your nearest Save-A-Lot or other similar store. By going to a store and buying non–name brand foods, you're saving money that can be used for other items. As for me, $50 worth of food at Save-A-Lot will last me for up to two or three months. Or if you're really low on cash and want to go back, just sell the food items that you don't like to your friends. Someone will buy it from you, eventually.

> "Work in the food services. I worked in catering on the weekends for three years and ate for free. I also got to bring home leftovers for my roommates."
> —senior, Northeastern University

—freshman, Xavier University

* * *

I tried to make this page fruit-flavored, but publishing hasn't advanced that far yet. There's also the risk that you'd eat this entire book. Now, some strategies for eating more for less:

- Get a part-time job where you can get paid and eat well for free. Waiting tables at a sorority, serving at a local restaurant, or working in catering can be a huge help. The best of these is the catering options. When the parties are all over, the people working the events can sometimes take the food home or it eat following the event. If you can work part-time on the weekends, you will save so much money. Typically, it's the weekends that cost the most. The reason—school cafeterias don't always serve all meals on the weekends. Ordering out can get expensive. Plus, you have the added expense of whatever you do on the weekends.

- Get a few friends together and shop at a warehouse club like Costco, Sam's Club, or BJ's Wholesale Club and split the bill. You can eat for weeks. In addition, there are canned foods, soups, pastas, and other non-refrigerated items where all you have to do is add water.

- Always use coupons—there are so many deals out there if you take advantage of them. You can find a book of coupons in the student union or a high-traffic area. Ask about student discounts or discount cards. If the coupon is a buy one get one free, find someone to go in with you or buy one and keep the other one for another meal.

- When your schedule doesn't allow you to get to the dining hall, a lot of times you can get meals to go. Ask the dining hall director if the meal plan includes meals to go. Also, ask about late night and weekend options to cut costs.
- Take a little bit of food with you from the cafeteria. Just put some fruit in your bag. If you don't have a bag, then put it in your pants. I'm not saying to steal food, but if you don't have time to sit and eat every meal in the cafeteria that day, rather than going hungry, take a bagel or Pop Tarts as a snack. And chew slowly. That can help, too.
- Bring food from home. If your mom or dad is a good cook, bring back frozen food. Even if they're not good cooks, bring food. Pack pre-cooked frozen food in one-portion plastic bags. Keep them in your freezer (assuming you have one), and use it when you're on the run.
- Go to functions on campus where there is food. You don't need to stay for the event. Just go long enough to eat (if you're poor and hungry).

If you find that you're too poor to eat and are going hungry, talk to the people in the dining hall or contact someone in financial aid. Explain the situation and see if you can get a meal plan. If it's a no go, see if you can get a job working in a cafeteria. And no, don't steal your roommate's food—not cool.

"Coupons have saved me. Every week there is a new book of coupons. If the place you're ordering from doesn't have coupons, ask if they'll accept a competitor's coupon. If they don't, just buy from the competitor. When dealing with 2-for-1 deals, buy both of whatever it is that's 2-for-1 and keep one for the next day. Look for daily specials—you can buy it cheap one day and eat it for many days. Also, bring food from home that's frozen. It seems like a pain to take, but when it's 3 a.m. and you're hungry, you'll be so happy."

—sophomore, University of Illinois

Bottom Line

You can eat cheap if you work on eating cheap. If you're really strapped for nourishment, get a job in food services. The catering jobs tend to yield massive employee leftovers.

Tip #96
Laundry Tips: This Page Is Not Fabric Softener

The Tip
Don't leave your clothes in the dryer after they're done.

The Story
I had someone steal my laundry after it finished drying. I've had friends who have had their laundry stolen, too. If your clothes are done and you leave them there, people will cut

them. That happened, too. There was one girl who left her clothes over night and someone cut them up. I've heard about someone urinating in a dryer once that had clothes in it, but I didn't actually see it. Bring lots of quarters and don't leave your clothes sitting there. Bring Downy balls and the premade tablets. Do it off campus because the one on campus can be broken and you end up spending $10 and then find out that it's broken.

—student, Southern New Hampshire University

> "About laundry, I recommend the Tide laundry cubes. Wash whites and darks separately. There's nothing more depressing than having tons of laundry money, but no quarters."
> —junior, Hollins College

* * *

If you're reading this and you're desperate for clean underwear, you can tie two strings to this page and use it as underwear. Better yet, you can use each page of this book as underwear, which should take you through two semesters.

For those who are actually looking for laundry tips, please follow these helpful suggestions and your whites will stay white, your darks will stay dark, and nothing and no one will bleed:

- Don't wash dark and light colors together. They will bleed and then you'll end up wearing mostly pink and gray clothing (not a problem if that happens to be your school's colors). And wash on permanent press (cold water works best).
- Use the detergent tablets. They save space when it comes to storage and they're lighter and easier to carry than the 200 ounce jug of detergent.

- Investigate a Laundromat near campus if the washing machines in the residence halls aren't maintained well. Some Laundromats have food, music, and drinks. It's also a way to meet scantily clad people with no clean clothes to wear.
- Avoid shrinkage—read labels carefully. When in doubt, don't toss it in the dryer. Hang-dry what might shrink. Fold clothes immediately.
- Never leave your clothes in the dryer unattended—clothes often get stolen if they sit in the dryer long enough. And if they get stolen, you're left looking over members of the same sex from head to toe—not because you're interested in them, but because you're wondering if that person is wearing your pants.
- Do laundry at slow times—not on the weekends.
- Don't overstuff your machine. If there's no room to agitate, your clothes won't get clean and you'll get agitated.
- Quarters are gold—save quarters, take quarters from home, give that extra three cents so you can get two quarters instead of forty-seven cents back.
- The laundry room is a great place to start a conversation with someone. The best lines: 1) Can I borrow your fabric softener? 2) Gee, that smells terrific! 3) Excuse me, is this your thong or mine?

Ways to avoid having to do laundry:
- Date someone who loves doing laundry.
- Take advantage of the inside-out method—this is the act of turning clothing inside out to get an extra wear (socks, underwear, T-shirts).

- Take your laundry home and just ask a parent to do it.
- Borrow a roommate's clothing.
- Bring it to a Laundromat that does it for you and charges by the pound.
- Avoid working up a sweat or soiling your clothing (by keeping your body under control and wearing the same clothing dozens of times).

> "Bring rolls of quarters with you for laundry. On campus, everyone is always looking for quarters for the laundry machines, and usually the bookstore and cafeteria are reluctant to give them out. Often it's hard to get off campus, and I found that a roll or two of quarters really came in handy."
> —graduate student, Washington University

Bottom Line

When doing laundry, brush your teeth and fix your hair before heading to the laundry room. It might not seem romantic, but two people in a hot room for hours with the aroma of Snuggle fabric softener sheets is a recipe for love.

Harlan's Tip Sheet

Money, Laundry, and Cheap Eats Resources, Websites, and Additional Info

Financial Aid Office:

>The office that handles student requests for financial assistance with tuition and college costs. This is the place that handles the money.

Financial Aid Advisor:

>The individual that will help answer your questions regarding availability of money, loan options, and paperwork questions.

FAFSA:

>Free Application for Federal Student Aid. This is the government form that must be filled out for financial aid. Contact your financial aid advisor with particular questions. www.fafsa.ed.gov

Financial Aid/Scholarships/Grants/Loans

>Scholarship Searches: Use free searches. One frequently mentioned to me: www.fastweb.com.
>
>Check out the College Board's website for information on aid and links: www.collegeboard.com
>
>Visit Sallie Mae's lending online: www.salliemae.com
>
>Citibank has a helpful website worth visiting: www.studentloans.com

Credit Card Information:

The Federal Trade Commission has helpful information on understanding credit and credit cards.

http://www.ftc.gov/bcp/menu-credit.htm

Buying Books:

Do your own keyword search. Use "New and Used College Textbooks." There are several major online textbook services out there. The ones students mentioned most:

www.half.com (part of eBay)

www.bn.com (see tab marked "new & used textbooks")

www.amazon.com

www.ecampus.com

www.textbooks.com

Laundry Tips:

Never do laundry on the weekends (it's too busy).

Don't leave your detergent or basket (I'll steal it).

Get rolls of quarters at the grocery store service desk or at a bank.

What They Don't Tell You

Dear Harlan,
Does the freshman 15 really happen? I've heard many rumors about people going off to college and when they come back a few months after being a freshman, they've gained fifteen to twenty pounds. I want to know so I can be prepared when I start college to not start packing on the pounds!

—Fearing the Fifteen

Dear Fearing,
It's true. It happened to me. Actually, I still have my freshman 15. I keep it in a jar in the refrigerator as

a constant reminder of just how easy it is for me to lose control. I haven't eaten pizza, wings, or subs past midnight since my freshman year in college (and no, it's not really in a jar—it's in Tupperware). See Tip #97 for more...

Dear Harlan,

I'm a sophomore in college in New Mexico. I recently came home after attending one semester at the University of Arizona because I felt like I did not fit in there. I was having trouble making friends, so I moved back in with my mom. Now, I regret the decision. I'm unhappy here. I do not know anyone. I am wondering if I should transfer somewhere else and give the whole college experience another chance or if it is too late.

—Stuck at Home

Dear Stuck,

The college brochures never tell you...but college can suck at times. No one tells you because then you wouldn't go to that college. But clearly, it can be a tough transition that takes work, time, and effort on your part. The problem with transferring after one semester is that when the problem isn't the college, the problem travels with you. You can transfer from college to college to college, but until you figure it out...see Tip #102 for more.

Tip #97
The Freshman 15...Or, Um, 45

The Tip
Remain active, be wary of the cafeteria buffet, and don't drink too much.

The Story
I was a ballet dancer for fourteen years. When I moved out of state for college I didn't realize that my dancing had kept me in shape all those years. I didn't participate in anything active besides walking to class or to the cafeteria, which by the way was a huge all-you-can-eat buffet every day! The partying was happening every night. I did not do too well in my classes my first year, and I also gained forty-five pounds. Try dealing with the humiliation of going home on vacation and hearing all or your old friends say, "Your face has filled out," "Are you pregnant?" etc. Now that I'm a fifth-year senior, I've lost most of the weight but I wish I had never gained it in the first place!

> **CAUTION:**
> If you're like me and have a history of emotional eating or if you have an eating disorder, all the changes that come along with going to college are triggers for emotional eating. Come to college prepared on how you'll find balance, who you can turn to for help, and how you'll manage yourself.

—senior, St. Cloud State University

***

I gained my freshman 15, lost it, and then kept it (it's in a jar in the freezer). Actually, I did gain and lose it, but I didn't keep it.

I have no idea how it happened, but eating breadsticks, wings, pizza, drinking an occasional beverage at 3 a.m., and then sleeping resulted in the addition of a few pounds. On top of that, I frequently took advantage of the all-you-can-eat option available in the cafeteria. See, my mom

> "Always take the stairs if possible. Do not eat french fries every meal of the day. Take only one dessert."
> —freshman, Radford University

never did a lot of cooking with a deep fryer, and those chicken fingers and french fries were tempting. We also didn't have a soft-serve ice cream/yogurt machine with ten different toppings next to the kitchen table.

Easy access to food combined with the lack of movement and all the changes that come with college make consuming calories easier than ever. So much of college is built around social calorie consumption. If it's not social, it's emotional eating. Craving comfort can easily lead to junk food. Had I not been overweight in high school and overly aware of my eating habits, I can only imagine the poundage I would have been packing.

> "Exercise regularly to avoid the freshman fifteen, the sophomore seventeen, the junior twenty... Eating late at night, drinking, and eating too much helped me put on a few."
> —senior, University of Pittsburgh

It's easy to gain weight in college. BUT it's also easy to not gain weight. If you eat during normal hours, exercise regularly, and snack smart, then you don't have to worry about gaining weight. Most meal plans offer a healthy option (a trough of frozen yogurt is not a healthy breakfast), or at the least, a salad bar is available. If you don't have a low-fat dressing option, use the oil and vinegar. (BYOB: bring your own balsamic.)

Should you overindulge, work out. Most campuses have state-of-the-art recreational facilities. There are often classes that you can join for free (spin, cardioboxing, martial arts). Even better—become an instructor. Then you have no choice but to go.

Another way to stay active is through sports (this does not include the Madden NFL video game). If you find that you're having a hard time managing your weight, figure out what you're doing differ-

> "Stock your dorm room with food. My food is what is keeping me from the freshman fifteen! I always have healthy snack foods like fruit and nuts in my room to bring to class with me and eat while doing homework. Instead of eating pizza, I'll eat some dried fruit."
>
> —freshman,
> University of North Carolina–Chapel Hill

ently. Also, look into seeing a nutritionist on campus. If you really want to gain some control, try Weight Watchers (they also have an online program). One Weight Watchers program assigns each food a point value—you're only allowed so many points in a day. If you eat more points than you're allowed, you gain weight. Even if you're not looking to lose weight, it's helpful. If you're supposed to eat twenty-seven points of food and you eat one hundred points in a day, you'll understand why there's a problem.

Bottom Line

Eating a large pizza, a dozen breadsticks, fifteen wings, a bag of chips, a pound of chocolate-covered peanuts, a bag of dried fruit (to be healthy), and drinking a six-pack of thick malted beer before bedtime will make your pants tight.

Tip #98
The Student Body Image

The Tip

Hang out with people who are obsessed with their bodies, and you will become obsessed with yours.

The Story

When I was in high school I didn't worry as much about what people thought. When I got to college, it was all I thought about. It had a lot to do with the people I'd hang around with. They were obsessed with how they looked. It started to affect what I did and how I thought. Like, they said that they were going to the gym every day—I'm like, "I have to go." Then they eat nothing and I'm like, "I have to eat nothing." It's hard to eat when no one else is eating. What I learned is that I had to find a way to get away from it, if even for a short period of

"There are two mints you should always take: breath mints and compliments."
—sophomore,
University of Massachusetts–Dartmouth

time. I found another group of friends through campus organizations and in classes. I learned that it's all about how I feel about myself, not how they feel about me. It's important to have a wide variety of friends. If you don't, you start acting like the group you hang out with. It becomes easy to get obsessed or lose yourself in the process.

—junior, University of Connecticut

* * *

I have ears that protrude (please see photo on back cover). Several years ago, a reader wrote to me suggesting that I would be far more handsome if I surgically pinned my ears back. I ran the letter from "Doris in Dallas." My reply went something like this:

Dear Doris,

Yes, I'm aware that my ears stick out. And when I forget about them, there's occasionally someone to offer a friendly reminder, suggesting that I have them surgically stitched closer to my head (the same people who offer comments regarding other people's weight, hair, and wrinkles). Thank you, but I don't want to change. If someone doesn't like me because of my ears, it's not a loss. As for women, I've had extremely attractive women find me (and my ears) extremely attractive—and not just women with ear fetishes (are there such women?). Some even tell me that my ears are fun to play with.

And for those flat-eared people looking to change, there's no surgery I know of to have your ears pushed out. I appreciate your letter, and I love that you enjoy the column. Maybe, one day, you'll love my ears, too. I do.

It's taken me a while to see, but my ears are an asset. They separate me from all the flat-eared men of the world. They're attractive. At least that's what people have told me. Following my reply, I was flooded with ear-adoring mail from men and women around the country. Some sent their pictures. Some shared stories of what they wanted to do with me and my protruding ears (don't imagine). I even had a man in Dallas offer to host me in his hot tub if I was in town (never took him up on that one).

I've seen and heard firsthand that other people will love those things that we don't necessary love. It's not just ears; it happens

> **"It's pretty hot when a girl is confident. The thing that bothered me about one of my past girlfriends was that she was so obsessed with her weight that it interfered with the relationship. When I told her that she was beautiful, she would never believe it—but it was true."**
> —senior, Western New England College

with butts, boobs, noses, hair, lack of hair—whatever it is that you don't think is attractive, can be. The only catch is that you have to believe it's attractive (which can be a tough sell to yourself).

When it comes to body image, we are our own worst enemy. Most of us harbor a skewed image. And most of the time, it's not the most flattering image. If you want to reflect an image that will make you attractive, here's how you can do it. Stand in front of the mirror wearing the tightest thong possible. Don't look away. The things hanging out of your thong are the things you need to embrace or change in a healthy way. The things you can't change—embrace them. Trust that someone will love them. Until you can be comfortable with your reflection, it's hard to expect anyone else to be. If you find that you can't love or even like what you see and can't change it, then get help—a good therapist (or even a bad therapist) can help you change your focus and love the things that are hardest for you to embrace as just another part of you that makes you, you. Until you can love your reflection, it will be too hard to take risks because you'll be too afraid that someone will reflect something in yourself that you can't *bare* to see.

Bottom Line
No matter the size of your bottom line, someone will want it.

Tip #99
Exposing the College Eating Disorder

The Tip
If you see someone who you think has an eating disorder, don't just look the other way or make comments. Help that person.

The Story
People have a tendency to get scared when they see someone they know suffering from an eating disorder. I never thought I would be someone who would become anorexic. My sophomore year, I was put into the hospital. I'm five

feet, seven inches, and weighed close to ninety pounds—down from 124 pounds back when school started. When it was obvious that I was losing weight and getting way too thin, my friends in my sorority didn't help. They once put a flyer in the hallway that had information about eating disorders, or made flip comments, but that's as far as they went. No one really talked to me. I think they were too scared and didn't know what to do or how to help. If you see someone in trouble, tell that person. If they don't listen, then call that person's parents and alert people on campus—that person needs your help more than ever. After transferring to another college, I'm finally getting better. I hope my story can help others.

—junior, University of Missouri–Kansas City

***

I'm always struggling with this one. In high school, I gained fifty pounds (I was was five feet, two inches, and 192 pounds). I then lost it all, and more, my sophomore year and kept it off. In college, I gained a few pounds, but nothing too dramatic. I had a good idea that drinking beer, eating a pizza at three in the morning, and not working out would mean gaining weight. That said, it's not hard to work out, it's easy to make healthy choices, and you can avoid gaining weight. Just be careful. It's easy to get carried away or obsess about it.

The lack of control that's part of college, the constant pressure to look a certain way, and the abundance of all-you-can-eat, high-calorie foods make a dangerous recipe that can lead to an eating disorder (if you don't already have one). There are so many triggers. On top of that, spending so much time away from home (this includes commuter students) means that it's easy to hide an eating disorder from family or close friends (who can see you and stop you). It can get dangerous extremely fast.

Rather than obsessing or worrying, get familiar with your campus's recreational center before leaving for college. Pick a sport or cardio class. Make "being active" part of your daily routine, so that you can eat a little more without seeing it, feeling it, or worrying about it.

If you're coming to college with an eating disorder, find support on campus before setting foot on campus. If you're someone who develops an eating disorder, get help sooner than later. If you're forcing yourself to vomit, binging, not eating, or binging and then exercising excessively (bulimia doesn't always include vomiting), it's a sign that you're in trouble. Visit the counseling office and speak with a therapist. Explain your situation. And if you're someone who has a friend who develops an eating disorder, don't turn your head and look the other way. Be a good friend and get involved. Talk to the counselors at the health center. Talk to your friend's parents. Talk to your friend and make sure he or she gets help.

If you do gain weight, I'm a huge fan of Weight Watchers. It's just a great way to measure how much you're eating. You can follow the program online or you can find a meeting near campus (sometimes they'll bring the meeting to you if there is a group of people interested). They didn't pay me to say this. It's just what I use to keep myself at a healthy weight. If you're looking for support or want to share your stories, please post them in the Naked Roommate forums (www.TheNakedRoommate.com).

Bottom Line

It's way too easy to develop an eating disorder, or trigger an old one, in college. Be aware and get help before you're forced to get help.

Tip #100
Depression: The "Other" Major

The Tip

Asking for a little help does not make you weak.

The Story

I have been told by many that I am a very strong person. I'm nineteen and living in what seems to be more like a soap opera than real life. I never wanted to admit that I could have depression. Then, the beginning of this semester, I started to notice behavior I could not ignore.

National Depression Screening occurs in October of every year. Here's the URL for the website: http://www.mentalhealthscreening.org.

I would often overreact (often hysterically) to everyday stressful situations. I was sleeping—a lot—planning to wake up at 7 a.m., but often missing entire days of classes and increasing my homework and adding stress. I was eating all the time and gaining weight. I didn't want to do the things that made me happy.

All I wanted to do was sit in my room and sleep, or sometimes just stare and think. I decided it was time to take action. As a resident advisor, I was aware of all the resources

on campus for people in "my situation," never thinking I would be the one in need of them. Frantic and stressed, I did something that was extremely hard for my hard-headed, independent personality: I called the counseling center with the words "I believe I have depression, and I am ready to seek help." Now, with my depression medication and weekly counseling sessions, I feel like my old self again. My motivation is back, I am not unnecessarily emotional, I am happy. Although I am still dealing with the hole I've dug myself into due to my class absences, late assignments, and missed tests, I am looking forward to the future, as I can feel myself

DE-STRESSING

In coping with stress, some people find writing in a journal, exercising, or talking with friends helpful. But for clinical depression you need some form of treatment (usually medication and short-term psychotherapy) to start feeling better soon.

—National Institutes of Mental Health

getting better and better each day. It takes courage to admit you have a problem, and to be serious about wanting to fix it. I now feel stronger than ever.

—junior, Bowling Green State University

* * *

things not mentioned in the college brochure   393

This will not be a depressing tip about depression. I promise. I wouldn't do that. In fact, to help you make this tip happier, I'm adding some suggested background music to play while reading this tip:

Jimmy Cliff:
"I Can See Clearly Now"
The Beatles:
"Here Comes the Sun"
R.E.M.:
"Shiny Happy People"
Hanson:
"MMMbop" (MMMaybe not...)
Brady Bunch:
"It's a Sunshine Day (Everybody's Smiling)"
Harlan Cohen: "My Roommate Stu" or "The Syphilis Song"

If you think you suffer from depression in college, there are some things to be happy about. Never before have there been more resources, treatments, information, and support available for you. On most campuses, there is at least one full-time therapist, and therapy is often covered by your health insurance.

Depression in college happens—a lot. According to the Higher Education Research Institute, more than 55.3

percent of first year students "occasionally" felt depressed and 12.1 percent "frequently" felt depressed. New friendships, relationships, living arrangements, financial burdens, classroom stress, temptations, and emotions can be the ingredients that trigger depression. Factor in that your support system for the past eighteen years is either far away or not what it used to be, and some will be sent spiraling to a bad place. The problem is that it's easy to pretend to be happy without anyone else knowing something is deeply wrong. And the people who know you best aren't close enough to see you're in trouble and save you.

Suicide

Suicidal feelings, thoughts, impulses, or behaviors always should be taken seriously. If you are thinking about hurting or killing yourself, SEEK HELP IMMEDIATELY. Contact someone you trust to help you: a good friend, academic or resident advisor, or:

- staff at the student health or counseling center
- a professor, coach, or advisor
- a local suicide or emergency hotline (get the phone number from the information operator or directory)
- a hospital emergency room
- call 911

The first step in overcoming depression is recognizing it. It's normal to have some signs of depression some of the time, but five or more symptoms for two weeks or longer, or noticeable changes in usual functioning, are factors that should be evaluated by a health or mental health professional. (Also worth mentioning—people who are depressed may not be thinking clearly and need help to get help.)

The following are symptoms of depression:

- Sadness, anxiety, or empty feelings
- Decreased energy, fatigue, being "slowed down"

- Loss of interest or pleasure in usual activities
- Sleep disturbances (insomnia, oversleeping, or waking much earlier than usual)
- Appetite and weight changes (either loss or gain)
- Feelings of hopelessness, guilt, and worthlessness
- Thoughts of death or suicide, or suicide attempts
- Difficulty concentrating, making decisions, or remembering
- Irritability or excessive crying
- Chronic aches and pains not explained by another physical condition

"It's hard to tell who's depressed because you don't see them around and when you do they can act completely different..."
—junior, Western New England College

Over the past couple of years, there has been more and more attention focused on depression and suicide in college. If you're having thoughts of suicide or death, I'm begging you (seriously, and I haven't begged you in this entire book) to get help. If you think that you're going to do something terrible to yourself, get help. Contact the counselors on campus, call your local hospital, contact a crisis hotline, and get some help.

If you have a friend that you think might be depressed, contact the people I just mentioned and find out the best way to approach your friend. I've talked to so many survivors of attempted

"No one has it all together. I finally realized that everyone is flawed. The idea that no one is expected to be perfect in all situations has been one of the most valuable concepts for me."
—sophomore, Brandeis University

suicide—every single one is so thankful to still be here. Their families are thankful. Their friends are thankful. The dark cloud that hangs over you today will clear tomorrow—BUT YOU NEED TO BE HERE for it to clear. PLEASE, PLEASE, PLEASE, get help. Your friends, family, and the world need you.

Addiction (Alcohol, Sex, Gambling, Facebook, MySpace, Etc.)

Depression is naturally depressing. And a lot of times, people want to get away from the heaviness and find unhealthy methods to cope. Drugs and alcohol are some of the most common methods to help numb the pain and run from reality. Then there's sex addiction (online porn, masturbation, risky sexual encounters)—it's not about intimacy, it's about masking

> "My ex-boyfriend has been calling me crying. He's at a school where he really didn't want to go. He's been hanging out with friends from home. I've told him that he really needs to get some help."
> —freshman, Indiana University

the real emotions motivating the behavior. There's gambling addiction—more college students than ever are turning to gambling. It seems harmless, but it can cost students their future. I was recently at a campus where the president of the sophomore class robbed a bank at gunpoint to pay for his online gambling debt. Another student killed his roommates rather than pay gambling debts. Online gambling, casinos near campuses, and poker games down the hall are habits that can turn into a serious addiction (see hotlines at end of chapter). Then there's video game addictions, Facebook and MySpace addictions (not yet clinically recognized), and other Internet addictions (be careful of The Fifth Wall). In excess, these are unhealthy escapes that are taking you away from reality to help you cope with a deeper issue.

If you feel like a particular behavior is running your life, getting in the way of daily activities, or becoming the focus of your day, that habit might be more than just a diversion. If people are bringing up the habit, it's a problem. If your habit is getting in the way of your responsibilities and relationships, it's a problem. If you can't stop doing it, it's a problem. Get help before the problem takes over your life.

Bottom Line

The depressing news: depression can be depressing. The happy news: there's more help than ever before to help you get beyond depression. It's confidential, part of tuition, and can carry over into the rest of your life.

Tip #101
Sexual Assault

The Tip

When going out with friends to bars or parties, never leave without everybody you came in with, and keep track of each other throughout the evening. And never give out your number. Even violent crazies can come off as normal at first.

The Story

This is a story about keeping track of friends. My friend was close friends with a guy she's known since they were in kindergarten (good friends, never more). During their first year of college he invited her to come visit him because they were having a big party. She and one of her friends came to stay with him, thinking that since they had been good friends for nearly thirteen years it'd be okay. But his "friends" ended up drugging the girls. As far as she knows, he let them do whatever they liked. My friend ended up waking up the next day on a totally different floor than her clothes, surrounded by five or six passed out drunk guys.

—college withheld

* * *

I'm not trying to freak you out, but bad things can happen on college campuses. The National College Women Sexual Victimization Study estimated that between one in four and one in five college women experience completed or attempted rape during their college years. Most of the time, it's with someone the victim knows. Some of the time, alcohol is involved. Whatever the circumstances are, it's never the victim's fault. It's never, never, never your fault.

While there are things you can do to minimize your risk, sometimes it just happens. Still, these are some things to keep in mind:

- Never go home with a stranger.
- Never take open cups or drinks from a stranger.

- Never let your friends go home with a stranger. Watch out for your friends and do not let them do something with someone that you think is unsafe.
- Never walk home alone (even on a safe small campus).
- Never ignore your gut feeling.
- Never be afraid to defend yourself.

If someone you know has been sexually assaulted, or if you've been sexually assaulted, go to the hospital and get examined. You can decide to pursue legal charges later, but first, get help. Call your local hospital, call a local crisis hotline, or call the RAINN hotline (in the U.S., call 1-800-656-HOPE).

> "I always wanted to be away from home, but once I was away, I realized that I wanted to be closer to home."
> —junior, College of Charleston

A great book that comes highly recommended is *I Never Called It Rape* by Ellen Beattie. Find support, take time to heal, and then if you're strong enough, you can help other victims on their journey toward recovery. And for those men who are victims of sexual assault—and it happens to men too—get help and seek support.

And to all those who are doing the assaulting—please just stop. It's so not worth ruining your life and the victim's life. If someone you're with is too drunk to say no, and you have sex with that person, that's rape. If someone says no, you must listen. Otherwise, you can call it what you want, but the law calls it rape.

> "I really wanted to transfer because I didn't really like any of the people I was meeting, but all of that changed when I met this sophomore guy in my dorm."
> —freshman, Bucknell University

Bottom Line

Sadly, it can happen to you (men and women). Be aware. And should something bad happen, get help. And again, when it comes to sexual assault, I can't say it enough: it's NEVER, NEVER, NEVER the survivor's fault. Never.

Tip #102
To Transfer or Not to Transfer

The Tip
Try to make it work—you might be surprised what you discover.

The Story
I came to college ready to transfer, but found something great here. In high school, I was hoping to go to Ohio State University, but didn't get in. I was really depressed, but figured I'd go here and then transfer after a year.

"I transferred five times before finding what I finally wanted."
—junior, Clemson University

This has been an awesome surprise. It's the opposite of what I thought I had wanted before leaving for college. I've been so surprised how much I like the personal attention of a smaller college. It has helped me to develop close relationships with my professors. My religion professor has become a mentor and friend. I have dinner with his family. I tried to make it work, and I haven't left. I found what I was looking for here without ever knowing what it was that I wanted. It's important to try to make it work before giving up on a college.

—senior, Marian College

* * *

Take a good look around—according to ACT, Inc., about one in four students who start college will not return to the same school their sophomore year. I never planned on it happening to me, but it did. Like breaking up with a beautiful girl, I rejected my first college. It wasn't her, it was me. No, that's not just a line. I mean it. It was the timing. I just never found my place. I knew what I needed. I knew what I wanted. I wanted and needed a fresh start. And with that, I transferred to Indiana University and began a relationship that hasn't stopped.

It wasn't until my second college experience that I learned how to get comfortable with the uncomfortable that is the college experience. I just wonder—had someone told me how to get comfortable in college, had someone told me how to find my place, had someone told me that college can naturally be hard at times, had someone shared with me everything in these pages, would I not have transferred? Then again, I might have had to live it to know firsthand what felt right for me.

Before transferring, make sure that you're transferring for the right reasons. If it's not the right fit socially, academically, emotionally, spiritually, or geographically, figure out what isn't right and where you can thrive.

Make sure you know exactly why you're leaving and what will be different at your next school. If you can't clearly identify the reason(s), like bad body odor, the things that you're trying to avoid will stick to you and follow you from campus to campus to campus. One student I spoke with at Clemson University who had transferred five times finally realized that the problem wasn't the college—the problem was her. She came to the conclusion that what she was looking for wasn't at one particular college—it was inside herself. Then again, you might find that college itself isn't the right fit. That's cool. It happens.

Like I said, transfer for the right reasons. Avoid transferring to run from a problem or to run to a place because it's in your comfort zone. It takes time to make your current school comfortable. Also, make sure that you're transferring to a college that will accept your transfer hours. If the academic office at the college you're considering gives you a hard time, plead your case. Transferring all your credit hours can be the difference between graduating in four, five, or six years.

For the transfer students reading this: when you arrive at your new school, take advantage of all the orientation and welcome events. Even if you've experienced them all once before during your first freshman year, do it again. The students and professionals you'll meet are the people who will make your new college home. Should you have a tough time adjusting, you'll know of people you can lean on along the way.

A few things to keep in mind before transferring:

- Financial reasons? Make sure that you've talked to the financial aid office and pleaded your case. Also, investigate scholarships, grants, and work-study programs.
- Academic reasons? Make sure you're really leaving to find a better program and that you're not just using it as an excuse to leave an uncomfortable situation. Also, make sure you know what academic credits can and cannot be taken with you (think five-year-plus plan).
- Lack of opportunities? Make sure to contact the specific coordinators of the clubs and activities that interest you. Make sure the programs are strong (for example, if you want to debate, shop around for the best debate program).
- Social reasons? Give it at least a year. Be careful not to run to be with old friends, avoid letting a significant other dictate your moves, and make sure you've followed the first twenty tips in this book. These are the secrets to finding your place. When you leave for your new college, make sure you know why it will be different and what you'll do differently once you get there.

Bottom Line

Know exactly why you're transferring. Otherwise, you might just transfer the problem to another campus because the problem might just be you.

Tip #103
Safe, Schmafe

The Tip
Never walk home late at night alone.

The Story
After three years of walking around on my own, something happened. One night, after having one too many drinks and getting split up from my friends at a campus bar, I decided to walk home on my own. On the way through a not-very-good area, a man came out of nowhere (he had probably been visible the whole time, but I never noticed him), grabbed my arm, and tried to pull me off the street. Everything after that is kind of blurry. I know I ran and got away, but by the time I got home, I was sobbing and scared. This was an hour that I can't account for. All that happened is that some guy scared the hell out of me, but in the intoxicated state I was in, it could have been so much worse. No, I never walked home alone again. Now, I'll call a cab or cling to the people I'm with.

—senior, University of Minnesota–Twin Cities

* * *

Suppose you were crazy (this assumes you're not crazy) and you were looking to catch people off guard. You might consider heading to a college campus. It's the place where most people walk around with a false sense of security, and often in a reduced state of alertness. And it's not psychos that are the main concern—consider the drunks and possible sex offenders who go to college. On campus, there is often the "it will never happen to me" mind-set, but it's going to happen to someone. Who's to say it's not going to be you? I'm not trying to make you paranoid, but don't give anyone the benefit of the doubt. Nice people are often not-so-nice people in disguise.

If there is one class you should take in college, it's a self-defense class (for women and for men). A lot of campuses offer them as electives. Sometimes they're not affiliated with the college or university. You'll see them advertised on campus kiosks. (A great idea is to host a course as a residence hall program or sorority event.) I have friends who took part in one of these programs while at Northwestern University in Evanston, Illinois. It was the IMPACT program. Sessions take place over two weekends. The training combines mind, body, and spirit to teach women that they do have choices in the event of an attack. Participants are involved in simulated attacks to test their skills. There are IMPACT courses all over the country. If you have the opportunity to take a self-defense class as an elective, take it. The more difficult of a target you are to a potential assailant the less desirable a victim you become.

> "We've definitely done things we would not have done sober—like getting a ride home from guys we've never seen before. We're just lucky that nothing happened. It's scary to think what could have happened. A weekend hasn't gone by that one of us has been sober enough to know everything that happened the night before."
>
> —two junior females,
> University of Massachusetts–Dartmouth

I never thought it would happen to me, but it did. I was mugged—at gunpoint. (Yes, it makes it so much more dramatic, but it's true, there was a gun.) I was walking through a safe college neighborhood with a friend one night. We were one street off of a busy street. A man walked by us and pretended to go into an apartment. He then started following us. We moved faster. He started to move faster. Being the helpful guy that I am, I turned around to ask him if he needed some help with something. That's when he pulled out a gun. He said, "This is a stickup." (Yes, he actually used that line, which indicated that he was a novice, or just not a very creative mugger.) He appeared nervous, just a little less nervous than me. My friend was about ten steps ahead of me and kept walking. The guy told me to get on the ground. I was lying facedown on the cold concrete sidewalk. He ripped my chain off, took my wallet, and told me to shut the (insert expletive) up. Like a true amateur, he finished his mugging by directing me to count to one hundred. I started counting and heard a car pull up and a door close. He was gone. When I got to twenty-five, it was all over. I lost $28, my innocence, and a pair of underwear (I got nervous). Actually, I'm kidding about the underwear, but it did scare the crap out of me. I never thought it could happen to me. We never do.

> For more information on IMPACT, visit http://www.impactchicago.org/resource.html

Bottom Line

Yeah, it happens to people like us.

The Tip
If you are a commuter student, make an effort to join a club or activity on campus. Also, make friends with people in the dorms; it gives you a place to crash for the night.

The Story
I don't feel excluded, but I need to branch out a little more. I'd like to have more friends in different disciplines. I get to campus at 7:30 a.m. and stay until 4:00 p.m. I joined choir even before getting there. I have a lot in common with the people in the music building. It's fun to get to know a lot of people. I'm taking all sorts of classes and I'm talking to all the people in my classes. I have so many people I can say hi to. And one of my friends from high school lives in the dorms, so I can crash there. I have requested permission to do so and it was happily granted. I was hanging out there and the friend I know from high school's friend came by and we ended going to a party. And now when I see her on campus we talk a lot, and I talk to her friends (who happen to be in music). I also play pool in the pool room. That helps.

> "Every time I'm in the student center, waiting for my mom to pick me up, I meet people. Commuting makes it harder to feel connected to campus. I haven't experienced the total college experience. I need my independence to grow."
> —sophomore, University of Houston

—freshman, Mesa State College

Commuting can go both ways—it has its perks, but it presents some unique challenges.

First, you have to get to and from campus. Then you need to study for classes (making it that much harder to study with other students in class). Then you need to figure out how to feel like you're a part of campus. Things like seeing a professor during office hours aren't always so simple. Getting involved in clubs, activities, and organizations needs to be planned. On top of that, a lot of commuters have other responsibilities—a job, children, or other people to take care of at home. College becomes more like a place to visit or work than a home away from home. Unlike students who live on campus, commuters need to go that extra mile to get involved and feel connected to campus life. That's why if it's at all possible, try to find a way to live on campus. Talk to an advisor in the financial aid office and see if you can find a way to make it work. You don't even need to live on campus every day and night. If grant money or scholarships are not available, and a student loan is out of the question, consider becoming a resident assistant (free room and board). Talk to whoever handles RAs in the residence life office. If that's not an option, find out if there are any jobs on campus that can help with the expenses. If you just can't do it, then try to get a part-time job on campus. If you have to work—and most commuters need to work—at least try to work on campus. This way you can make friends with people who live on campus. They can be your connection to campus life and even offer you a place to crash. If a job isn't something that excites you, then make it a point to stay on campus as long as possible. Get on campus early and stay all day. Just be there as if it's a job. Then try to get involved with at least one organization or activity.

One way to feel connected on campus is to seek out other commuters. There is often a club or organization for them. By connecting with commuters, especially the upperclassmen, you can meet people with whom you have something in common and can map out strategies for how to get the most out of college life.

Attention First-Generation Students

First-generation students are students who are the first in their family to attend college. You guys and girls are often the most at risk of not making it to graduation (scary, I know). Whether you're commuting or living on campus, make sure you seek out people on campus who can help you and advise you during the college process. Because your family members haven't been there and done it, it's a MUST to seek out people on campus who can help you along the way. You can find mentors and assistance in the new-student office, multicultural centers (whatever your ethnic roots, there should be a group on campus), the counseling center, and in the classroom. You can also connect with other students in the Naked Roommate forums (www.TheNakedRoommate.com).

Bottom Line

Commuters have to go that extra mile (or one-hundred-plus miles) to get involved. If you must commute, try to go to class, work, and hang out on campus. Find a few good friends and find a place to crash.

Tip #105
Diversity: Sexual, Religious, Racial—It's All Good

The Tip
Have your own experiences before you pass judgment on other people based on their skin color, religion, or origin.

The Story
I had never met an Indian person before coming to college. I know that sounds weird, but it's true. I met her in Interpersonal Communication my freshman year. She sat next to me and we were assigned to work together on a group project. We got along well and became friends. A couple weeks later, she took me out to dinner to an Indian restaurant. It was so cool. She told me all about her culture. She had never met anyone who was Jewish before. After we went to dinner, she was like, "My parents don't really like Jewish people, but I'll tell them that I do." It was a little weird to hear that her parents wouldn't like me and didn't even know me—I've always been friends with everyone. I guess I can understand a little bit. I have a few friends who only hang out with white people. They're not rude. They just don't make an effort. They've grown up that way and are stuck in their ways. It's sad—it's really sad.

—freshman, Southern Indiana University–Evansville

Diversity is a word thrown around college campuses. My definition of diversity on campus is pretty straightforward. It's appreciating differences and being open to learning about something unfamiliar. The problem with new students and diversity is that everything is so unfamiliar during the first year that it makes dealing with unfamiliar people, lifestyles, religions, and cultures a little overwhelming at times. The knee-jerk reaction is to run the other way when faced with diversity issues. It's a normal and natural reaction. But try not to run away to your comfort zone. Instead, stand still. Take a good look at what you're faced with and then try to learn from it. Experience it firsthand.

> **"It's not always like the brochures. It helps to seek diversity. It can be easy to stay in your own group of friends. At a big college, people tend to stick close to each other. Having a part-time job that puts me in the middle of campus has helped me to branch out and find different friends from different places."**
> —junior, University of Wisconsin–Green Bay

Still, there will always be those who feel the need to run the other way, and that's fine. Just don't be hateful, hurtful, or hostile. Quietly walk the other way and hide in your comfort zone. But don't stay there forever. That would just be living in ignorance. As you get more comfortable with yourself in college, take a step beyond your comfort zone. Make an effort to get to know people who are different than you. Push your boundaries. Experience diversity. It's a chance to learn about things you never imagined. It's an opportunity to learn about yourself, and another person's culture, lifestyle, or religion. These are the conversations, experiences, and moments that you'll take with you forever, far beyond college.

And for those people who are judged, stereotyped, and run from, you have every right to feel offended and to be disappointed, but appreciate where it comes from. Use the resources, support services, and power on your campus to help educate others.

Bottom Line

When something makes you want to run, ask yourself what you're running from. If the answer is based on stereotypes and secondhand information, stop running. Experience it for yourself. When you do, you'll be shocked what you discover.

Harlan's Tip Sheet

Things Not Mentioned Resources, Websites, and Additional Info

Campus Counseling Center

Free counseling is often available for any of the issues mentioned here. It's confidential and if you exceed the number of free sessions you're allotted (assuming there is a limit), you can usually get help on a sliding scale (which means you pay what you can afford). From one-on-one counseling to group therapy, talk to the people who can help.

Recreational Center/Gym/Field House:

Inquire about organized classes to help you stay in shape. If your school doesn't have a recreational center or gym, ask about student discounts at the gyms near campus.

Sexual Assault Hotline or Counselor:

Check to see if your campus has counselors available. You can always dial 911 or call your local hospital.

Nutritionist/Registered Dietician:

See if your health center has a nutritionist on campus to help with balancing your diet and managing your weight.

Addiction

Alcoholics Anonymous
www.alcoholics-anonymous.org
Gambling Anonymous
www.gamblersanonymous.org
Sex Addicts Anonymous
www.sexaa.org

Depression

National Hopeline Network
24-Hour Suicide Hotline: 1-800-SUICIDE (784-2433)
Half of Us
www.halfofus.com
National Mental Health Information Center
www.mentalhealth.org/ (to more links)
Campus Blues
Deals with more than just depression:
http://www.campusblues.com/ (to more links)

Sexual Assault

RAINN—the Rape, Abuse & Incest National Network
(RAINN) is the nation's largest anti-sexual assault
organization

    www.rainn.org

National Sexual Assault Hotline

    1-800-656-HOPE

    CDC Website with Links

    www.cdc.gov/ncipc/factsheets/svprevention.htm

National Domestic Violence Hotline and Website

    1-800-799-7233 or 1-800-787-3224 (TTY)

    www.ndvh.org

Anorexia/Bulimia/Eating Disorders

The National Women's Health Organization

    www.4woman.gov/faq/anorexia.htm

National Eating Disorders Association

    www.nationaleatingdisorders.org

National Association of Anorexia and Associated Disorders

    www.anad.org

The Body Dysmorphic Website

    a comprehensive site for those victims of BDD

    www.bddcentral.com

Weight Loss

Weight Watchers:

A great online program that is reasonably priced. Sign
up for a trial and cancel if you can't pay (then do it on
your own). It's what I use: www.weightwatchers.com
(I pay for it).

South Beach:
www.southbeachdiet.com

Diversity Issues

On campus, contact the dean of students office
ACLU: American Civil Liberties Union
www.aclu.org
PFLAG: Parents, Families & Friends of Lesbians & Gays
www.pflag.org

It's Almost Time to Say Good-bye

Dear Harlan,
How is college? Is it fun like everyone says it is, or will I want to come back home? How was your first year in college? Was it hard? Were you scared to finally be on your own? Did you have a nice roommate? Did you have trouble getting to know people? Was it difficult to get around campus? How did you know if you picked the right school to go to? How will I know? As you can see I have a lot of questions on my mind. I would be grateful if you could help me out.

—Baby Love

Dear Baby Love,
I feel like I'm back in college during finals...

So, Baby Love, I think at this point in the book, I've covered most of your questions. The answer is that so many of these questions you ask can't be answered until you get to campus. I can tell you more about my experience, but my experience isn't going to be your experience. What was normal for me might not be normal for you. But when it comes to the big picture of what's to be expected, I think you can leave for school with a good sense of what's ahead of you. And what awaits you is a story yet to be written—a story filled with unexpected twists, wild turns, new emotions, new experiences, different kinds of people, laughs, tears, smiles, and memories that will last you a lifetime. I hope this book helped you, and I hope it will continue to help you during your college adventure. And then, I hope you'll share what you've learned with other students (see Tip #107).

ANSWER KEY:

College is a once-in-a-lifetime experience.

It's fun, but not always happy fun, if you know what I mean.

My first year was hard, but that's what helped me to write this book.

I was so scared, I tried to keep my long-distance girlfriend so I wouldn't be alone—until she dumped me.

My roommate was nice (nicer when he was messed up), but we didn't connect.

I had trouble really getting to know people, but that takes time.

Getting around campus was easy, once I figured out how to get around campus.

If you can't be true to yourself, then it's not the right college. That's the test.

Tip #106
The U of No Regrets

The Tip
As awful and painful as mistakes can be, they're the reason we grow to be better people. I wouldn't change a thing.

The Story
I sat for a long time trying to figure out what it is that I would do differently when looking back at my college life. If I were to change the past, and erase all the trials and tribulations that I've experienced in life, as nice as that would be, I wouldn't have turned out the way that I am today. When it comes down it, as painful as the past might have been at times, each experience has been necessary to help me grow into the person I am today. And that's not something I'd ever want to change.

—sophomore, Suffolk County Community College

* * *

I try to live my life by a thing I call The No-Regret Rule. Whenever I have to make a difficult decision, I ask myself the following question: "What is it that feels right for me right now, at this very moment in my life?" I ask myself that question because I know that I will change over the years, and there's a good chance that later in life I'll look back at a decision I made and think, *I should have done that differently...*

We all do it.

As your college journey is about to begin, or as it continues, you'll have a lot of tough choices to make—who will be your friends, how you deal with difficult roommates, what major to pick, to hook up or not to hook up, to get into to drugs or not, to remain a virgin or lose your virginity, to pledge a fraternity or sorority, to drink or not to drink, to get help if you're feeling down and depressed or not—the questions will swirl around your head day after day. And you're going to have to make decisions. When you do, this book will be here.

"Just chill—it will all come together."
—senior, Allegheny College

The purpose of *The Naked Roommate* is to help you to make the best decisions—no-regret decisions. I only hope the information throughout this book will help guide you to the best choices for you. I hope what I've written on my side of the page will help you. I hope the tips and stories shared from students will help you. I hope the resources, support services, facts, stats, websites, and hotlines will help you. The information in this book is all about helping you to get the most out of college life. It's the book I wish someone had given to me. Now you have it and more information than any college student has ever had as part of college life. So now, when you ask yourself the question, "Is this the right choice for me?" you'll know more than you ever wanted to know or needed to know to make the best choice throughout your college experience—and beyond.

Bottom Line

Be true to yourself. Be your personal best. If you don't know who you are or what is your best, figure it out. Do this and leave college with more than a degree, but an understanding of what you love and what you don't love. Then you can spend the rest of your life doing what you love to do. There's nothing greater you can take with you from college than this—it's called passion.

Tip #107
Your Tip Goes Here

The Tip
Enter your tip here.

_____

_____

_____

_____

Note: As you go through your college experience, keep this space in mind. When something throws you, shocks you, depresses you, confuses you, alarms you, makes you laugh, makes you smile, makes you cry, or makes you scream "Why?!", send the tip and the story to me via www.TheNakedRoommate.com or just send an email to harlan@helpmeharlan.com (subject: Naked Roommate Tip). Your experience can help literally millions of others.

The Story

Enter your story here.

If your tip is already in the book, send me your story that corresponds to a current tip. Don't hold back any details! The more information the better the tip and story.

_____

_____

_____

_____

_____

_____

_____

SEND TIPS AND STORIES VIA:
   www.TheNakedRoommate.com
   www.HelpMeHarlan.com
   EMAIL: harlan@helpmeharlan.com (subject: TNR Tip).

Naked Bonus #1
The Naked Blog
(from www.TheNakedRoommate.com)

The Roommate Honeymoon Ends

As September rolls…

Attention Readers: Post your naked comments by visiting The Naked Blog at www.TheNakedRoommate.com

How to Avoid Getting Your Long Distance Relationship (LDR) Puppy Shot

Tears streamed...

Attention Readers: Post your naked comments by visiting The Naked Blog at www.TheNakedRoommate.com

A Very Good Year to Be Gay

A man can't be a lesbian...

Attention Readers: Post your naked comments by visiting The Naked Blog at www.TheNakedRoommate.com

The Naked Rear End

Get the Nakedness Delivered Weekly

Sign up for a weekly dose of the nakedness via the Naked Roommate eNewsletter (yes, it's free via email). Visit TheNakedRoommate.com to sign up for the naked dispatch and browse recent naked issues.

Facebook, MySpace, and TheNakedRoommate.com

Harlan on Facebook:
http://indiana.facebook.com/profile.php?id=6855003

Harlan on MySpace:
http://www.myspace.com/harlancohen

Naked Roommate Home:
http://www.TheNakedRoommate.com

The Naked Author Speaks

Harlan can speak—he speaks at home, he speaks on the phone when ordering food, and he can speak as part of your convention, organizational event, campus program, retreat, or school assembly. Whether delivering a keynote about the sport of taking risks, facilitating a leadership training workshop, or helping students make the most of life on campus, Harlan's unmatched expertise, unique humor, and universal message has made him a favorite presenter across the country. Each of Harlan's events is customized to fit your needs and incorporates live music on the guitar (yes, he sings), audience participation, and the latest stats, facts, and trends. The following is a sampling of Harlan's events, keynotes, and programs:

New Student Issues

- The Naked Roommate:
  And Everything Else You Might Run Into in College
  (high school and college event)
- Your Kid's Naked Roommate:
  And Everything Else Your Son or Daughter Might
  Run Into in College (parent event)
- The Naked Roommate Living on Your Floor
  and Everything Else You Might Run Into as a Resident Life Professional (staff training)

Dating/Relationships/Sexual Health/Alcohol
Awareness

- Dating in the Nude: Exposing the Secret Truth
  about Dating and Relationships
- Tapping the Keg of Truth: Exposing the *Why*
  behind College Drinking

Leadership Workshops/Keynotes
(for professionals and/or students)

- Training for The Sport of Taking Risks:
  How to Always Win, Regardless of the Score

For additional information regarding Harlan's speaking events, please visit him at www.HelpMeHarlan.com or www.TheNakedRoommate.com.

The Naked Author in Your Newspaper

Harlan is one of the youngest, one of the most respected, and one of the only men writing advice. He is creator and author of the syndicated Help Me, Harlan! advice column and has been referred to as the Dear Abby of the next generation, only younger, hairier, and a man. Help Me, Harlan! can be read in local daily and college newspapers around the globe and is distributed by King Features Syndicate.

If you would like to read Harlan's advice column in your local newspaper, please email your newspaper editor and demand that they run Help Me, Harlan! (Demand it nicely.) Feel free to send a note to syndication@helpmeharlan.com and we'll pass along the word for you. In the meantime, Harlan can help you online if you visit his website, where he publishes recent columns after they first appear in print.

The Naked Author Sings

Harlan is proud to announce the release of his album *Fortunate Accidents*. Based on themes addressed in *The Naked Roommate* and in his syndicated Help Me, Harlan! advice column, this musical journey explores the complexities of love, loss, and life in a professional studio recording. *Fortunate Accidents* features such classics as:

"My Roommate Stu"
"The Chlamydia Jive"
"Girl Walks Bye"
"The Syphilis Song"
"Open-Toed Sandals"
and many more…

Sample songs online at: www.TheNaked Roommate.com. *Fortunate Accidents* is available via Harlan's website, on iTunes, and at CDBaby.com

About the Author

Harlan's writing career began at Indiana University's school newspaper, the *Indiana Daily Student*. He shifted his path toward advice after interning at *The Tonight Show* with Jay Leno in the summer of 1995. That's when Harlan came up with the idea to write his column after meeting a writer who had penned an advice column in college. Upon returning to IU, he immediately launched his Help Me, Harlan! column. At first, he wrote questions and answers to himself, and helped himself. Then "real" letters started rolling in. He consulted experts on and off campus to help with his replies. This balance of honest advice, helpful resources, and humor turned the column into an instant success on campus. Help Me, Harlan! soon spread throughout the country and beyond.

He is the author of two books on college life, a contributor to *Chicken Soup for the Teenage Soul III,* and an occasional contributor to the *Chicago Tribune*. He penned the On Campus column for *The Wall Street Journal Classroom Edition* for two years and has been featured as an expert in *Seventeen, CosmoGirl*, and *Psychology Today*.

When not writing advice, Harlan can be found speaking across the country, appearing on radio and TV, expanding his websites (HelpMeHarlan.com and TheNakedRoommate.com), playing original music as heard on his new album *Fortunate Accidents*, and working on his next book. Harlan is the founder and president of Rejection Awareness Week and The International Rejection Project. He resides in Chicago, Illinois, with his wife, whom he met after discovering the secret truth of dating and relationships as revealed to him while conducting relationship research for his advice column.

Index

Death
    alcohol-related, 309–12
    drug-related, 331, 332–36
Debit cards, 365–68
Decision making, 419–21
Department offices, 142
Department websites, 211
Depo-Provera, 282
Depression, 37, 97–99, 246, 392–98, 414
Desperation hookups, 219
Diaphragm with spermicide, 279
Digital cameras. *See* Fifth Wall; Technology
Dining. *See* Eating
Directions, on-campus, 29–31
Diversity, 151, 153, 411–13, 416
Doors, locking, 93
Dormitories. *See* Residence halls
Dorm rooms, 60. *See also* Residence halls
Drinking. *See* Alcohol
Driving while intoxicated, 312–15
Drop/add, 211
Drugs, 323–37
    addiction to, 397
    alcohol and, 306, 335
    avoiding, 327–32
    cigarette smoking, 342–44
    grades and, 178
    Greek organizations, 153
    overdosing and death, 332–36

roommates and, 93–96, 98
sex and, 265
tip sheet, 344–45
types of, 336–41
Drunk driving, 312–15
Drunken dialing, 292, 301
Drunk hookups, 219
Dues, for Greek organizations, 159

E
Eating, 371–74
    alcohol and, 295–96, 297, 316
    body image and, 386
    campus arrival and, 29
    credit cards and, 361
    drugs and, 330–31
    freshman 15 and, 383–86
    homesickness and, 37
    residence halls and, 55, 60, 66
Eating disorders, 98, 389–92, 415
Educators. *See* College educators; High school educators
Electives, 207–10
Email. *See* Fifth Wall; Technology
Emergency contraception, 285, 286
Emergency contraceptive pills (ECPs), 286
Emotional abuse, 240–41
Essay tests, 176
Exam. *See* Tests

You still reading?

So, I'm done. I've written enough. I have nothing left.

Please, put your shoes back on, button your pants, and get back to what you were doing before you got comfortable and started to read this book. Now, get going to college or to class or to work. I'm here if you need me. And just know that whatever happens or doesn't happen in college, you're never alone.

Have an amazing college experience!

Thanks,
Harlan